Chuck Close | Life

Chuck Close | Life

CHRISTOPHER FINCH

Prestel

MUNICH · BERLIN · LONDON · NEW YORK

Front cover: Chuck Close in front of *Self-Portrait I*, 2009.
Oil on canvas, 72 x 60 in. (182.9 x 152.4 cm). Photo by Michael Marfione
Frontispiece: Chuck Close working on *Keith* in his studio at 27 Greene Street, 1970.
Photo by Wayne Hollingworth

Prestel, a member of Verlagsgruppe Random House GmbH

PRESTEL VERLAG
Königinstrasse 9, 80539 Munich
Tel. +49 (0)89 24 29 08-300 | Fax +49 (0)89 24 29 08-335

PRESTEL PUBLISHING LTD.
4 Bloomsbury Place, London WC1A 2QA
Tel. +44 (0)20 7323-5004 | Fax +44 (0)20 7636-8004

PRESTEL PUBLISHING
900 Broadway, Suite 603, New York, NY 10003
Tel. +1 (212) 995-2720 | Fax +1 (212) 995-2733

www.prestel.com

Prestel books are available worldwide. Please contact your nearest bookseller or one
of the above addresses for information concerning your local distributor.

Library of Congress Control Number: 2009943596

British Library Cataloguing-in-Publication Data: a catalogue record for this book is available
from the British Library. The Deutsche Bibliothek holds a record of this publication in the
Deutsche Nationalbibliografie; detailed bibliographical data can be found under:
http://dnb.d-nb.de

Editorial direction by Christopher Lyon | Edited by Mindy Werner
Editorial assistance by Ryan Newbanks | Proofreading and indexing by Ashley Benning
Design by Mark Melnick | Typography by Duke & Company, Devon, Pennsylvania
Origination by Reproline Mediateam, Munich
Printed and bound in Germany by Passavia Druckservice GmbH & Co. KG, Passau

FSC
Mixed Sources
Product group from well-managed
forests and other controlled sources
Cert no. SGS-COC-003859
www.fsc.org
© 1996 Forest Stewardship Council

Verlagsgruppe Random House FSC-DEU-0100
The FSC-certified paper *Fly* has been supplied by Papier Union.

ISBN 978-3-7913-3677-0

Contents

Preface

One day in late October 2004, I called Chuck Close from the steps of the Metropolitan Museum of Art, where I had just attended the press view of an exhibition surveying the career of one of his predecessors, the early American portraitist Gilbert Stuart. The purpose of my call was to arrange for a studio visit, but in the course of the conversation Chuck proposed the idea of my writing a book about his career. When I pointed out that there were already several volumes dedicated to his work, he countered that they were either catalogues of single exhibitions or were limited to a specific area of his art, such as printmaking. What was yet to be done, he said, was a comprehensive book that covered his complete oeuvre in every medium.

One reason he thought of me as a logical candidate for this project was that I had been a witness to his career from its beginning. I had met Chuck and his wife Leslie in 1968 when I was an associate curator at the Walker Art Center in Minneapolis, and had been instrumental in the Walker purchasing his first major painting to enter a public collection—the now iconic *Big Self-Portrait*. When I settled in New York the following year, I became a frequent visitor to his SoHo loft, hung out in the same bars and restaurants, and on Saturdays we often toured the galleries together, logging innumerable hours of conversation and debate about art and everything else from politics to movies.

This was a dramatic period, full of cultural and social turmoil, during which SoHo was transformed from an urban wilderness colonized by painters, dancers, and musicians—who at first were little more than squatters—into one of the centers of the international art world. Chuck was at the nexus of that ferment, and I was a privileged eyewitness. I had ongoing access to his seminal photorealist paintings (a term he dislikes) as they were being committed to canvas and saw how he took a leadership role in the art world protests that followed the tragic shootings at Kent State. He was a witness at my wedding and a couple of years later painted a major portrait of my wife, Linda, which is now the pride of the Akron Museum of Art. I have been a close observer of his career ever since.

A day or two after that initial phone conversation, we discussed the idea of a book over lunch, and a few months later I had a detailed proposal for a monograph ready to submit to publishers. The most interesting response came from Christopher Lyon of Prestel Publishing, suggesting not one but two books, the first the comprehensive study of his art that Chuck had envisioned, to be followed by a full-scale biography. Unlike almost any other major living artist, the dramatic arc of Chuck's life justified such a concept, not only because his work has been interwoven with his life in an unusually rich way, but because at the center of both is a traumatic event that would have destroyed most careers and which Close overcame with a determination and flourish that can only be described as inspirational. This momentous episode would, of course, have to be addressed in both books, but only in an exhaustive biography could it and other key aspects of his story be treated as fully as they deserved to be. A degree of overlap between the books would be inevitable, since to some extent the biography draws upon research and quotes used in the first book, *Chuck Close: Work* (published in 2007). *Chuck Close: Life*, however, stands by itself as a book that is complementary to the earlier volume but far more complete with regard to biographical material.

When embarking on the biography, I was encouraged by the knowledge that Chuck Close is a pack rat, one of those people who holds on to the ephemera of his past—childhood snapshots, elementary school report cards, high school yearbooks, even his grandmother's old magnifying glass—all preserved as meticulously as the catalogues and reviews that form a record of his adult career: a biographer's dream. Before I started work on either book, he handed me a typewritten family history compiled by his Great Aunt Bina, forty-five single-spaced pages packed with invaluable information about everything from his family's migration from Nebraska to the Pacific Northwest to the circumstances surrounding Chuck's birth. I included a few tidbits in *Chuck Close: Work* and then put her typescript aside to draw upon at length for this biography.

As I embarked on *Chuck Close: Life*, its subject produced other treasures, such as his baby album—scrupulously and tellingly annotated by his mother—as well as access to some of his oldest friends whose generously shared reminiscences facilitated my reconstruction of Chuck's life in Everett, Washington, in the 1950s. In addition to all these resources, Chuck made himself available for innumerable hours of questioning, patiently going over the details of traumatic events in his past as well as the complexities of his relationship with his mother, a difficult woman who was in crucial ways responsible for much of who he is today. All this enabled me to reconstruct his early years in great detail, so that whereas his life prior to settling in New York occupied a single chapter of *Work*, it takes up eight chapters of *Life*, tracking the evolution of Chuck Close the artist as he advanced, sometimes painfully, from the Everett Public School System, through Everett Junior College and the University of Washington, and finally on to Yale, where his colleagues in the MFA program constituted a golden generation that included such future luminaries as Richard Serra and Brice Marden.

While writing *Chuck Close: Work*, I soon realized that I had been flattering myself in thinking that my knowledge of his art was reasonably comprehensive. I had previously written about several of its aspects, notably his paintings and dot drawings, but now I was hit by just how many facets there are to his work. Close might have one primary subject, the human face, but he brings to it an infinite variety of approaches. (I can imagine a story by Jorge Luis Borges in which an artist named Chuck Close fills a studio with endless portraits of the same sitter, each of them entirely different.)

Something similar happened when I began working on *Chuck Close: Life*. Here was someone who had been a friend for forty years, and whom I thought I knew pretty well, but the gaps in my knowledge of his past were enormous. These lacunae were filled during the course of the aforementioned long sessions of informal dialogue. We would sit in the artist's studio or in some NoHo bistro for hours at a stretch, talking about anything and everything—old friends and current art world gossip, Yankee games and auction prices—pausing for an espresso or a drink then almost at random turning to matters directly related to the book. It was during these rambling conversations that—to paraphrase Chuck—the process really began to percolate, as we reached back to the roots of our friendship and became so relaxed that, when we did turn to matters connected with the narrative, rich nuggets would emerge. It was during conversations like this that he would suddenly recall the art epiphany he experienced at a Billy Graham rally in Tacoma, or an incident involving Robert Rauschenberg and a chicken in a New Haven lecture hall. This kind of enjoyably discursive dialogue, especially when exploring his early years, enabled me to piece his life together as if reassembling an ancient artifact from shards—or accumulating a narrative by means that have something in common with the incremental process used to produce a Chuck

Close portrait. This process continued for three years, with some of the most critical material emerging during the final weeks before my deadline.

At the outset of his career, Chuck described his paintings as "mug shots," preferring to think of them as "heads" rather than portraits in the traditional sense. Over the past four decades, he has moved away from that concept—at least in its most literal form—demonstrating that there are many valid ways to make a portrait if pursued with rigor and integrity. One rule he has adhered to from the beginning, however, is that he never sets out to flatter. In a recent interview, he talked about his regard for his sitters when considered in this light.

"It's an act of tremendous generosity and bravery to submit to my photographs. ... Anyone I've painted has [given me] an extraordinary gift by lending me their image, with no control over what I'm going to do with it."

This book is the result of a huge act of generosity on the part of Chuck Close. He gave of himself magnanimously, as did many other people who unstintingly shared their recollections and reflections with me, enabling me to create this portrait of the artist. I hope I have done them justice.

Prologue

At five o'clock in the afternoon of December 7, 1988–the forty-seventh anniversary of the attack on Pearl Harbor–Chuck Close finds himself in Yorkville, the old German neighborhood on the Upper East Side of Manhattan. At the age of 48, Close has established himself as one of the most accomplished painters of his generation, already the subject of a major museum retrospective and a full-scale monograph. His most recent exhibition, at the Pace Gallery, was rapturously received by both critics and his peers.

Well over six feet tall, slim but broad-shouldered, with a full beard and thick glasses, Close is a familiar presence in art world haunts from the bistros of SoHo and Tribeca to the galleries of Fifty-seventh Street and Madison Avenue. Yorkville, however, is off the beaten path for him. He is here, and more conservatively dressed than usual, because he's on his way to Gracie Mansion–the official residence of the mayor of New York–for the annual awards ceremony of the Alliance for the Arts, at which he is to be a presenter.

Close is feeling under the weather. For a couple of weeks now he's been suffering from a miserable respiratory infection, accompanied by a hacking cough. On top of that he woke up this morning with severe chest pains, but was not especially worried by this because he has a history of angina-like episodes, none of which has ever progressed to anything worse, or led to a credible diagnosis of a heart condition. He puts them down to stress but likes to add, "Denial runs in my family."

He's a little early so he stops into a neighborhood tavern and orders a scotch, hoping the drink will make him feel better. Instead he feels worse. He's nauseous and, by the time he leaves the bar to walk the last few blocks to Gracie Mansion, the chest pains have returned. It's dark by now, and the day has turned cold. He walks past storefronts trimmed with Mylar icicles and blinking Christmas lights, past Chanukah candles glowing in apartment windows, arriving at Gracie Mansion a little before six. There he's shown into a reception area where hors d'oeuvres are being served. He sees people he knows but, although normally gregarious, is in no mood for casual socialization. The chest pains have become worse and he is beginning to take them more seriously. On the program he's he has been handed, he's listed as the third presenter. Even assuming everything goes smoothly, that's almost an hour away. Close approaches the woman in charge of the event, explains the situation, and requests that he be moved to the head of the list. She tells him that's impossible.

As waiters circulate with canapés, Agnes Gund—a prominent collector and a trustee of the Museum of Modern Art—approaches Close and tells him she is pleased to have run into him because she has been meaning for some time to ask him if he would accept a commission to paint her portrait. As a matter of principle, Close never accepts commissions. He paints friends and family, and then only when and whom he chooses to—one of the ways in which he distances himself from the traditional role of the portrait painter with its feudal baggage of artist and patron. Under normal circumstances, Close would point this out politely and with a palliative dose of charm, but in pain and with claustrophobia pressing in on him, his reaction to Gund's request verges on rudeness. Surely she knows his policy on accepting commissions? It's no secret, after all. His curtness, so out of character, takes the collector by surprise, and she backs off.

At 6:10, as scheduled, the mayor—Ed Koch—appears to introduce the awards ceremony. By now, the chest pains have become almost unbearable. As Koch begins his introductory speech, Close leaves his seat and once again confronts the woman in charge of scheduling. He makes it clear that the moment for protocol is past. He needs to get medical attention as soon as possible. If he is to present the award, he must be moved to the head of the list; otherwise he will leave immediately. This is a demand rather than a request and is finally agreed to. An offer is made to call an ambulance, which he refuses, but a police officer is alerted to accompany him to Doctors Hospital, which, fortuitously, is just across the street from Gracie Mansion. Even so, Close must wait through the mayor's speech, and Koch famously relishes every minute in the spotlight, playing this evening to an audience of fewer than a hundred people with a born performer's hunger for applause, his timing as measured as Jack Benny's. At last he's finished, and Close is introduced. He makes his way to the dais and reads the citation.

"Louis Spanier, visual arts coordinator, community school district thirty-two, is being honored for bringing an appreciation of the visual arts to students in the Bushwick area of Brooklyn . . ."

The pain and the constriction in Close's chest are such that he has difficulty getting the words out. He makes the presentation, and then instead of returning to his seat, hurriedly and unsteadily leaves the room. Accompanied by the assigned police officer, he makes his way on foot the short distance to the Doctors Hospital emergency room, where—a miracle for New York City—not a single patient is waiting. Close is attended to immediately. He is given massive doses of painkillers, and intravenous Valium for sedation.

Fully conscious, Close requests that his wife, Leslie, be alerted. She hears the phone as she awaits the elevator outside the couple's Central Park West apartment, on her way to the Pace Gallery Christmas party. She jumps into a cab and heads for the hospital, not as alarmed as she might be because she too has been through this before. Like her husband, she initially puts this latest episode down to the effects of stress and fatigue, but the scene that greets her at the emergency room quickly dissolves any vestige of complacency. The urgency communicated by the staff immediately brings home the seriousness of the situation, and to make things worse no one can tell her exactly what the problem is. They are testing for cardiac arrest but cannot confirm that that is the explanation. Only one thing is clear—the situation is critical.

There is a feeling of helplessness that comes in a moment of crisis like this—a sense of being in the way yet needing to be there, of wanting answers to questions that may be unanswerable.

Suddenly Close goes into convulsions. Long and frenzied, it seems they will never end, but then just as suddenly his body is still, unnaturally so, just lying there, dead weight, flesh without animation.

Still fully conscious, Chuck Close is paralyzed from his shoulders down.

Part I

Four generations: the infant Chuck Close in the arms of his maternal great-grandfather, Benjamin Albro, with Chuck's mother, Mildred Close, left, and Blanche Albro Wagner, his maternal grandmother, 1940.

Chapter 1

Born on the Fifth of July

It is unusual, to say the least, for a living artist's face to be featured on billboards, but not long ago commuters from Long Island, and travelers en route into Manhattan from Kennedy and La Guardia airports, were greeted at the entrance to the Midtown Tunnel by a towering black-and-white likeness of Chuck Close dressed in a black leather jacket and a white tee-shirt adorned with a facsimile of one of his many portraits of the composer Philip Glass. Had it not been for his unsmiling expression, it might have seemed that he had been appointed the city's official greeter, an adjunct to the Empire State and Chrysler buildings. Nor did it stop there—a companion billboard was the first thing you saw as you emerged from the IRT subway station at Sheridan Square and, 2,500 miles away in LA, another overlooked the Walk of Fame on Hollywood Boulevard, while a Godzilla-scaled photomural climbed the side of an office building on the Sunset Strip. Sponsored by the Gap to promote the Whitney Museum Biennial Exhibition, the image used at all these sites was also featured on the back cover of *The New Yorker* and prominently in other periodicals; but then it's not unusual to find Chuck Close's likeness on the pages of publications ranging from *New York Magazine* to *Interview* to *W,* and he has produced enough self-portraits—around one hundred so far, including paintings, prints, drawings, and photographs—to have merited a full-scale traveling retrospective that consisted of nothing else. To those who follow the American art scene, Chuck Close's face is as familiar as any since Andy Warhol's.

Faces are the artist's business, and a biographer must contend with the fact that this subject has already accumulated and presented an extensive visual autobiography which commenced in 1967 when he conceived the iconic *Big Self-Portrait* now hanging in the Walker Art Center in Minneapolis—a painting nine feet tall, severely black-and-white like those recent billboards, a vision of the young artist as outsider, cigarette smoldering between lips parted into the hint of a sneer, the cumulative effect proto-punk and confrontational. That at least was the impact the painting had until, with the passage of time, reverence crept into the artist-viewer relationship, as it inevitably does, altering the experience as it alters that of reading a Kerouac novel half a century on or watching a *nouvelle vague* movie at some revival house. The experience is still powerful, but has undergone a sea change.

The image most associated with Close's likeness today is that of the New York sophisticate, the insiders' insider. He seems to know everyone and to be at every major opening, every A-list party, feted and showered with awards and honorary degrees. He was the first artist to be appointed a trustee of the Whitney Museum (and is one of very few to have had retrospective exhibitions at the Whitney, the Museum of Modern Art, and the Metropolitan Museum). He is active in the American Academy of Arts and Letters, a member of the New York City Cultural Affairs Advisory Commission, and sits on the boards of a number of organizations concerned with the well-being of education and the arts. He is, in fact, the consummate New York cultural establishment figure, to the extent that it has become difficult to understand just how shocking–transgressive even–paintings like *Big Self-Portrait* seemed when they were first shown. (*The New York Times* critic Hilton Kramer characterized Close's debut exhibition as, "The kind of garbage washed up on shore after the tide of Pop Art went out.")

Given his present eminence, and his current identification with New York, it may come as a surprise to some that Chuck Close was born a continent away from Manhattan. He did not, in fact, set foot in the Big Apple till a few weeks before his twenty-first birthday nor take up residence there till he was twenty-seven. That was when, in a downtown loft as bare of luxuries as any *Trilby* era Montmartre garret, he began *Big Self-Portrait*. From his student days, when he first encountered the work of Willem de Kooning and Jackson Pollock, making it in New York had been his goal, but–like Pollock, like Robert Rauschenberg, like Jasper Johns and so many other major American artists whose names have come to be associated with the Big Apple–Chuck was in fact a product of what would appear to be an unpromising provincial backwater, in his case the industrial fringes of Puget Sound.

Thus, there are almost three decades for a biographer to explore before the artist's visual autobiography was definitively launched. Chuck Close is a self-made New Yorker, and a master of the New York School of painting, but beyond that he is an American artist, in the sense that Vermeer is Dutch, and Cézanne French—representative of an entire culture.

Chuck Close can point to forebears from Ireland, Denmark, Quebec, and elsewhere, but from the mid-nineteenth century on his family was the product of the rural Midwest, of farms, floods, droughts, and modest railroad towns where livestock was loaded for transport to stockyards in Omaha and Chicago. Like other families that had had enough of tornadoes, blizzards, and backbreaking dawn-to-dusk work harvesting sweet corn or sugar beets, the Closes, Wagners, and Albros who are Close's antecedents migrated westward, finding their way to the Pacific Northwest and the burgeoning cities and towns clustered around Seattle.

Chuck was cheated by a few hours of having the archetypal birth date for an American artist. On Independence Day, 1940, in Monroe, Washington, a small mill town on the Snohomish-Skykomish river system, Mildred Emma Close, age 27, was full-term with a child who—uncharacteristically in light of later developments—seemed in no great hurry to make an entrance onto the world's stage. The baby's arrival had been predicted for the middle of the previous month, but

The house in which Chuck Close was born,
134 South Madison Street, Monroe, Washington

the evening of the 4th arrived with no sign of an impending birth. As darkness fell, Mildred's husband, Leslie Durward Close, set off a barrage of fireworks and firecrackers. According to family legend, this was the trigger. Early on the fifth, Mildred went into labor. A local physician–Dr. Cooley–was summoned, and in the bedroom of his parents' tiny clapboard cottage at 134 South Madison Street–which had been scrubbed and sterilized daily for weeks in anticipation of his arrival–Charles Thomas was delivered, his weight at birth a healthy nine pounds.

His father immediately phoned Mildred's parents in Everett, fourteen miles downstream, and within a few hours her mother, Blanche Ethel Wagner–who had been frantic with worry because of the extended pregnancy and the thought of her daughter giving birth without her–arrived at the cottage in a black Ford sedan driven by her sister, Bina Almyra Albro. (Much of the information in this chapter derives from a detailed typewritten account of Chuck Close's antecedents prepared at his request, in the early 1980s, by his Great Aunt Bina Albro.) Many years later, Bina reported that she would never forget her first impression of Charles Thomas, "still red and such a big lump of a baby that no one would mistake for a girl . . ."

This last observation was prompted by the fact that, in anticipation of the imminent arrival, both Mildred and Blanche had spent a multitude of hours sewing and embroidering baby clothes. It seems, however, that they had been expecting–perhaps even hoping for–a girl since Bina would recall that many of these garments were hardly appropriate for a boy. She remembered in particular the spectacular, long christening gown, trimmed with yards of lace. Despite protests from his father that this garment (though in fact traditional) was highly inappropriate for a boy, the baby wore it for his October 6 christening, at Monroe First Methodist Church, through which he slept soundly. Afterward there was time for a single snapshot before his father insisted that the infant be changed into something deemed more appropriately masculine.

Bina was asked to become the baby's godmother. Her contribution to the layette was a white reed basinet, hooded and lined with shirred Japanese silk and furnished with a matching lace-edged coverlet. The shirring had been done by women at the factory where Bina kept the books, a business devoted to the manufacture of funeral caskets.

Both of Chuck's parents were migrants to the Pacific Northwest from the American heartland. An only child, his mother, Mildred Emma Wagner, was born in

October 1913, to Blanche Wagner, at the Birdwood ranch a dozen miles northwest of North Platte, Nebraska.

Birdwood was the home of Blanche's parents, Benjamin and Emma Albro. Aunt Bina—born in a sod homestead in 1902—lived there at the time of Mildred's birth, as did Theodore—"Teddy"—Bina's younger brother, born in 1910 when his mother was forty-two years old. Emma had believed herself to be past menopause and did not realize she was pregnant until a week or two before giving premature birth to a baby weighing less than two pounds. Incubators were such a novelty in those days they were a popular feature of the midways at spectaculars such as the St. Louis Louisiana Purchase Exposition, and even entertained gawkers at

Close's maternal grandparents, Charles and Blanche Wagner, with Mildred Emma Wagner, Chuck's mother, c. 1915

Coney Island's Luna Park. The Albro clan had no access to one so they made do with a washbowl full of olive oil placed on the hot water reservoir of the kitchen range to keep it warm. When Teddy turned blue he would be immersed in the oil, except for his face, and gently massaged until his color improved. Then he would be taken out and wrapped in flannel. Uncle Teddy not only survived but grew up to be a strapping adult, six foot two inches tall.

Millie's father, Charles Henry Wagner—whose own father had been born in Denmark—originally came to Birdwood to help on the ranch, Blanche having fallen in love with him while teaching in a one-room schoolhouse in northern Nebraska. As described by Bina, Birdwood sounds idyllic—a setting waiting to be painted by a Regionalist artist such as John Steuart Curry, the big house located among a grove of trees near a lake created by the damming of a creek. In fact, though, life was far from arcadian. The children were expected to help with chores—from milking, to mucking out the horse stalls, to cooking for seasonal migrant workers housed in the haylofts—though Benjamin never forced them to do jobs unsuited to their age and physical limitations. The brutal Nebraska climate made for a life that was harsh and sometimes cruel, and however hard they worked, the Albro/Wagner clan did not enjoy much security because they were tenant farmers, owning little beyond their animals, farm equipment, and household belongings. Not long after Millie was born, Birdwood was sold from under them.

Mildred Close's graduation photo,
Auburn High School, c. 1930

There were subsequent attempts to scrape a living from the land, and Benjamin's prize mules continued to win ribbons at county fairs, but disaster was never far away. Bina would remember her father standing out on the porch of one farmhouse, watching as a hailstorm destroyed the entire corn crop.

When Millie was five, Charlie and Blanche Wagner found their way to Ravenna, a small city on the trunk line of the Chicago, Burlington & Quincy Railroad. The Burlington provided Charlie with work as a brakeman. Millie, meanwhile, was able to start school in a setting rather more sophisticated than the one-room schoolhouses that older family members had had to make do with, and also began to take piano lessons, quickly displaying a gift for the instrument. In 1918, Bina Albro moved in with the Wagners, and the following year, Benjamin and Emma finally joined the others in Ravenna, where Emma would die two years later.

Among the perks of Charlie's job on the Burlington were free railroad passes. Not long after Emma's death—in the summer of 1922 or 1923—the three Wagners took a trip west to visit Blanche's sister Mabel, who had moved to Washington State. Charlie and Blanche fell in love with the Pacific Northwest.

"Who wouldn't," Bina wrote, "after living in Nebraska?"

It did not take long for the Wagners to decide on a permanent move, with Bina accompanying them while her father and Teddy remained in Ravenna for

Mildred Close in recital dress, late 1930s

one more year until Teddy completed middle school. In the late spring or early summer of 1924, with minimal belongings strapped to Bina's old Model T tourer—spare tires and rolled bedding bulging from the driver's side, a trunk clamped firmly to a rack suspended from the back of the car, pots and pans dangling—the quartet set out westward along dusty prairie and mountain roads, many of them unpaved, sleeping in tents at primitive auto-camps, making meals in the communal cookhouse or over an open fire. It was an odyssey undertaken by tens of thousands of Americans in the twenties and thirties, a journey that acquired mythic status in the pages of John Steinbeck's *The Grapes of Wrath*.

After many flat tires and patched inner tubes, Bina, Blanche, Charlie and Millie made it to their destination, bones aching from potholes and cramped quarters but without having encountered any major crises. Jobs were not easy to come by, but eventually Charlie found work at the Fleischmann's yeast plant in Sumner, not far from Seattle, and the Wagners plus Bina settled nearby in Auburn, then a small community of truck farmers, where Bina was hired by the casket manufacturing factory.

Benjamin and Teddy finally joined them in the Northwest, driven out there by another of Benjamin's sons, Floyd, in what Bina describes as "a makeshift camper" constructed on the body of a small roadster that had been retrofitted with an improvised flatbed at the rear and a prairie schooner–style canvas canopy. The reason for this jerry-built rig was that Benjamin had broken his leg and was forced to travel on his back on a mattress strapped to the flatbed. Bina was able to find her father a job with the casket company, and soon she was able to buy a home for her parents in the city of Everett, north of Seattle.

The Wagners remained in Auburn, some fifty miles away, but stayed in close contact. The latter part of the 1920s was a reasonably settled and prosperous time for the Wagners with Millie adapting readily to her new surroundings. She was a strong, healthy child, Bina would remember, and strong-willed too. She seems to have done well in school and to have displayed considerable gifts as a pianist, studying with the top teachers in the Seattle area. Undoubtedly she dreamed of having a career as a concert pianist, but any such ambitions had to be put aside because of the onset of the Great Depression, which plunged the Wagners into dire financial circumstances once again. Losing their house in Auburn, they eventually moved in with the Albros in Everett, where Bina was able to use her influence to find Charlie an opening at the casket factory as well. She reported, however, that the long months out of work, and the stress of losing his home, had taken its toll, writing that, "having to start over again just seemed to change him."

A teenager at the time, Millie must have felt her father's pain; his chronically high strung and phobic wife certainly did. "As she grew older," Bina writes, "[Blanche's] nervousness and fears increased." She became very possessive towards her daughter, which may have put a further damper on Millie's musical ambitions since her mother had a horror of her loved ones moving away from home. Millie, however, was a tough-minded young woman, determined to avoid developing any of her mother's fears. Chuck describes his mother as being "counter-phobic"–someone who consciously neutralized any tendency towards phobia by becoming a risk-taker. She would prove less successful in eliminating from her own makeup Blanche's possessive instincts.

Shortly before she graduated from high school, while the Wagners were still hanging on in Auburn, Millie met Leslie Durward Close during choir practice at the local church. A recent arrival in town, and ten years older than Millie, Les was a personable young man who, according to Bina, "dressed quite well." He made a good impression on Millie's parents, and soon Les and Charlie joined forces to hunt for jobs, agreeing that they would never sign on with the WPA or any such federally sponsored relief agency, disdaining government handouts— always referred to as "the dole"—as beneath the dignity of honest working men. (Later, Les—who was in fact sympathetic to the Roosevelt administration—did take a WPA job, helping to create an entirely unnecessary island in the middle of a lake.)

After graduation, Millie moved to Everett to live with Bina and her grand-father on the theory that she would have a better chance to acquire paying piano students there. Les remained in Auburn and took Millie's place in the Wagner household, renting her former room. Before long the Wagners made the move to Everett, and Les came too, managing to earn a meager living performing vari-ous freelance jobs. He developed a considerable reputation as a "douser," or water diviner, using forked twigs to determine the spot where a well should be sunk. (Chuck, who later went along on such expeditions with his father, recalls that he never failed to find water.) More profitably, Les established a name for himself as a window dresser, arranging displays for stores in downtown Everett as well as in nearby smaller towns. He must have shown imagination and flair since at the height of the Depression no retailer was likely to hire an outside window dresser unless the results generated cash flow.

One of Les's major commissions during this period was to completely revamp the vitrines of the Lloyd Hardware Company, a big, bustling store at the major intersection of Hewitt and Broadway in downtown Everett. Lloyd's had many windows, which Les fitted with shelves, steps, and platforms that permitted the installation of livelier, multilayered displays. This led to him being hired as a clerk in the store at $15 a week. He continued to do displays for other stores in his free time, and by 1934, three years after they first met, Les and Millie decided that, between his earnings and her piano lesson fees, they were doing well enough to get married. As much as the family liked him—in truth, he was already practi-cally a member—the idea met strong resistance, with everyone urging the couple to wait for better times. When it became evident that their minds were made up, plans were put into motion for a July 3 wedding, which took place in Millie's parents' house. Blanche made Millie a white satin wedding dress that Bina describes as "lovely." Because the house was tiny, and perhaps because times were hard, the guest list was restricted to a few friends and family members.

The Wagner/Albro concerns about the prudence of the marriage proved unfounded, and the couple got by modestly but comfortably in Everett until a more desirable opportunity prompted them to pull up stakes once more. One of Les's freelance window-dressing jobs was with another large hardware store, this one upriver in Monroe. Les was offered a full-time position there, a better-paying proposition that called for him to do sheet metal work, lay linoleum, install countertops, and the like.

It was thus that Les and Millie Close were living in Monroe when Millie became pregnant.

Leslie Durward Close,
Chuck's father, foreground,
with mother Lulu May Reno Close,
half-brother Orville Guilander,
and father Thomas B. Close,
c. 1907

By comparison with the saga of the Wagner/Albro clan, scant information has survived about Leslie Durward Close's background. What can be said with confidence is that his grandfather was George Close, who, in the 1840 census, was listed as living in Kane, Illinois, a small town in agricultural Greene County in the western part of the state. Leslie's father, Thomas B. Close, was born there in 1869, and married Lulu May Reno, who had previously been married to Jesse Guilander and by whom she had a son, Orville—Leslie's half-brother, seven years his senior—who spent his entire life farming in western Illinois. Les himself was born in Kirkwood, Missouri, a residential satellite of St. Louis, but was brought up on the family ranch, where as a very young man—while in the fields harvesting grain—he suffered a ruptured appendix. The weather was stifling hot and the nearest hospital miles away. By the time he saw a doctor, he had developed peritonitis—inflammation of the tissue that lines the walls of the abdomen. Surgery was performed that resulted in the formation of adhesions—bands of scar tissue that can cause intestinal blockages. From that point on, Leslie Close's health was compromised. He was unable to continue with the chores generally assigned to a farmer's son and instead learned to help his mother in the kitchen, cooking for the family and the ranch hands. Further medical problems, including a heart condition, would pursue him to the Pacific Northwest when he moved there in his late twenties.

After that move, his ties to his family back in the Midwest seem to have become tenuous. The unstinted enthusiasm, and perhaps gratitude, with which Les embraced the Wagners and the Albros suggests that they provided him with something he might have been missing, a secure family environment in which

Young Leslie Close standing behind his father, Thomas Close, left, and half-brother, Orville Guilander, Kane, Illinois, c. 1915

he felt he belonged. The warmth the Wagners and Albros exhibited towards him was itself an expression of something that seems to have sprung from rural America at its best. Les was not exactly the man from nowhere, torn from the pages of a James M. Cain novel, but he had arrived in their life without references, forming a romantic attachment to the Wagners' considerably younger teenage daughter; the family had accepted that and trusted his intentions.

(In some respects, the situation resembled the one that Chuck Close would find himself in when he grew up and took a bride.)

It would emerge many years later that there was a secret in Leslie Durward Close's past. He did not hide it from Millie, and it was known to her parents and to Bina, but it was strenuously concealed from his son for more than forty years.

Chapter 2

Learning to be Unafraid

In the aftermath of the attack on Pearl Harbor, the Close family's life was up-ended once again. Leslie had been a member of the Coast Guard Reserve, but his poor health prevented him from playing an active role in the war. Soon after the outbreak of hostilities, however, he was taken on as a civilian employee of the military at Paine Field in Everett. Built as a WPA project, Paine Field had been appropriated by the Army Air Corps at the outbreak of war, the squadrons based there being charged with defending the nearby Bremerton shipyards as well as the Boeing plant and airfield in Seattle. Leslie Close was hired as foreman of the sheet metal shop, a job well suited to his blend of practical and imaginative talents.

The bread-and-butter part of the job involved carrying out work for the buildings that were being erected to accommodate the Air Corps personnel and equipment, but the job also provided the opportunity for him to exercise his imagination, solving problems that arose under extraordinary wartime circumstances. A number of these solutions resulting over the next several years in patented inventions ranging from a large-scale filter laundry system that could handle mess shirts, service issue underwear, and fatigue jackets in unprecedented quantity, to a "roof jack"—a form of flue that made heating Quonset huts more efficient—to a luminous paint that when applied to the tarmac made night landings possible without the need of runway lights. These inventions did not make him rich, though the military presented him with a check for $100 for his contribution in designing and building the filter laundry system, said at the time to have saved Paine Field $4,000, and the improved roof jack, which saved the government millions when installed around the world, earned him a letter of commendation from the Secretary of Defense. To make ends meet, Les still dressed windows and accepted dousing jobs in his spare time.

Chuck Close dressed as a magician, c. 1947

The fact that Leslie was now employed at Paine Field meant that the Closes were living near Millie's parents once again—next door in fact—so that from the age of eighteen months Chuck basked in the adoration lavished on him by Charlie and Blanche, and in her more restrained way by Bina, too.

Mildred, Leslie, and Chuck Close in his grandparents' yard, summer 1941

Chuck's early childhood seems to have been largely unclouded. There might be a war on, and money tight, but he was in a manifestly loving environment, and never lacked for anything. Despite wartime shortages he always had playthings since his father—a classic *bricoleur*—was able to renovate old toys or to create new ones from scratch, including a rather modernistic looking bicycle. In fact, Chuck—initially known in the family as Charlie, like his grandfather—was always more than adequately supplied, as is recorded in the birthday and Christmas gift lists in a baby album—*All About Our Baby*—meticulously kept up by his mother, not just for his first year but for seven. Early gifts included rubber Mickey Mouse figures, toy soldiers, a xylophone, a "magic slate," modeling clay, a red wagon, and for his third birthday, a Jeep (though Millie would insist that the boy's favorite toys were the bottles, containers, and cooking utensils he found in her kitchen). Later birthdays brought a racing car, a baseball bat, a soldier's costume, a wristwatch, a toy telephone, and a toy typewriter, these items inevitably supplemented with more practical gifts such as shirts, shoes, pajamas, pillow cases, and soap.

One Christmas, Chuck received so many presents that they filled a laundry basket to overflowing.

Chuck belonged to a generation whose parents had survived the Depression and were determined that their children should have the advantages they had lacked. If anything, he was the object of excessive attention. His grandmother was possessive and perhaps prone to smothering. While Millie probably did her

Leslie Durward Close, May 1945, in a photo taken for a patent application for a filter laundering system

best not to emulate her mother in this regard, she was tightly focused on her son's progress in the world, wanting and in fact demanding the best for him. That focus is amply illustrated by the baby album, which is scrupulous in its attention to detail, with Millie always referring to herself in the third person as "Mother."

> Spent 4th birthday in California, very lonesome for Daddy. Mother bought
> him some tinker toys, paints and paint books and kaleidoscope.

Certainly this was a prophetic choice of gifts for someone who would later make paintings that have a decidedly kaleidoscopic aspect. Elsewhere in the album, important developments are duly noted. We learn, for example, that Chuck took his first steps on May 11–Mother's Day–when he was ten months old. We are told that on his first visit to the dentist he was "a good boy." He is in fact so frequently referred to as a good boy that it's a relief to discover that his first spoken sentence was "I don't want to."

Bina's manuscript describes Millie as, "a hardworking person, intelligent and very efficient.... I'm sure many of her friends thought she had a college education.

... I'm sure she was not ashamed of [her background,] but I do know that it takes an extra effort to overcome the effect of spending your 'learning' years with a family that had not had the advantage of a decent education. She succeeded ... mainly because she had the self-assurance to use the knowledge she gained through her study and reading."

Chuck with his mother, c. 1943

Bina touched on some of Millie's faults, too, saying, "She was not always easy to live with. She was inclined to dominate and take charge—often because she did know more than some about a subject or could do some job more quickly." Offsetting this, Bina detailed many instances of Millie's devotion to her family, always making herself available to look after sick relatives, or to pitch in whenever there was a problem of any sort to be dealt with. Bina reported too on the physical ailments that must have had an impact on Millie's personality. These included severe migraine headaches—something she had in common with her father—and like her mother, she was subject to heavy and painful menstrual periods, sometimes hemorrhaging, which led eventually to a hysterectomy. Bina describes her as "having the ability to tolerate a great deal of pain and also a great determination to survive."

In 1946 Paine Field reverted to civilian control, but Leslie Close was given the opportunity to continue his civil service career at McChord Field, a U.S. Air

Force base in Tacoma. This entailed another move, a ninety-minute drive from Everett along Route 99, with the family first renting in one of the sprawling government projects that had sprung up near the base, and later relocating to 3317 South Monroe, a modest tract home in a section known as Oakland where their neighbors were predominantly working- and lower-middle-class families,

Chuck stands outside of his grandparents' home on Cady Road, mid-1940s, on a bicycle made by his father

many dependent on paychecks from either the Pacific Match Company or Nalley's Fine Foods, the big local employers.

(When very young, Chuck ran away from home, inspired by a billboard that announced "You Are Entering Nalley Valley," this being the name given by the locals to the area where the company was headquartered. Once there, he expected to find himself in the arcadian world portrayed on the billboard—a cartoon paradise populated by Disneyesque bunnies, squirrels, bluebirds, and adorable baby deer—and anticipated feasting on the potato chips that had made the Nalley name familiar throughout the Northwest. He was disappointed to find only food processing plants and warehouses.)

By now Chuck had begun school, and it was here that he would first face the difficulties that would dog him for years but that ultimately may have contributed to his success as an artist and to his ability to cope with an encounter with near tragedy.

Early report cards, however, shed little light on these latent problems. He began kindergarten in September of 1945, before leaving Everett, but that report card, signed by his first teacher, Evelyn Shockby, concerns itself primarily with attendance and categories of behavior such as habits regarding health ("Showing by his alertness that he has had sufficient sleep"), citizenship ("Showing care of his own belongings"), and of gaining new experiences and conveying old ones ("Expressing his ideas through playing in sand, building, drawing, painting, and modeling"). Interestingly, this last sub-category is one of only three out of twenty in which he failed to attain a perfect score. (His worst was for "Using a hand-kerchief when needed.") Additionally, the teacher noted that he had "a marked ability to depend on himself."

Christmas, c. 1946

When he progressed to first grade in Tacoma, his teacher Fern Schachterle commended "Charlie" for his effort and for his ability to express his thoughts. In the second quarter he was praised for his improvement in reading, which has some relevance given that it would soon become apparent that—although the terms weren't in use at the time—Chuck suffered from chronic dyslexia and from a perceptual disability called prosopagnosia. It would be in the higher grades that dyslexia would shadow his life more definitively, but it manifested itself from the outset. He remembers having difficulty learning to read and problems with math-ematics—even with adding and subtracting—and from the time he first learned to write, he would sometimes produce mirror writing, now seen as characteristic of many dyslexics. (Leonardo da Vinci, retrospectively diagnosed with the disorder, is famous for having employed mirror writing in his notebooks.) Chuck also displayed the ability to write upside down as fluently as he wrote normally.

Prosopagnosia is a condition that makes it difficult to recognize faces. In extreme cases, it can mean that the victim does not recognize members of his own family and, in very rare instances, cannot recognize his own face in a mirror. Chuck does not suffer from the condition to anything like that degree, but the move to Tacoma, which involved meeting new people, alerted him to its existence. He was outgoing and made friends easily, but he found that, when re-encountering a recent acquaintance in the playground at Oakland Elementary School, often he would be unable to identify him or her even though the face might seem vaguely familiar. Adding to the problem, he had difficulty remembering names. Embarrassing situations were inevitable, and he quickly learned to compensate, using non-facial characteristics—a hairstyle, a way of dressing, an individualistic gait—as aids to identifying people. (Typically, a victim of prosopagnosia has no difficulty recognizing things other than the topography of individual faces.)

To have difficulty placing faces is an interesting condition for a future painter of portraits to be afflicted with. Chuck discovered early on, however, that usually he could "learn" a face more easily if he could see it represented in two dimensions, as in a snapshot, for example. Even this was not foolproof, but it certainly inclined him towards an interest in planar representations.

An ability to reduce topography to two dimensions proved to be a solution to one function of his dyslexia. When traveling through an unfamiliar neighborhood, searching for a specific destination, dyslexics are apt to turn left when they should turn right. The projects where the Closes lived when they arrived in Tacoma were laid out on serpentine streets that looped back on one another—potentially very confusing—but Chuck found he could find his way anywhere by picturing the layout of the streets as if represented in the form of a map or an aerial photograph. (Today, he claims that he can draw a plan of every room he has ever been in.)

On top of these challenges, Chuck suffered from a neuromuscular condition and problems with his eyesight. Although strong and well-built, Chuck had difficulty lifting his feet when walking, being inclined to swing his legs from the hips rather than bending the knees in the normal way. This was a nuisance when climbing stairs and, worse, he was unable to run any distance without his legs "seizing up," so that sometimes he tripped over himself and fell. Additionally, he was unable to make effective use of his arms when they were raised above shoulder height so that he could not, for instance, climb a rope or learn to swim the crawl.

Chuck's mother was very much aware of these challenges, which led to numerous visits to doctors' offices, including a specialist in Seattle. There were as many theories as there were appointments. No definitive diagnosis was made, but the possibility was brought up that the condition might result from his heart not pumping enough oxygen to adequately supply his muscles. This was borne out by tests in which it was evident that his muscles rapidly lost strength as he exercised them. (Any hint of a malfunctioning heart must have terrified Millie, given her husband's health problems.) Many years later retrospective diagnoses, such as myasthenia gravis, were put forward, but even then there was no consensus.

The eyesight problems may have been related to the larger neuromuscular condition. Chuck was very nearsighted, suffered from a severe astigmatism, and his right eye "drooped" as did his right eyelid. From an early age he wore corrective lenses in heavy frames that might have caused his contemporaries to ridicule him as a classic "four-eyes," the automatic butt of ritualized cruelties. By the time he was in the early grades at elementary school, however, Chuck had acquired reserves of self-confidence and determination that spared him from this fate. In part, at least, this must be attributed to the fact that his parents offered support that went far beyond simply encouraging him to do his best. It is impossible to know what exactly it was that Millie envisioned for her son, but all the evidence points to the fact that from the beginning she imagined him becoming someone special. Whenever he showed a spark of creative ability, it was nourished. At the same time, she refused to coddle him or allow him to succumb to the family history of phobia. From the time he was little, and despite his eyesight and neuromuscular condition, she would encourage him to do things that seemed risky and even dangerous. If he balked, she would call him a "pantywaist."

"If I wanted to jump off the garage roof," he remembers, "she would tell me to go ahead and do it. She never said 'You'll hurt yourself' or 'You'll poke your eye out.'

"She'd grown up aware that her own mother was chronically phobic—and hating it. I suspect she was phobic, too, but she met hers head-on—refused to give in to them. If she was afraid of something, she went out and did it, and she was determined that I would deal with things the same way. As a result I grew up without knowing when it was appropriate to be scared. I loved to take chances—it gave me an adrenaline rush—and that sometimes became an issue when I was raising my own kids. I'd be in the playground, encouraging Georgia or Maggie to jump off the jungle gym—not even thinking of it as risky—and other parents would look at me as if I was out of my mind."

He recalls how, when he was still very young, the family was hiking on the cliffs one day when his mother set out on a narrow track of loose shale, little more than a ledge with a steep drop on one side. When Chuck balked at following her, she said, "You know how to walk, don't you? You walk okay at home. What's so different about this?"

Her husband too was not one to display or promote excessive caution. Chuck recalls how, when they were camping in the mountains, his father decided to photograph a large brown bear. He walked up to it and released the camera's shutter inches from the bear's snout. Then, to show there was nothing to be afraid of, he reached out and touched the bear's nose, retreating—but not hurriedly—only when the bear snarled.

Learning to be unafraid was an important legacy, but the diligence with which Chuck's parents encouraged him to cultivate creative skills was just as crucial.

One way in which he learned to compensate for his lack of athletic prowess was by becoming an entertainer. He might have a problem seeing and hitting a curveball, but he was able to develop the sleight of hand skills needed to perform conjuring tricks, so that—wearing a costume devised by his mother from a thrift shop coat and a battered top hat—he became a magician. (This marked the beginning of a preoccupation with costume as a form of self-expression that would continue through his college years.) Meanwhile, his father built him a puppet theater for which Chuck devised spectacles to entertain his school pals. A nascent sense of showmanship enabled him to draw his contemporaries into these performances—a talent that later would prove invaluable as an adjunct to his painting skills, as anyone who has witnessed his interaction with an audience, or even seen him interviewed on television, can attest. Instead of being an outsider, he became one of the more popular kids on the block. It was, in his own words, a matter of maximizing his skills and minimizing his deficits, a balancing act that would define his progress in the world. He already knew, instinctively, that he had to find a way to beat the system.

Though he loved to perform, his biggest passion was for making art, and he claims that by the time he was five years old he knew that he wanted to be an artist, and specifically a painter. When he was six or seven, he asked his parents for "real paints." The Genuine Weber Oil Color set—its fat tubes bulging with pigments suspended in luscious poppy and linseed oils, the smell so seductive—was ordered from the Sears, Roebuck catalogue, but the easel that accompanied it had been lovingly constructed by Leslie Close at the McChord Field sheet metal shop.

There is no entirely satisfactory way of accounting for how a child acquires the ability to convincingly represent the world on a sheet of paper—to take the first steps towards a mastery of pictorial illusion, an almost magical skill not accessible to most adults. This is not to suggest that Chuck immediately drew or painted like an accomplished artist, but rather that from the outset he strove to do so, and with considerable success. His precociousness at representing objects in two dimensions extended, for example, to an early intuitive understanding of perspective. In a 1987 interview conducted for the Smithsonian, he recalled an occasion when that particular accomplishment got him into trouble at school:

> It must have been somewhere between first and third grades. . . . Everyone made a drawing of their own house and colored it the color their house was, etcetera. I made a drawing of our house in perspective. The teacher wanted it to be . . . wrong. She didn't know how to draw in perspective, so she kept telling me that mine was wrong. . . . I had the sense of outrage . . . I knew I could do it and that I was right and that somebody else who did not understand the system could force me to do it the wrong way.[1]

More usually, though, his budding skill with pencils and paintbrushes won plaudits and presumably encouraged him in his early enthusiasm to become an artist. Beyond that, and his parents' support, it's not easy to see where the impetus might have come from. Most of his first five years had been spent in Everett—population a little over 30,000 in the 1940 census—a gritty working-class town with docks, lumberyards, and the world's largest paper pulping mill, a sprawling, throbbing monster that filled the air around the clock with the stench of the sulfates used to "cook" logs into pulp. (Chuck recalls the odor with extreme distaste, which makes it surprising to discover that he has produced a substantial body of work utilizing pulped paper.) Still, it would be unfair to dismiss Everett as merely an industrial eyesore blighting the picturesque shores of one of America's most beautiful waterways. The city had plenty of character—and was home to its fair share of characters—but it was not the kind of community where it was commonplace for children to be funneled towards the arts. It was devoid of galleries and museums, and Chuck's family did not associate with the kind of people—mill owners, or the professional classes—who might have had "real" paintings, however conventional, on the wall. In those days, though, billboards, as well as magazine illustrations and advertisements, often reproduced hand-painted images of a sort that were in fact more likely to capture the imagination of a very young aspiring artist than the work of Picasso or Poussin. Chuck readily acknowledges the early influence of commercial art on his development.

His other hometown, Tacoma, was larger than Everett and could boast an art museum—founded in 1935 as the Tacoma Art Association—which over the years occupied several temporary homes, including a former jailhouse. Basically, though, Tacoma was another hardscrabble, blue-collar town that had come to prominence as the western terminus of the Northern Pacific Railroad, which, along with the city's location on Puget Sound, made it an important shipping center. As with Everett, the lumber industry played a major role in the local economy and provided patronage for what cultural activity there was.

When it came to indigenous culture, Tacoma and Everett were virtually twins. The same gleaming Studebakers, Hudsons, and DeSotos graced the billboards, along with the same bowls of steaming Campbell's Soup and the same skillfully rendered, much-larger-than-life, frosty cans of Olympia beer. The same scrupulously cared-for Fords and Chevys sat in the driveways, and the same eagle-embellished mailboxes awaited the arrival of the same magazines—*Look*, *Collier's*, *Ladies' Home Journal*, *Good Housekeeping*, *Life*, *Popular Mechanics*, *Reader's Digest*, *National Geographic*, *The Saturday Evening Post*, *Boy's Life*—carrying the same ads for Maytag and Whirlpool appliances, Perma-lift girdles and Peter Pan bras, Pillsbury cake mixes and Sealtest ice cream, Old Gold cigarettes and Old Forester bourbon. The Madison Avenue ad agencies of the period employed artists who knew how to render the fresh cheeks of a doe-eyed teenager so enticingly that you longed to kiss them—but only after you'd sipped from the fluted bottle of Coke, dripping with icy condensation, that she caressed with her pretty fingers. Along with the genre covers of *Collier's* and the *Post*, and the slick illustrations for short stories about cowpokes, coeds, cops, con men, corporate romances, and court room shenanigans, these advertising images provided the young provincial artist with his own museum without walls.

For Chuck, an eye-opening experience came courtesy of, of all unlikely events, a Billy Graham Crusade. He was taken to one of the evangelist's rallies at the field house of the University of Puget Sound. While the Reverend Graham preached, and members of the congregation prepared to commit themselves to Christ, Chuck was riveted by what was happening directly behind the evangelist. Three large white panels had been set up, abutting one another so as to form an elongated rectangle similar in proportion to a CinemaScope movie screen. As the rally unfolded, an artist covered their surface, from left to right—at astonishing speed—with biblical scenes culminating in the Crucifixion, rendered in chalk in a vigorous chiaroscuro style that Chuck describes as Rembrandtesque.

And when the Reverend Graham's exhortation ended, the house lights were doused and black light was directed onto the panels behind him. The biblical scenes were miraculously replaced by a huge and melodramatic rendering of the Four Horsemen of the Apocalypse, complete with intimations of thunder and lightning.

"That did it," says Chuck. "I was sold. I joined the line of people giving themselves to Christ, except I was trying to get as near to the stage as I could to get a better look at the art. That was the first time I experienced the emotional impact art can have."

At home, too, Chuck witnessed the making of things that could be thought of as art, though at that time they probably would have been dismissed as examples of household craft and nothing more. Sixty years on he remembers watching his grandmother crochet, fascinated by the slow, incremental process of creating individual squares of looped yarn—each a unique and distinctive invention—which she piled into stacks on the floor before eventually assembling them into banquet-sized table coverings, a process not dissimilar to the incremental way in which he builds his paintings today. He recalls too how the completed table covering was blocked and starched by being soaked in sugar water and stretched on a frame in the backyard.

Undoubtedly, too, Leslie Close's ability to turn his hand to almost anything, and to do so with dexterity and flair, was another crucial example for his son. The work Chuck Close has produced as a mature artist has always been characterized by superb craftsmanship—a respect for skillful fabrication for its own sake—that must have derived to a significant extent from watching his father constructing toys and other more practical objects in his garage workshop, or in the more fully equipped shops at Paine Field and McChord Field. Leslie Close's legacy to his son was considerable. Tragically, it would be cut short.

Chapter 3

Life Lessons

Nineteen fifty-one was a difficult year for the Close family. Leslie, who turned forty-eight years old that July, remained in nominal charge of the metal shop at McChord Field, but recurring health problems meant that he was frequently absent from work. Ten years his junior, Millie continued to give piano lessons but was increasingly obliged to devote her attention to her husband's medical issues, and now to her son's, too. Chuck was still enrolled at Oakland Elementary School but was unable to attend classes most of that year, suffering from nephritis, an inflammation of the kidneys. In those days, the prescribed treatment for this condition was total bed rest—it would last for several months in his case—combined with a salt-free high protein diet. Since the Closes had to weigh every dollar they spent, this typically meant eating unseasoned horsemeat twice a day. (Horsemeat was widely available in the United States in the period following World War II.) Isolated from the world of his contemporaries, Chuck, who would turn eleven that summer, was forced to entertain himself as best he could, and his severe dyslexia meant that losing himself in a book was not an option. His escapes were the radio, comics, drawing paper, and a boxed set of eighty Mongol colored pencils.

Decades later, collectors and curators visiting Close's New York studio were likely to find *The Edge of Night* or *As the World Turns* playing on a small black-and-white television set strategically placed alongside the canvas he was working on. Soap operas, peripherally absorbed, took the edge off the monotony of the repetitive, almost mechanical, process involved in producing meticulous, hand-made enlargements of photographic images. His addiction to the soaps began in Tacoma during this bout with nephritis. In 1951, the Closes did not own a television, but daytime radio dramas like *Stella Dallas* and *Young Doctor Malone* still enjoyed a sizable audience and played on plastic Philco portables and veneered

Motorola radio-phonographs in kitchens and living rooms all over America. Improbable as it may seem, for the better part of a year the future painter of ruthlessly detailed–some would say pitiless–supersized portraits, waited anxiously every afternoon, along with millions of housewives, to learn if Helen Trent could triumph in her pursuit of romance "at the age of thirty-five . . . and even beyond. . . ."

His portal to the airwaves was a smallish, wood-grained set on a bedside table within easy reach of where he sat propped up against a nest of pillows, sometimes thumbing through a comic as he listened. (Uninterested in action comics and superheroes, he preferred the "funnies"–*Nancy and Sluggo, Scrooge McDuck*, or the Dell comics featuring Looney Tunes characters like Bugs Bunny and Sylvester.)

In the evening, came the more age-appropriate action serials–*Sky King, The Lone Ranger, Sergeant Preston of the Yukon, The Green Hornet*–and later still spookier mysteries like *Inner Sanctum* (which he found thrillingly scary). And, just as he would one day paint with the television playing–the image on screen largely ignored–so often he would sit up in bed and draw, creating his own world as the networks delivered tales of adventure and intrigue punctuated by commercials for Wheaties, Beech-Nut gum, and Palmolive shaving cream. He could even cross the invisible barrier and enter that world by means of a microphone that his father had rigged to the radio's speaker, allowing Chuck to assume the guise of an announcer or to impersonate Walter Winchell greeting all the ships at sea.

This confinement lasted through an uncharacteristically hot summer, into the fall and the long, wet Pacific Northwest winter, beyond the Christmas holidays and deep into the New Year.

Chuck's nephritis was by no means the only thing Millie Close had to worry about. Far more serious was the deterioration of her husband's condition. The adhesions and other complications that followed his ruptured appendix had guaranteed that good health could never be taken for granted. In the early years of his marriage he contracted rheumatic fever, apparently from a strep infection that had been inadequately treated. Although he was nursed back to health by Millie and her parents, this caused permanent damage to his cardiac system, and on one occasion he suffered a heart attack while working at the top of a telephone pole, surviving only because of his safety harness. The medication used to control his heart condition began to cause blood clots that by 1951 were causing frequent hospitalizations followed by periods of home recuperation. (Years later, Millie would tell her son that on four or five occasions doctors had told her that she should prepare for the worst.) On top of his heart problems, an accident in the sheet metal shop at McChord Field—Leslie had fallen backward and cracked his skull against the concrete floor—had caused a concussion and injured his spine. Even before this, he had suffered from a chronically bad back, and now he was obliged to wear a brace that ran from his neck to his coccyx, a device so substantial it could be seen through his suit.

The ill health that had been a constant of the Closes' seventeen-year marriage probably explains why they elected not to have more children. By 1951, a recurring pattern of incapacity was beginning to cast a pall over family life since Millie was all too aware of how precarious the situation had become, and Chuck, although protected from the worst news, must have sensed it as well.

Until illness intervened, both Les and Millie had been active in the community. Millie in particular was a dynamo, focused and determined, especially where her son's well-being was perceived as being at risk, so that almost inevitably she had become president of the school PTA, and even the leader of Chuck's Cub Scout pack. Although she actively encouraged him to be independent and fearless, there were times when she could not resist fighting Chuck's battles for him. She was the sort of mother whom principals dread seeing in their office, and the kind whose offspring are in corresponding dread of the potentially embarrassing consequences of such interventions.

On the surface, the Closes were regular folk, much like their neighbors. They attended the local Methodist church, and much of their social life involved church activities. They lived modestly and retained a close relationship with Millie's parents and Bina, traveling regularly to Everett to see them and receiving frequent visits in return. In fact, however, the dynamic of the Close household was not as typical as it appeared to be from the outside. The parlor grand piano that took up a sizable part of the tiny living room was symbolic of aspirations towards culture that were not routine in South Tacoma. Those aspirations arose principally from Millie, but were fully embraced by Leslie who—perhaps because of his early experience helping his mother in the kitchen at the ranch—was anything but the prototypical fifties husband with rigid ideas about a woman's place in the world (though he might have drawn the line at encouraging Millie to take a job outside the home). There was a sense of equality to the Closes' marriage that sometimes expressed itself in a mild form of gender reversal that was unusual for the period. For all his skills at the workbench, Leslie liked nothing better than to bake and cook so that on weekends he could often be found rolling pastry while Millie performed some traditional male chore such as changing the piston rings on the family's green 1941 Studebaker (though she would do so under her husband's tutelage).

Still Life by Chuck Close, oil on canvas board, c. 1950

Millie also had a highly developed sense of social justice that on a number of occasions led her to take up unpopular causes. In the wake of Pearl Harbor, for example, she had been outraged at the internment of Japanese-Americans, some of whom had been her schoolmates in Auburn. Not one to be shy, she took part in a protest on the steps of the State Capitol in Olympia, bravely expressing her opinions at a time when anti-Japanese feelings had reached the rabid stage. Chuck would grow up greatly admiring his mother's political independence and her willingness to take stands against injustice.

As already noted, both Millie and Leslie were unusual too in the lengths to which they would go to encourage their son's precocious artistic ambition. There was more than a little of the classic stage mother in Millie's makeup—she was after all a frustrated artist. It was her husband, however, who had taken the practical step of finding Chuck an art teacher.

Les had been in the habit of interrupting his four-mile morning commute to McChord Field to eat breakfast at a small diner on Route 99, usually ordering

Mount Rainier, Curve in the Road, Fall, c. 1950

bacon and eggs with hash browns and toast slathered in butter. (Given the date, he was probably unaware of any connection between his dietary preferences and heart disease or stroke.) Chuck remembers the diner fondly as a place where you mixed your own soda from seltzer and syrup, but more significantly there were paintings on its walls that appeared to be the work of someone who had received professional training. At some point, probably in the winter of 1948–49, Les made the acquaintance of the artist, a youngish woman who lived just across the highway from the diner. Discovering that she had attended the Art Students

League in New York, he asked her if she would consider giving his son lessons, which she agreed to do.

Once a week for two and a half years, beginning when he was eight, Chuck would be dropped off at the ramshackle building—not much better than a flophouse, he recalls—that his teacher shared with several other women. As might be expected of an alumna of the Art Students League, his instructor had a solid command of academic technique, and her pupil remembers being set to work on still lifes and, sometimes, when the weather permitted, landscapes painted *en plein air.* There were also, he reports, figure drawing sessions for which some of his teacher's housemates posed nude or partially clothed. He also recalls that men sometimes came to the door during his lesson and were sent away and told to return later. Clearly this was not a run-of-the-mill Truman-era Tacoma household. It may not have borne much of a resemblance to the luxurious Parisian *maisons closes* once frequented and portrayed by Degas and Toulouse-Lautrec, but Chuck remains convinced that the classroom in which he received his earliest art training probably doubled as a bordello.

The lessons at the decrepit house across from the diner came to an end in 1951, interrupted by the onset of nephritis and by the growing concerns about Leslie Close's health. The problem with blood clots continued, and in the early weeks of 1952—just as Chuck's health was finally showing signs of improvement—Leslie suffered a particularly bad attack that led to hospitalization and a prolonged period of recuperation at home, so that Chuck and his father were undergoing bed rest in adjacent rooms.

The layout of 3317 South Monroe Street was not unlike that of a New Orleans shotgun house, with the living room, master bedroom, and Chuck's bedroom lined up like so many boxes placed end to end, connected by doors that, when open, provided a direct line of sight the length of the building. To reach Chuck's room from the living room, it was necessary to pass through his parents' bedroom. The bed in Chuck's room was placed with its head against the back wall, so he could see directly through the facing doorway. The bed in his parents' room, however, had its headboard up against a sidewall, meaning that all Chuck could see of it through the open door was its foot.

One afternoon towards the end of February, always a gloomy time of year in the Pacific Northwest, Chuck was alone in the house with his father, the door between the rooms open. Probably the radio was silent because of Leslie's condition, or at least turned down very low. It can be presumed that the box of Mongol pencils was somewhere nearby along with a drawing pad and a pencil sharpener. As he lay there, Chuck heard his father trying to get out of bed and sensed something was wrong. Alert now, Chuck saw his father pitch forward, framed by the proscenium arch of the doorway—falling out of sight to the left—and he heard a sickening thud as his father's skull came into violent contact with a chest of drawers. Weakened by his months in bed, Chuck moved as fast as he could to his father's aid, finding him in a pool of blood with a gash to his head. Since no one else was at home, yelling for help would have been useless. Chuck tried to revive his father—attempted to assist him to his feet, but was unable to budge him. Leslie Close had suffered a massive stroke.

It's difficult to imagine a more traumatic event for an eleven-year-old to have experienced. While his comatose father clung to life in a Tacoma hospital, Chuck was cared for by his grandmother, who came down from Everett. Millie kept a vigil at her husband's bedside, where Bina spent as much time as she could comforting her. Chuck was not told how serious his father's condition was, but he had witnessed the fall and its immediate aftermath and he overheard the tears and the whispered conversations, and remembers blurting out, "He's going to die, isn't he?"

His father never regained consciousness, but his damaged heart displayed surprising resilience, keeping him alive long enough for the doctors to find it worthwhile to cut away a circular section of skull to relieve pressure on the brain. On Saturday, March 1, 1952, at the age of 48, Leslie Durward Close died. Three days later, he was buried in Tacoma's Evergreen Cemetery.

Since Bina still worked for the casket company, the coffin was rather grand, with a plush silk-satin lining. No viewing had been scheduled, but when the family entered the funeral home, the lid of the coffin had been left open so that Chuck saw his father there, barely recognizable—almost a stranger—with pancake makeup on his face and his fingers—which held his Bible—swollen so that his wedding ring cut into the flesh. Strangest of all for Chuck was the skullcap—made from the same material as the lining of the casket—used to cover the shaved area where the disc-shaped section of skull had been removed.

Seeing that Chuck was upset, his grandfather sought to reassure him, clumsily explaining that Leslie's soul had "escaped" the body so that now there was nothing left but its shell. (Charlie Wagner was a man of few words—many of them swear words—and may in fact have suffered from Tourette syndrome.) Attempting to make his point more concrete, he rapped on the corpse's skull with his knuckles. The hollow and surprisingly loud sound this produced further traumatized the already distressed boy.

That night, Mildred Close insisted that her son share her bed, an arrangement that would continue for some time to come. No impropriety should be read into this, but the inappropriateness of the arrangement was not lost on the boy.

"It was," says Chuck, "a long time before I understood the Freudian implications, but at the time I was very uncomfortable about it. After all, I wasn't a four-year-old—I was almost twelve. I sensed this was not right, but my mother didn't catch my discomfort—it went right by her. When it came to things like that, she was emotionally tone-deaf."

Presumably Millie must have excused this sleeping arrangement to herself, if she even felt the need to do so, as a way of blunting grief, but the Freudian aspect of the situation is inescapable, and it would not just disappear as Chuck entered adolescence. It seems fair to say that it was at this point that Millie's already fierce involvement with her son crossed a line and became overtly unhealthy. The oedipal dimension of the arrangement cannot have failed to have had an impact on Chuck's development, both emotionally and in terms of a sense of guilt where his father's death was concerned. He would carry that guilt with him into his adulthood, though he would eventually resolve it in a way that would prove crucial to his very existence.

The events and emotions that surrounded Leslie Close's death tightened an already taut bond between mother and child, one that in time would threaten to strangle both of them. Until then there had been a third person in the equation, and an ailing one at that, in need of a significant portion of Millie's love and attention. Now there was just Chuck, and where he was concerned, Millie's devotion and barely suppressed desire was inseparable from vicarious ambition. She had not had the opportunities she felt herself worthy of. She had spent her life looking after other people. Now she intended to make sure that her son enjoyed his full measure of opportunity, and she looked forward to sharing completely in his successes.

Chapter 4

Everett

One consequence of Leslie Close's death was that, within a few months, Millie and Chuck moved back to Everett. This was partly because Millie could no longer afford to keep the house on South Monroe Street, but doubtless she was also anxious to be close to her family in this trying period, and in fact she and Chuck moved to 6608 Cady Road, next door to her parents, buying the house with Blanche and Charlie's help, the Wagners having moved from 6608 to 6612, the house that Millie and Leslie had rented during the war years. This was in South Everett, about three miles from downtown and not far from a section called Lowell, in those days a rough neighborhood, its focal point a hill lined with the dilapidated frame homes of machinists and shingle weavers who worked in the mills.

Cady Road was a cut or two above those ramshackle hillside streets and living there seemed like an ideal arrangement, since Millie would now have to find a full-time job and, living so close to his grandparents, Chuck would have somewhere to go when he came home from school.

There was a downside to this, however. In her manuscript, Bina describes how Chuck's grandmother became "possessive and concerned" about the entire family, but especially about Chuck and Millie. Despite her ailments and her tendency to be high-strung, Blanche had once been able to hold down a job at a department store, where she had been a corset-fitter, but around 1950 she began to display early symptoms of Parkinson's disease, and after that became reluctant to stray far from home. By the time Millie and Chuck returned to Everett, this had reached the point of full-blown agoraphobia. Blanche still went to church every Sunday—but had to be driven there, even though it was only a block away. Occasionally she would allow herself to be taken to the homes of family members such as her older sister Mabel, who lived a short drive away in Renton. Otherwise she never left her house, so that her husband was obliged to handle chores such as grocery shopping.

Charlie Wagner had his own problems. Not long after Chuck's father died, Charlie, then in his mid-sixties, had a serious accident in a drying kiln at the lumber mill where he worked, falling onto an eight-foot rotary fan. As he fell, he had the presence of mind to thrust his left arm out, knowing that the fan would turn off automatically as soon as it bit into any part of his flesh. This probably saved his life, but his arm was severed almost completely above the biceps, though it remained joined to his shoulder by a flimsy web of tissue. This mishap occurred in an isolated section of the mill, so there was no one around to help. Charlie stuffed his left hand into the side pocket of his jacket and made his way to his car (this involved crawling out of the housing of the kiln). With his arm now hanging out of the driver-side window, he drove—shifting and steering with his right hand—to Everett General Hospital, bypassing Providence Hospital (which would have been closer) because he did not want to be cared for by nuns. He managed to make his way to the entrance of the emergency room before collapsing from a massive loss of blood. Astonishingly, given the period, surgeons were able to reattach his arm. He recovered only very limited movement, but nonetheless eventually returned to work.

As an example of an individual's determination and ability to overcome life-altering trauma, this certainly made an impression on the young Chuck Close, and it is reasonable to suppose that it contributed to the battery of resources he would draw upon decades later when faced with his own life-altering crisis.

Charlie's accident undoubtedly had a negative impact on his wife's already nervous disposition and intensified her possessiveness towards her daughter and grandson. According to Bina, this meant that Millie and Chuck never had any time to be alone together to "do the things that [they] liked to do." Millie would occasionally take Chuck away on camping trips, an activity they had enjoyed with Leslie, but expeditions of that sort were apt to make Blanche sick with worry (her concern perhaps amplified by her awareness of Millie's propensity for risk-taking). The pressure on Millie must have been enormous, and Chuck too must have found it suffocating at times, yet there can be no doubt that this remained a very loving environment in which to grow up, and Chuck adored his grandparents, especially his grandmother. He was showered with praise for his talents, and this seems to have gone a long way towards offsetting the academic problems he encountered at school, and certainly did no harm to his ego.

Despite her caveats, Bina paints a picture of a tight family unit, three generations gathered around the radio, and later the television set, enjoying prizefights and baseball games together—a tradition in the Albro family that went back to Nebraska days. There was no TV in his own house, but Chuck would watch shows like *The Mickey Mouse Club* at his grandparents'. His strongest memory of early television is of becoming caught up in the 1954 Army-McCarthy hearings, which precipitated Senator Joseph McCarthy's downfall. His grandfather, he recalls—a firm believer in the threat posed by "commies" and fellow travelers—thought McCarthy was a great man.

More routinely, one can imagine Chuck coming home from school and sitting at his grandmother's table, working on his latest drawing while subliminally taking in the deliberation with which she crocheted square after square.

"It had a calming effect on her," he says. "It was an antidote to her nervousness. Time was not important—the process would take however long it was going to take, and I learned from that."

Millie, meanwhile, was faced with having to find work. She had no practical training or experience of any kind and she first found a retail job at a J.C. Penney department store, but in her spare time she would drop in on Bina at the casket factory and practice on the office machines there. After a while, she acquired the necessary skills to become a civil servant in the office of the county assessor, and later secured a position in the medical supply department of the hospital at Paine Field, the facility having reverted to military use once more. Later still, she would study successfully for a real estate license.

Upon his return to Everett, Chuck enrolled at South Junior High School, still suffering from the aftereffects of his bout with nephritis, meaning that for the time being he was excused from gym and sports, which must have come as a relief since he would need all his energy and concentration to deal with regular classwork. His health remained such a concern that for a while he was forbidden to walk between the school's main building and its annex, which were separated by a steep incline.

Chuck describes his academic problems as having been centered on difficulties with memorization. It was not a question of having a poor memory—he had an excellent memory for everyday events and many kinds of information—but rather of being unable to retain data that was presented in the way that was considered "normal" within the educational conventions of the era, in textbooks or on a blackboard. Such difficulties tend to have a way of reinforcing themselves since the inability to master them inevitably triggers anxiety, in turn making the task that much harder. In grade school Chuck had had a hard time memorizing such things as names and dates, leading some staff members to assume that he was a malingerer, but in general he had been able to get by. As with many dyslexics, however, he found that in middle school the challenges increased, which he attributes to the fact that he now had to cope with tests and exams that brought into play the phenomenon of success being measured in the cruel form of marks and grades. At the same time, the lessons being taught became more elaborate, requiring the ability to process more complex ideas.

In those days, there was no school psychologist to turn to for advice, so Chuck had to improvise ways of proving to the teaching staff that he was not just lazy and stupid. He had learned that it paid to make sure that he was *seen* to be alert—by being the first to raise his hand when a question was asked, for example—and he continued to use his abilities as a budding visual artist to enhance his work and make an impression on teachers. At South Junior High, he would marshal these talents to more deliberate effect as he wrestled with the increasingly demanding assignments. Success often depended on whether or not the teacher he was dealing with was willing to go along with his strategies. In seventh grade, he had the good fortune to have a homeroom teacher who was especially sympathetic to his efforts. It was during that year that he responded to a history assignment by producing a ten-foot-long illustrated map that presented the story of the Lewis and Clark expedition in a way that was far more effective than any written essay could have been. Not surprisingly, this was extremely well received, and the thirteen-year-old must have found great satisfaction and encouragement in realizing that when his strategy worked he was capable of earning a level of praise that his contemporaries could not hope to achieve by writing a conventional paper. His growing mastery over visual material could be a source of power.

Sometimes.

In eighth grade, he ran up against a by-the-book pedagogue named Ruth Packard, who was impervious to his attempts to impress with his creativity.

"I wanted to kill that woman," Close remembers. "She was rigid. I would try everything I knew to get her to bend, but she wouldn't give an inch."

The unrelenting Miss Packard handed him straight Ds, which led to Chuck being directed to a stream of low achievers.

It was Ruth Packard who insisted that he would never be able to tackle algebra, trigonometry, chemistry, or physics. It meant that he was put in classes with "the dumbest of the dumb—hicks from the lumber camps that came to school in bib overalls." Instead of chemistry and physics, they studied "general science," and instead of algebra and trigonometry, "general math," with curricula that were so dumbed-down it was virtually impossible to fail. As for literature, Close reports, "They'd give us a year to read a single book. In fact, you didn't have to read it because you could go out to a drugstore and buy the Classic Comics version. In that environment, I was the star student."

All students were entitled to music classes and art classes several times a week, a fact to which Chuck attaches enormous significance.

"It's one of my strongest beliefs," he says, "that kids should have access to art and music programs, preferably five times a week. At a recent dinner party, I had a big fight with [New York City] Mayor Bloomberg, and the [New York City] Schools Chancellor [Joel I. Klein]. The city has been shifting funds from the arts to remedial education, which I believe is disastrous. They both argued that this was the way to deal with the dropout rate. I told them they were crazy. Arts programs give kids a reason to stay in school. If kids with problems discover there's something they're good at, they're much less likely to drop out. I know this from personal experience. I dread to think what might have become of me if I hadn't had those classes to look forward to."

The art and music classes at South Junior High not only gave Chuck a reprieve from his general science and general math classmates, they also brought him into contact with mainstream students. It was in the art room that he began to hang out with Donn Trethewey and Larenzo Stair, who would become lifelong friends.

Trethewey remembers first becoming aware of Chuck, in seventh grade, on Sadie Hawkins Day, "a day in which costumes were allowed, in fact invited, to be worn, and a day when girls could ask guys to be their lunch dates. Heady stuff..."

Trethewey came as a hobo, wearing "the same costume that appeared every Halloween." Chuck made more of a splash. He arrived at school that day in a Tarzan costume, sewn from leopard skin fabric, with Jingles, his pet squirrel monkey, perched on his shoulder. (He had bought the monkey with money he had saved, most of it earned by picking strawberries. He had it for a couple of years before it became sick and died, possibly from ingesting DDT along with the fruit that formed the bulk of its diet.) Chuck's flair for the theatrical was readily apparent, and his contemporaries evidently attached far more significance to this than to the fact that his grades were terrible, as is borne out by Larry Stair's recollections.

"Chuck could walk into any room, any group, and act like he belonged," he recalls. "He always had a way of talking from an area of knowledge, or plausible bullshit, [and] that ability certainly required intelligence and garnered my respect.... [He] was not in my homeroom at Junior High so I never thought twice about any academic problem [he might have]. I just knew he had talent and a good sense of humor. I don't think there was a conception of dyslexia in that era, or other diagnoses ... especially by any school nurse or psychologist hired by the Everett School District...."

Chuck with pet monkey, c. 1954

"[Chuck and I] tended to group together because we did have similar humorous insights and aesthetic interests that separated us from the Purple Gang bad boys, unless they were talking about girls. Then we listened in. We both needed all the help we could get there."

Trethewey agrees that the concept of learning disabilities had not crossed the threshold of anyone's consciousness at South Junior High, and concurs that Chuck had a good deal going for himself socially, not the least of which was his casually flaunted self-confidence. His new friends were not even aware that he rubbed shoulders daily with academic bottom-feeders. Nor did these friends have much knowledge of his family background, in part because they lived some distance from South Everett so that there was not much socializing after school.

"I doubt," says Trethewey, "if any of us knew of [Chuck's] dad passing away.... Few of us knew Chuck was an only child."

The ninth grade art teacher was Helen Cook, whom Chuck remembers with approval as having provided him with encouragement. Both Donn Trethewey and Larry Stair self-deprecatingly recall spending much of their time that year rendering Korean War dogfights between F-86 Saber Jets and Russian-built Mig-15s, while Chuck more ambitiously made "cartoonish character drawings," says Trethewey, adding that Chuck spoke at that time of having ambitions to be a political caricaturist. (This would have been at about the period he was mesmerized by the Army-McCarthy hearings.) Both Close and Trethewey recollect being asked to do a lot of craftwork—assignments such as die-stamped belts and designs burned into wood. Close remembers that Miss Cook required everyone to produce an "art scrapbook" in which they made a record of the year's projects. Chuck

Chuck Close and his dog Laddie, behind the house on Cady Road, Everett, c. 1954

included in his some of the nude drawings he had made during his private art classes in Tacoma. Surprisingly, Miss Cook acknowledged them with equanimity, while they of course made Chuck the envy of his male classmates.

It was readily apparent that Chuck Close was more serious about making art, and more ambitious than any of his classmates, but Stair and Trethewey too seem to have progressed that year beyond their dogfight periods, becoming along with Chuck charter members of the South Junior Art Club where somewhat higher aspirations prevailed. For the three of them, it marked the beginning of a close association that would continue for almost a decade and friendships that would last much longer.

After school, back at Cady Road, Chuck honed his skills with a self-devised program of extracurricular studies, analyzing and imitating the work of illustrators who came into the house by way of magazines ranging from *Collier's* and *The Saturday Evening Post* to *Boy's Life* and *Look*. This was a golden age of American illustration, with artists such as Robert Fawcett, John Gannam, Steven Dohanos, and of course Norman Rockwell, at the height of their powers. Chuck wanted to figure out how they achieved their effects—how each of them marshaled his own bag of tricks to conjure up the illusion of form and space on a two-dimensional surface. It is easy to imagine him poring over one of Gannam's watercolor illustrations, absorbing the way in which the artist rendered a satisfying sense of reality with studied economy of means, or looking through his grandmother's magnifying glass—which he inherited when she died, and still treasures—at the details of a Dohanos *Post* cover painted with an exacting technique virtually identical to that employed by painters who twenty years later would be hailed as the pioneers of photorealism.

Close notes the influence at the time of the illustrators who made up the faculty of The Famous Artists School, a correspondence course launched in 1948 and advertised in many of the magazines where their work appeared, as well as on matchbooks.

"I remember being sent away to Bible camp. I didn't play sports and do all those things you're supposed to do in those places, but there was this fat kid there who had the Famous Artists course and we'd hide out in a cabin and pore over it for hours. Later I got to meet some of those guys and I'm still friendly with Will Barnet who was one of the faculty."

Not surprisingly, in view of later developments, Chuck's favorite illustrators were the artists who painted portraits for the cover of *Time*, notably Ernest Hamlin Baker and Boris Chaliapin. These men were the heirs to an academic tradition that had become largely discredited in the world of high art, but flourished in this journalistic context.

Close devoured their paintings in reproduction, learning everything he could about the way in which the likeness of a politician or an entertainer could be engineered. He applied the same analytical keenness to reproductions of old master paintings in books borrowed from the library, and in the family copy of *The Childcraft Encyclopedia*. (There were in fact very few books in the house, and then mostly the anthologies of concise versions of best sellers published by *Reader's Digest*.)

Today Close is convinced that his hunger to understand the mechanics of pictorialism had much to do with his dyslexia and his prosopagnosia. Even in two dimensions, he had some difficulty recognizing faces, but understanding how an artist like Chaliapin created a likeness—for example, by distributing light and shadow to obtain a chiaroscuro effect—was helpful. Analyzing how a painting was built taught him to break down a whole into component parts that could be more easily digested. This would have broader implications too, since, as he grew older and his difficulties at school increased, he discovered that by breaking academic tasks down into their component parts he could master them more easily. The incremental process by which he would make paintings as an adult is clearly prefigured in his early struggles to overcome his perceived learning disabilities.

For Chuck, painterly illusion was a conjuring trick he wanted to master for himself, but, not long after moving back to Everett, he had an experience that momentarily challenged his infatuation with that kind of visual magic. His mother took him to the Seattle Museum to see "real" paintings. There he encountered his first Jackson Pollock, a smallish drip painting, on loan to the museum, which shocked him profoundly. It was, he says, as if he had heard profanities shouted from the pulpit of a church. This was not art, it was sacrilege! Transgression had its allures, however, and he soon found himself dribbling paint onto his own carefully rendered earlier works.

It was while at South Junior High that Chuck began to find his mother's often-overzealous interventions in his affairs difficult to tolerate. Sometimes she merely caused him embarrassment. When, for example, parents were asked to bring in baby pictures, she brought a snapshot of Chuck seated on the potty. That level of discomfort, however, was no worse than the humiliations Chuck was exposed to in gym classes, when he was finally given medical clearance to participate, or in English classes (because of his inability to memorize), but other episodes involving Millie were harder to take.

In seventh grade Chuck was enrolled in a woodshop class taught by a man with a sadistic streak, given to mocking his students, and—when he felt his authority was challenged—to pulling down their pants and whacking them across the behind. (Astonishingly, this seems to have been tolerated by the school administration because woodshop was an all-male class.) At this point, Chuck was still under the doctor's care in the wake of his nephritis, and one of the precautions that had been advised was that he should wear long johns at all times, to keep warm. In the woodshop, students were seated on high stools while they were given instructions on how to use a rasp or a miter box. On this particular day Chuck was wearing scratchy long johns that were causing him considerable discomfort. A couple of times he hopped down from the stool, to try to adjust the offending garment. This irritated the teacher. The next time Chuck descended from the stool, the man confronted him, bawled him out, then pulled down his pants and struck him across the rear. As if this was not humiliating enough, he then went on to ridicule Chuck's underwear, encouraging the rest of the class to join in the hilarity.

Chuck tried to keep this from his mother, but she sensed that he was hiding something and eventually got the story out of him. She promptly confronted the principal and demanded that the offending teacher be fired. The very public commotion that ensued was far more embarrassing to Chuck than the workshop incident itself, which would soon have been forgotten. Now he felt himself singled out as a troublemaker. Given his multiple difficulties, academic and otherwise, the last thing he needed was to have a spotlight directed at him. He resolved never to tell his mother about any of his problems again.

It's interesting to try to reconcile the boy who could show up on Sadie Hawkins Day in full Tarzan costume with a monkey on his shoulder—and with the chutzpah to carry it off—and the kid who under other circumstances desperately did not want to draw attention to himself. Chuck was living in two different worlds, in one of which he was in control and wanted to stand out from the crowd, in the other of which he was a potential victim who tried to avoid trouble by blending in with the background. It would be his task over the next few years to resolve the conflicts latent in the gulf that existed between these two sides of his personality.

When he moved on to Everett High School, Chuck remained in the lowest track that took general science and general math. Larry Stair and Donn Trethewey, although they had not sunk that low, were also considered to be underachievers whose grades were unsatisfactory, a fact in which they seem to have taken some pride. The trio continued their friendship in art class which, according to Stair's recollection, was used as a holding pen for misfits and miscreants of all kinds.

"Ms. Mabel Thorsen," he says, "was our first high school art teacher. The most notable memories from that class were the jokes and abuse [she] received from the academically challenged 'students' she was assigned to baby-sit. The boys would blow up prophylactic balloons and play room volleyball with them. Poor Ms. Thorsen had no clue. Folded paper airplanes were launched daily, some even on fire."

In less permissive classrooms, Chuck tried to buckle down to learning. His greatest problem remained his inability to retain information. He used mnemonic tricks to memorize key words, and before a test he would engage in a study ritual that, as he explains it, depended in part upon establishing a state of sensory deprivation. This involved spending hours in a bathtub filled with lukewarm water, a plank placed across it to hold books and file cards, the bathroom in darkness except for a single lamp focused on the notes he was memorizing by rote. (This watery routine inevitably conjures up Jacques-Louis David's 1793 painting of the dead Jacobin revolutionary Jean-Paul Marat, assassinated in his bath. Marat worked and received visitors in the tub because of a painful skin condition. Close reports that the hours he spent partially submerged had the effect of giving his skin the texture of a prune.)

If the test he was studying for took place the next day, as scheduled, Chuck generally did reasonably well. If it was postponed by just twenty-four hours, it was back to the tub. Friends like Stair and Trethewey continued to be unaware both of these learning difficulties and the strategies he employed to counter them. They did take note, though, of the fact that he would employ visual means to respond to assignments whenever possible—but even so they did not make the assumption that this was a matter of necessity being the mother of invention.

"When a project was due," says Stair, "Chuck's were almost always visual solutions that were always unique if not always successful. I just thought he was creative. . . ."

Chuck's well-developed social skills ensured that he remained popular, especially within a group of like-minded boys. No matter how poor his grades, he was fully integrated into campus life, having created niches for himself in various school activities. He built and painted sets for school plays, produced posters for a variety of clubs and events—often working with Stair and Trethewey, which helped further cement their friendships—and contributed cartoons and caricatures to school publications. Also, he had inherited his mother's musical talent, even though he fiercely resisted her attempts to teach him the piano (in part because he found it impossible to coordinate right and left hands on the keyboard). Instead, he chose an instrument she did not play, the saxophone, mastering it well enough—manual coordination did not prove to be a problem in that instance since, he explains, both hands do the same thing—to hold down the lead chair in a number of school groups, from the orchestra to the marching band. Everett High was an entirely white school, but its marching band took its cue from black models, straying from the classic repertoire to perform rock 'n' roll and rhythm 'n' blues numbers, complete with flamboyant choreography, this back in the days when Elvis's pelvic gyrations were still being denounced from pulpits in some parts of the country. Far from provoking moral outrage, the Everett Seagulls' exhibitionist pep band enjoyed a regional following, with the blue-and-gold uniformed strutters being invited to participate in events all over the Northwest and as far away as Northern California.

Chuck Close drawing caricatures
for the "Senior Hi-Jinx" review,
Everett High School, 1958

In addition to making and painting sets, Chuck himself occasionally appeared on stage. A photograph in the school yearbook shows him, dressed in a long smock, a top hat on his head, standing with a just completed caricature of a wavy-haired gent identified by Larry Stair as "Pufty" Cummins, a local sports hero who taught math, coached basketball, and later became the school's health education teacher. This picture was taken at the "Senior Hi-Jinx" review, where Chuck's turn consisted of making a series of rapid likenesses of staff members.

More surprisingly, given his later antiwar, anti–gun violence positions, Chuck was a marksman on the high school rifle team. By joining the gun club he automatically became a member of the National Rifle Association, and this membership entitled him to a seemingly endless supply of free ammunition. (At every opportunity, the point was driven home that Everett High School students represented the last line of defense against Communist incursion.) At different times, Chuck owned various small caliber weapons, including a .32 long barrel pistol. He remembers too a winter when he and other boys sold Christmas trees alongside the highway, for the benefit of Memorial Baptist Church, though in fact they spent most of their time in the nearby woods shooting at one another with BB guns.

He also participated in a volunteer program of aircraft spotting that involved learning to recognize American and Russian-built planes so that if an Ilyushin bomber should materialize in U.S. airspace—say, above the roof of the Everett police station, where the program was headquartered—it would not be mistaken for a B-36 and the citizenry could be alerted to head for the fallout shelters.

Chuck had a knack for striking up friendships in all sectors of the school's population.

"I got along with pretty much everybody," he says, "except maybe the jocks. I even got on with the biker crowd and could count on them to look out for me. But I really made a point of making friends with the freaks and outsiders—kids the others thought of as weird—because they were the people I found interesting. I got to be really friendly with an openly homosexual guy. I'm sure other people said I was gay, but I didn't care. Another friend, Lee Dalton—he became a scientist at Los Alamos—was the prototype geek, fat and awkward and really weird. I preferred to hang out with people like that."

There was time too for girls, though Chuck managed to avoid the fate that befell so many of his contemporaries.

"Maybe it was the long, wet winters," he says. "I was one of the few who wasn't married within a couple of years of graduation—[there were] a lot of shotgun weddings."

During his final year in high school, Chuck dated an attractive girl named Nancy Peterson, who shared his interest in art and displayed considerable ability of her own. Like Chuck, she received encouragement from John Hunt, a small, intense man who ran the art program for juniors and seniors. Nancy was always available when Chuck invited her to a movie or a church social, but proved resistant to his most ardent and persistent advances. It came as a shock to the Everett High population, and to Chuck in particular, when it was learned that Nancy and John Hunt had precipitously departed from Everett as a couple, apparently bound for Paris. Chuck had been dating Nancy up to the eve of her disappearance.

After that humiliating experience, Chuck turned his attention to Betty Cox, an attractive junior at Everett High who had studied piano with Millie. Close describes himself as being relentless in his pursuit of Betty, perhaps because he had been so recently burned. He sent flowers, saved up to buy her Chanel Number 5, and refused to take no for an answer.

Eventually Betty succumbed to this barrage and became Chuck's steady girlfriend for the next couple of years. Donn Trethewey remembers her as "a really pretty young woman . . . quite beautiful in a classic sense." He adds that Chuck tended to be "a bit quiet" when it came to his girlfriends. Trethewey, in fact, had no idea of the extent of the relationship until a decade or so later when he and Betty Cox worked at the same company for a while and she told him about it.

There were also summer jobs. Chuck's first, in junior high, had been picking strawberries. Later, in high school, he worked as a cleaner at a cafeteria in downtown Everett—its booths upholstered in pink Naugahyde—which he remembers for its excellent homemade pies and friendly management. As soon as he had his license, however, he decided he wanted a job driving a delivery van for a local meatpacking company. The company turned down his first application, but he pursued the job as doggedly as he had Betty Cox and eventually was hired.

Chuck employed some of the spare time he managed to salvage from this busy schedule learning to use his father's tools, which he had inherited, making himself useful around the house, and in the process acquiring many practical skills that would stand him in good stead in his future life, whether stretching canvases or refurbishing a loft (despite his repeated insistence that he is a hopeless klutz).

He recalls, "Anything that needed fixing, [my father would] always fix it. Anything that needed making, he'd make it. It was just taken for granted because he was so good at it and he enjoyed doing it. So he never really showed me how to do things, but from the time I was little I'd watched him in his workshop, and sometimes in the sheet metal shop, so I had some idea of what you were supposed to do."

Anyone who knows Chuck Close today is sure to be impressed by the sheer volume of his ongoing activities. If he's not painting or proofing a print or setting up a photograph or engaged in some other work activity, then he is in the middle of an interview, lunching with a visiting museum director, working the floor at a gallery opening, speaking his mind at a meeting of the board of some cultural institution, planning a trip to Russia, or on a dinner date with one of his grown daughters. He is seldom still—though in front of a canvas he is working on he can become almost serene.

Talking with his former schoolmates, the impression comes across quite strongly that—while the character of the activities may have been somewhat different—Chuck was already engaged in a headlong rush from one thing to the next, from class to band practice to target practice to a date. With his magic tricks, his puppet theater, and his exotic art classes, he had had a busy enough life even before returning to Everett; but one has a sense that the lonely months in bed with nephritis, and the loss of his father, had given added impetus to his desire to live life to the fullest. The urge to be with people, and to participate—more than that, to excel—can be seen as a key expression of his burgeoning ambition.

A little more than a decade after Chuck Close graduated from high school, Everett would find itself in the *Guinness Book of World Records* as home to the largest building in the world, by volume, in the form of the Boeing 747 assembly plant. The arrival of Boeing, on the perimeter of Paine Field, would inevitably change the character of the town. In the 1950s, however, Everett remained an old-fashioned blue-collar community, not yet fully recovered from the Great Depression—an industrialized urban complex contrarily located among some of the continent's most spectacular scenery.

The city occupies the Port Gardner Peninsula—a spur of land that has been described as being like the back of a whale—dividing Port Gardner Bay, to the west, from the mouth of the Snohomish River. Downtown Everett occupies the high ground that runs north-south, parallel to the waterfront, providing striking panoramas of the bay. As the city evolved, the scenic potential of the setting was subverted by the fact that the gargantuan Soundview pulping plant and a string of paper and lumber mills, including four Weyerhauser plants, sprang up along the shoreline, knit together by a railroad right-of-way that effectively separated the city from its beach. Members of the managerial elite lived on a bluff that overlooked the bay and the railroad tracks. (One prominent resident was Senator Henry "Scoop" Jackson, who shared his childhood home with his unmarried sisters.) However, even the privileged had to put up with the insistent noise generated by the unending industrial activity below and the stench that was a by-product of the pulping process. If the wind was blowing off the bay, a fine ash, resulting from the burning of sawdust, descended on gracious homes and railroad flats alike.

For all its man-made blemishes, the spectacular location made Everett different from other mill towns and gave it a distinct personality. This might be the kind of place that bright young men and women wanted to move on from, but it was not a place they would forget. They would remember touches of demotic poetry such as the World War II P-40 Curtis Warhawk fighter plane that topped Tony Dyre's Flying-A gas station, across the street from the Great Northern Railroad terminus. And Everett was not without citizens who aspired to more than a late model Bonneville or a built-in barbecue. When he was a junior in high school, Chuck encountered an unorthodox married couple who would have stood out anywhere as extraordinary exemplars for a young man of artistic bent.

This happened at a point when Chuck had reached the conclusion that his opportunities to further his art education at the college level were rather bleak, given his dismal grade point average. His career counselor suggested that he consider body and fender school, and when he took standardized tests issued by the University of Washington—equivalent to today's SATs—the conclusion reached was that he might just be able to scrape by in nursing school. (Inexplicably, he was awarded an F for art.) Faced with this prognosis, he began to look around for alternative ways to nourish his talent. One possibility he entertained quite seriously was becoming a Disney animator, and he applied to the studio. When he discovered that the apprenticeship involved years of chores, such as "cleaning-up" other artists' drawings, he cooled on the idea. Still, he was determined to find a way to become an artist of some kind, perhaps by apprenticing himself to a commercial art studio.

At this time, Chuck was still involved with the church that his family had attended for years, even teaching Sunday school. At a social event, one evening, he found himself in conversation with a woman named Marjorie Day who wore striking, oversized jewelry. Possibly, the meeting had been instigated by someone who knew about Chuck's ambitions—his mother being a likely candidate. In any case, he poured out the story of his desire to become an artist and his confusion as to what he should do about this since he would not be able to get into a recognized four-year college program.

"I can't add," he told her. "I can't subtract. I can't multiply."

Marge Day's response was to tell him, "Don't worry. There's an alternative. You don't have to multiply to be an artist." And she invited him to visit her house for dinner and to meet her husband. It was an invitation that was to have enormous and unforeseeable consequences. Close sums it up by saying, "Marjorie Day saved my life."

He arrived at the appointed time to discover a house that to someone brought up in small clapboard cottages must have seemed as exotic as something out of *A*

Thousand and One Nights. Long and low—a graceful, Richard Neutra–like West Coast gloss on International Style modernism—it was spectacularly sited near the edge of a cliff, with magnificent vistas over the bay which was carved into segments by a row of pine trees that might have been borrowed from a Japanese ukiyo-e print. Located in Everett's View Ridge section, the property was exquisitely landscaped in a style inspired by the gardens of the Alhambra in Granada, with carp-stocked reflecting pools at different levels. It was patrolled by peacocks that doubled as guard dogs, screeching loudly when any stranger approached the property line.

Inside the house, Chuck found an eclectic collection of modernist furniture—including the first Eames Lounge Chair he had ever seen—boldly abstract stained-glass windows, craft fabrics woven on hand looms, miniature metal sculptures (elements of which could be removed and worn as jewelry), Navaho rugs, pre-Columbian figures, and a mind-boggling profusion of exotic *objets* that the Days had brought back from their travels around the world. Remarkable as all this was, it was eclipsed by the appearance of the man Chuck had been invited over to meet.

Russell Day elevated the desire to surround himself with beautiful things into a secular religion, insisting that this, in combination with creativity, was what made life worth living. Like Oscar Wilde, he was his own greatest creation. There was nothing superficial about Rus Day, but he projected a studied flamboyance that must have withered the Protestant souls of the righteous burghers of Snohomish County. At his most conservative he could be counted upon to enliven his outfit with a shirt dyed to a hue that no one had ever seen before and an eye-catching, hand-printed tie. That, however, paled by comparison with his more extravagant outfits.

"He might wear a bright yellow jacket," Close recalls, "silk-screened with some abstract design. Or you might go to his house and find him in a shirt he'd stitched together from strips of different colored fabric. Everything was always carefully chosen to achieve the effect that he wanted. Usually he'd be wearing his own jewelry—men weren't supposed to wear jewelry back then—and then there was the wig! Rus was losing his hair and he bought himself a very expensive, very natural-looking toupee. But he didn't wear it every day to hide his baldness—that wasn't the idea. He would wear it only when he wanted to convey a sense of occasion, when he had to wear a tuxedo, say, or for a party. It was just another part of his wardrobe—a way of dressing up."

Slender, with fine-boned features, and a presence that combined confidence and defiance of convention, Rus Day was someone you could not avoid noticing.

"You *knew* when he had come into a room," says Donn Trethewey, who got to know Day a little later. "Rus projected passion."

Certainly Day made an immediate impression on Chuck Close, and he confirmed everything that Marjorie Day had told the aspiring painter—he *could* get an art education. Day was in a position to give this assurance because he was the founding director of the small but highly regarded art department at Everett Junior College (where his wife taught English), and Chuck could not be denied entry to the school because it had an open admissions program for local residents.

During the balance of his high school career, Chuck was invited to the Days' home several times, and when graduation approached, there was no doubt about what his next move would be, though his motivation was not entirely as high-minded as Rus Day might have liked.

"I enrolled at Everett Junior College thinking I'd be a commercial artist. I figured that a commercial artist might make enough money to buy a nice car—a T-Bird, or something like that—and that would get me girls. My mother was furious. She thought it was disgusting. For her, art had to be pure—all or nothing, no compromise."

In one way, Millie's disgust may simply have reinforced Chuck's determination to pursue the commercial art option, since by now he was finding her overbearing interest in his activities increasingly oppressive. If attending Everett Junior College had one drawback, it was that it meant living at home for another two years.

Chapter 5

Breaking Away

The campus of Everett Junior College, where Chuck Close commenced his higher education in the fall of 1958, was no Ivy League bastion, but freshmen that year were greeted by a spanking new, generically modern building that still smelled of fresh paint.

"Previous to that, the school hadn't been much more than a collection of Quonset huts," says Larry Stair, who enrolled as an art major that September, as did Chuck's other high school confederate, Donn Trethewey. "Now there were clean, bright studios and we were the first class to have a chance to get the place dirty."

The campus might have been modest, but the art department was exceptionally well equipped by any standard, a consequence of Rus Day's energy and passion. If there was a choice to be made between art supplies and jerseys for the football team, art supplies would win. Most important of all, the art department had a small but remarkable faculty, consisting of just three men—Day himself, Don Tompkins, and Larry Bakke.

Of the three, only Bakke—a native of British Columbia, and a recent graduate of the University of Washington—was primarily a painter. Day was a talented and versatile designer—a fine typographer, for example—with exceptional gifts as a jeweler, and especially as an artist working in glass (he would become a key influence on, and mentor to, Dale Chihuly, now regarded as America's premier glass artist). Day's own work is distinguished and inventive, but above all he was a seminal figure in the evolving worlds of design and art education in the Northwest. (Prestigious institutions tried to lure him away from Everett Junior College, but he resisted their offers, though he did teach summer school courses at UCLA for several years.) Tompkins was a protégé of Day's, and was himself an innovative metalsmith, like Day capable of blurring the line between craft and art. He was particularly adept at working with non-precious materials, such as bottle caps and broken glass, and in the sixties he would become one of the first jewelry designers to incorporate Pop Art elements into his work.

Close describes the curriculum at Everett Junior College as owing a good deal to the Bauhaus tradition. Day—Lazlo Moholy-Nagy's *The Language of Vision* was his bible—taught Art 101 through 103, along with design classes, and was famous for setting difficult assignments—Day described himself as a "fiend." Close claims that he still has nightmares about them.

Russell Day, c. 1970

In a 2008 interview published in *The Seattle Times*, Day talked about how he believed in putting his students through many kinds of problem-solving experiences, starting in two dimensions and progressing to three:

> We started with just taking color pieces out of magazines, and tearing them or cutting them up and creating a design that way. . . . They started with materials that were readily available and didn't cost anything, and eventually they got into more expensive and more detailed problems.[2]

One example quoted is "creating a three-dimensional design that uses reflected light and color while concealing the source of the color." Former students also talk about the assignment requiring them to produce as large a sculpture as possible from a single sheet of paper just 12 inches by 12 inches. Using origami techniques, one student managed to make a tower eight feet tall, and there is photographic evidence that others came close to matching this. Chuck remembers constructing his tower by pulling strips of paper through a hole bored in a piece of wood—a kind of hands-on extrusion process—producing tubular forms that were elegant but highly unstable. He did not succeed in making the structure stand on its own until moments before Day arrived for his critique. Miraculously, it remained vertical, until Day exited the room and a draft from the closing door flattened it.

Nor was it just that the assignments themselves were demanding. The critiques and discussions that followed were equally tough, with no quarter given, though, like other students, Chuck emphasizes that Day was always extremely fair, and somehow managed to avoid hurting people's feelings. There was even a touch of *The History Boys* about Day's classes.

"When he came into the room," Chuck recalls, "Rus used to pat the boys on the ass and say, 'I hope all you girls have been thinking about this assignment. . . .'"

All this should be understood in the context of the fact that the great majority of those who majored in art at Everett Junior College were from working-class or lower-middle-class families and arrived with no art background whatsoever. Mike Monahan, for example, had worked at Boeing for two years before enrolling.

"Baseball was all I really cared about till then," says Monahan. "The first time I heard of Beethoven or Rembrandt was when I got to Everett Junior College. [Before that] art was *Saturday Evening Post* covers and Bob Hale, the weatherman on Channel Five, who drew cartoons. Someone gave me one of those Famous Artists courses that were advertised in the magazines—with photos of Norman Rockwell and other illustrators. I didn't take it seriously, but those people didn't give up. Someone from Famous Artists knocked on the door and said, 'How come you didn't return your exercise?' Somehow, I don't quite know how, that got me to Rus Day, and—along with Larry Bakke and Don Tompkins—he opened up worlds I could never have imagined existed."

Monahan would quickly become part of the tight group of friends that included Chuck, Donn Trethewey, and Larry Stair, along with another new student, Joe Aiken, who used the occasion of a 2008 tribute to Russell Day to recall his trepidation at attending Day's design class for the first time:

> The reality was more exciting than scary and a true awakening for me.
> The classroom walls were filled with examples of visual design elements,
> images of modern architecture and crafts. Russell taught us a whole new
> way of seeing. . . .[3]

Chuck was considerably more sophisticated about art than the others in the group, though his knowledge was still quite limited when it came to contemporary painting. One thing that quickly went out of the window was any thought of becoming a commercial artist.

"I took one class and I knew that wasn't for me."

Chuck had become infected by Day's vision and enthusiasm and now threw himself into both classwork and consuming every scrap of information about twentieth-century painting that could be found in the school library, which included publications provided by the Museum of Modern Art in New York. Also in the library were copies of the short-lived magazine *It Is*, which featured coverage of the New York art scene. Chuck had already encountered Jackson Pollock, but now he became infatuated with the other Abstract Expressionists, in particular developing a lasting passion for the paintings of Willem de Kooning.

Why de Kooning? In part it had something to do with the fact that, of the major Abstract Expressionists, de Kooning was the only one who did not abandon imagery entirely. De Kooning had the ability to conjure up a human presence or a landscape with bold slashing strokes possessing a bravura, macho quality that was bound to appeal to a young man trying to break with convention at the end of the Eisenhower era. De Kooning would become Chuck's artistic father figure.

Suddenly Chuck found himself in an environment where he felt completely at home and where he could flourish.

"At the junior college level," says Donn Trethewey, "Chuck showed a remarkable change—as many of us did, but Chuck's [transformation] was the most dramatic. It was as if he saw far ahead of the rest of us. He seemed to know that he could not only do the work assigned, but he could do it well, and in profusion. The more work he did, the better he became. It was as if somebody had taken the governors off the carburetors. . . . The assignments were difficult and time-consuming . . . Chuck found out that he could surpass [the requirements] of the assignments and did so with increasing ease. His paintings took on a life of their own. His entire outlook began to appear boundless. And it was. . . .

"Chuck worked in a controlled frenzy. He painted with a studied abandon that was in direct contrast, for example, with my 'thoughtful' strokes."

Larry Stair recalls that it was not unusual to arrive at school to find Chuck working on three paintings at three different easels.

"He was insatiable."

Close himself recounts how sometimes, when it was time for the janitors to lock up for the night, he would hide on top of the lockers, emerging when the coast was clear to paint into the small hours.

Inevitably, exhaustion would set in from time to time. Trethewey recalls one warm evening when, *al fresco*, he and a group of students shared a bottle of scotch Chuck had brought in his briefcase. Afterward, they returned to the painting studio where a night school class was in progress, and Chuck turned his attention to the multiple paintings he was busy on at the time. It was hot and stuffy indoors, and Chuck's relentless schedule—with an assist from the booze—finally caught up with him. He fell asleep on his feet, and pitched forward onto an elderly female student perched sidesaddle on a drawing mule (a low easel with a bench-like seat) who was hurled to the floor, along with canvases, paintbrushes, turpentine, and some surrounding easels. The brand-new building's pristine floor was baptized with stains that remained there until some years later when the structure was destroyed in a fire.

Chuck's urge to hurry through whatever he was doing, so he could move on to the next challenge, occasionally got him into trouble. Photography was a requirement for art majors, and one assignment was to make photographs without a camera. Chuck threw himself into the project with his usual gusto, producing a series of X-ray-like "Rayogram" pictures by placing objects onto unexposed film, then exposing the film to produce reverse-silhouette designs. Working at his accustomed rapid pace, he fed his still wet prints onto the belt of the expensive, newly installed drum dryer and waited impatiently for the process to be completed so that the results could be admired. In his excitement, he neglected to remove the metal tongs used to handle prints from the belt—a piece of carelessness that resulted in their leaving a permanent indentation on the polished stainless steel drum, rendering it useless.

Chuck theorizes that there were two major reasons why he was fortunate to have attended Everett Junior College, rather than starting out at a four-year school such as the University of Washington. One is that he was part of a golden generation there. The students might have been raw when they came under Rus Day's tutelage but, in addition to Chuck, Trethewey, Stair, Monahan, and Aiken all went on to have careers in art, and all are still practicing artists. Then there was the quality of the teaching staff.

"If I'd gone to a four-year school I'd have spent the first two years working under student teaching assistants," says Close. "At Everett I had the full attention of three talented practicing professionals."

Painting classes were under the auspices of Larry Bakke. According to Trethewey and Monahan, Bakke's work of the period owed a good deal to the Abstract Expressionists he was always talking about, and Close agrees that Bakke's work was refreshingly different from the work of other "advanced" Pacific Northwest painters—typically artists influenced by Japanese art and by the Asian-inflected paintings of local heroes Morris Graves and Mark Tobey.

"Although, I believe, [Bakke's] work always started from some reference in the real world," says Monahan, "it rarely was obvious when the painting was finished. All work was started with a gestural drawing in a brushed line. Enclosed spaces became shapes that he would then develop in color. He would load his brush, then, using the lines from the drawing as a guide, make a gestural stroke or strokes until the brush was dry. He would then load the brush with a new color and attack the canvas in another area. He seemed to work on figure and ground simultaneously, often using the color stroke used for figure in one area and then repeating it for the ground in another. Although . . . this implies an overall effect like that of Mark Tobey or Jackson Pollock, he in fact achieved active areas by putting colors of similar value or hue in an area. He referred to this as color development. He believed a painting should be finished at any time (thus [he worked on] all areas of the painting simultaneously). He once said 'You do not start in the upper left-hand corner and when you arrive at the bottom you are finished.' Another time he said, 'A painting is never finished.'

"Another statement he once made, that relates directly to Chuck's work, is, 'You cannot make a portrait bigger than life-size. . . .'"

This last remark of Bakke's has obvious resonance, given the fact that Close is best known for portraits that are many times larger than life. It's worth noting too that starting at the upper left-hand corner and finishing when you arrive at the bottom of the canvas is a precise description of how Close now works. On the other hand, the desire to abolish any difference of emphasis between figure and ground is a concept wholeheartedly embraced by Close in his mature work. The way Close employs "families of color" in his prismatic grid paintings—relating one cluster of units to another in a chromatic sense—is something to which Bakke would be sympathetic. In 1958, however, Bakke's most notable gift to Chuck was his enthusiasm for the Abstract Expressionists.

Bakke was the only painter among the three teachers in the EJC art department. In light of his embrace of post–Pollock and de Kooning modernism, it might be thought that Chuck would have turned to Bakke as a mentor. Close says that he liked Bakke, respected his work, and learned a great deal from him, but adds that there was a certain tension between the two of them. Chuck's contemporaries at EJC readily admit that he was by far the most gifted of the students, and the most advanced, yet in two years Bakke never gave him an A for any assignment. No matter how outstanding the work was, or how much extra effort had been invested, Bakke would find some fault—saying, for instance, that Chuck had failed to stick strictly to the letter of the assignment. Like Day, both Bakke and Don Tompkins were known for being tough critics, and Chuck acknowledges that Bakke may have been trying to push him by not giving him an easy ride. (Bakke was demonstrably tough on other students too.) There is reason to suppose, though, that faced with the obvious talent of this precocious teenager, Bakke—himself only in his mid-twenties—may have felt threatened, or at least competitive, and subsequent events tend to bear this out. (A decade later, when Larry Bakke was teaching at Syracuse University, he led a group of students on a Manhattan studio tour. Reportedly, when he learned that Chuck Close's loft was next on the schedule, he told the bus driver to stop and precipitously disappeared.) At EJC, the teacher-student relationship would have helped mask competitiveness while providing opportunities for it to express itself in surreptitious ways. On the surface, relations remained cordial, but Chuck was hurt by Bakke's refusal to fully acknowledge his talent, and it is likely that Bakke interpreted Chuck's combination of confidence and precocity as inappropriate cockiness. Things were not helped when Chuck and Bakke submitted works to the same juried exhibition—Chuck even chauffeuring Bakke's works to the space where judging was to take place—and Chuck's work was selected while Bakke's was not.

It's not hard to see how, from Bakke's point of view, Chuck Close was a challenging student to deal with. His hunger to become an artist, and the sheer, whirlwind energy and ruthless intensity with which he pursued his goal, must have been bewildering and perhaps intimidating. Even more difficult would have been Chuck's almost casual ability to make paintings that "looked like art." The majority of undergraduate painting students struggle to produce work that approximates the output of professional artists, and many never get there. Bakke had gone through that evolution himself, much more successfully than most, but Chuck possessed a seemingly effortless knack of producing accomplished-looking work.

If you know what art looks like, he claims, then you can make something that looks like art. By this he means to be deprecating of his own early efforts—implying that if it "looks like art" it means that it resembles *someone else's* art: in other words, it is inauthentic, the result of imitation. Very few people have the talent to imitate convincingly, however, and it was Chuck's precocious ability to do so which could be threatening to someone like Bakke. Chuck could look at a black-and-white reproduction of a de Kooning painting, go to his easel, and approximate the idiom and execution almost as if he was able to enter into de Kooning's skin. To be able to do this amounts to something more than mere imitation. It means that the disciple has already—possibly without fully understanding what he is doing—absorbed what was original in the master's work *and* has the technical ability to implement the lesson that has been learned. No artist—if one makes an exception for outsider artists—arrives at originality without going through this phase. As will be seen, Chuck's immense facility with imitation (he would have made a master forger) eventually became a liability that may actually have delayed his arrival at a personal idiom.

On Bakke's behalf, it should be stated that he was an immensely popular teacher, both at EJC and at Syracuse University where he taught later on. Donn Trethewey remembers him standing at the back of the painting studio at EJC, arms folded, watching his students busy at their easels, and recalls how "one rather lazy afternoon, as we painted, or tried to paint, [he called out] loudly from the back of the room, 'Paint, paint, paint, as if your lives depended on it!'" Trethewey also remembers, with gratitude, that Bakke would play recordings of modern classics as they painted—Béla Bartók, Aaron Copland, George Antheil's *Ballet Méchanique*. "It was then that I and the others put it together; that it was all linked so beautifully." And he adds "Bakke's paintings had an effect on us all. Especially Chuck. I'd imagine the freedom Larry Bakke urged us to pursue was paramount. And his insistence that we go to the library and find, and study, and know the contemporary artists, and know that we too were artists."

Clearly, any edge of competitiveness that existed between Bakke and his most gifted student was only one aspect of a complicated relationship that was essentially beneficial, as Close readily acknowledges, invariably singling Bakke out as an important early exemplar. It's possible too that this early encounter with art world competitiveness may have helped him develop an edge that would become crucial a few years down the line.

It was Don Tompkins who was Chuck's real mentor. Chuck had no desire to follow Tompkins into the design field but appreciated the fact that "Don treated me like a human being." Although recognized as an innovative and influential metalsmith, Tompkins seems to have derived his greatest satisfaction from teaching. Chuck found him to be someone he could talk to, and who was always prepared to listen. The relationship extended beyond the classroom, Tompkins being the kind of teacher who liked to hang out with his students and share a few beers. He and his wife Marilyn would often have Chuck over to their house, and Tompkins would accompany Chuck to Seattle for visits to galleries and the Seattle Museum. Like Bakke, Tompkins—born in 1931—was just a few years older than Chuck. In his case, however, the closeness in age provided a basis for friendship rather than competition. (In the 1970s, Tompkins taught at New York University and for a while he and Chuck lived in the same building.)

As had been the case at Everett High School, Chuck cultivated the outsiders at EJC as well as his core group of friends, and singles out in particular a student named Don Campbell, whom he describes as having been completely out of place, an overweight rich kid with a sports car. Campbell produced outrageous work that nobody—neither staff nor students—knew what to make of. Disdaining oils, he made paintings from flypaper or pushpins or using a blowtorch. Chuck remembers him as being the kind of person who seemed to spend his life cooped up in a room, living inside his head. Chuck was as nonplussed as anyone else when it came to Campbell's work, but he enjoyed talking with him since he was more intellectual than any of the other students, read voraciously, and had a wide and eclectic range of interests. (Given his blowtorch paintings and such, one wonders if he might have come across Dada.) Campbell had an encyclopedic knowledge of jazz and rhythm and blues and early rock 'n' roll. Chuck would visit his house and drool over his vast record collection, but his fondest memory is of being taken by him to a concert, sponsored by the Negro Elks and starring Ray Charles, whose career had been launched in Seattle, an experience Chuck describes as unforgettable.

While at EJC, Chuck Close, like most of his fellow students, lived at home, and so remained subject to the close attentions of his mother, which continued to try his patience. The problem was that she did not want to let go. Everything Chuck did, she wanted to do. If he learned to sail, she had to learn to sail. If he took up skiing, she had to take up skiing, and when she did so, she wanted it to be a shared experience, often tagging along with him, though usually she at least made the concession of letting him bring a girlfriend along.

Despite these maternal intrusions, his social life changed and expanded. Since everyone now had his own car, trips to Seattle became routine. (Chuck owned a long line of clunkers, including a 1926 Model T, much like the car in which his family migrated west.) Nearer to home, as soon as they could pass themselves off as being old enough to drink, the art majors became acquainted with the bars and taverns of Everett's Hewitt Avenue. At one time there were thirty-four

Chuck Close and friends in a 1926 Model T decorated for the Everett Junior College Homecoming celebration, 1958

watering holes there, reveling in names like Sharkie's, The Cabin, The Purple Pennant, The Anchor, and My Office. The tipple of choice was "Oly"—Olympia beer—which, in the days long before the state of Washington became a mecca for microbrewers, could legally be served only at a strength so low that quite a few had to be consumed in order to produce much of a buzz, giving rise to the plausibility of something called the Hewitt Run in which the aim was to drink one beer at each of the bars along the strip. Even with low alcohol brews, however, this could prove a challenge, and there was one occasion when Chuck and Mike Monahan—after abandoning the "run" partway through—drove home in someone else's car. The next day, Chuck reported it stolen and turned himself in.

An occasional denizen of these Hewitt Avenue bars, though he was not there to drink, was a notable local eccentric named John Patric, who sometimes chose to call himself Hugo N. Frye (try saying it out loud). Like most American working-class communities, Everett could boast its share of memorable characters, and Patric was a larger than life example. His purpose in visiting bars was to distribute a muckraking newssheet known originally as *The Snohomish Free Press* (later changed, tongue in cheek, to *The Saturday Evening Free Press*), which he wrote and published himself. As a connoisseur of outsiders, Chuck could not fail to be drawn to Patric, a constant thorn in the side of the Everett establishment.

Patric had spent a chunk of the Depression era living as a hobo, but he went one better than the bums who rode the freight cars to Frisco and Chi-town by shipping out to the Far East and spending three years living off his wits in Japan, China, and Korea, claiming to have managed the entire trip, passage included, for $200. A memoir of his adventures in Asia was published in 1943 as *A Yankee Hobo in the Orient*, a book that combines Twain-like humor with strenuously expressed political views that might best be described as a willfully eclectic blend of anarchism and libertarianism, cogent although subject to repetition and overstatement.[4]

Even earlier he had had a mainstream journalistic career, starting out as a newspaper reporter, then contributing articles to magazines like *National Geographic* and *Reader's Digest*, but in 1957 he returned to his birthplace, Snohomish, a small town near Everett, the latter being the administrative seat of Snohomish County.

Patric habitually referred to his native turf as "Sodomish County," having so re-named it on account of the corruption he claimed to uncover under every rock from Puget Sound to Troublesome Creek. Certainly the city had a long history of class confrontation, frequently tainted by graft, with local union organizers pitted against the mill owners and the city's malleable political and law enforcement machines. The most notorious episode had taken place in 1916 when members of the Industrial Workers of the World (IWW)–better known as the Wobblies– came to Everett in support of a strike by local shingle workers. This climaxed in a shootout in which two sheriff's deputies and as many as a dozen of the IWW party were killed, with even more wounded, an incident that became known as the Everett Massacre.[5]

Forty years later, the kind of social animosities that had precipitated this event had to a large extent gone underground, but they continued to simmer beneath the surface and supplied Patric with ample material for his newssheet. Patric was so detested, even feared, by the local mandarins and their flunkies that in 1959, after nine issues of his irreverent publication had appeared, the police showed up at his home, smashed his typewriter, and had him thrown into jail, from which he was transferred to a state mental institution. This chain of preposterous events culminated in a trial in the Washington Superior Court that garnered national attention. During the course of these proceedings, Patric was branded a potentially violent, schizophrenic-paranoid type and a menace to society. Defending himself, he made a passionate and effective case for, as Larry Stair memorably puts it, "every American's right to be strange." After four days of testimony and ten minutes of deliberation, the jury found Patric sane, allowing him to return unrepentantly to his crusade against the corruption that he perceived as festering in every boardroom and municipal office.

After hearing Patric stories, and seeing him on the streets of Everett, Chuck decided this was someone he very much wanted to know. His opportunity came when he landed a job delivering meat to Snohomish, where he quickly located Patric's house which was engulfed in a jungle of overgrown vegetation. Once, when the neighbors complained about this, he "beautified" the property by buying apples and oranges and bananas from the supermarket and hanging them from branches with string, like ornaments on a Christmas tree. And John Patric himself was something to see—a Howard Hughes character with a straggly gray beard and long fingernails that had not been trimmed in years.

Chuck got to know Patric, and spent hours listening to his tales of corporate greed and governmental malfeasance, absorbing ideas and attitudes that would influence him throughout his life. He saw to it too that his mother made Patric's acquaintance, realizing that the pamphleteer's libertarian views would appeal to her antiestablishment streak. The outcome was that she became a member of the small coterie surrounding Patric, helping him bring out *The Saturday Evening Free Press*, each issue of which was laboriously set by hand using essentially the same methods employed by Benjamin Franklin in the days of *The Pennsylvania Gazette*. By introducing Millie to Patric, Chuck may have been implementing a hidden agenda, conscious or subconscious. The more Millie's energies were involved in combating perceived corruption, and helping to bring out *The Saturday Evening Free Press*, the less time she would have for meddling in Chuck's affairs.

Some years later, after her son had left the Pacific Northwest, Mildred Close ran for lieutenant governor of Washington State on the same anarchist/libertarian ticket as John Patric, who was running for governor.

During these junior college years, Chuck was consciously cultivating an image for himself, building on his already well-tested ability to role-play in ways that maximized his strengths. That talent depended on his ability to project confidence, often supported by a theatrical flair for costume. He had once been one of the shorter boys, but by now he had topped out at an imposing six feet three inches. He had the face of a character actor rather than a matinee idol, but he turned that to dramatic effect by growing a full beard as soon as he left high school, perhaps in an effort to offset his already thinning hair. This was the era of the James Dean wannabe, making smooth chins and slicked-back pompadours, accompanied by an existential pout, the template of the hour. In a city like Everett, for a teenager to sport facial hair—other than carefully manicured sideburns—was so provocative as to be seen as positively un-American, especially in combination with the derby that Chuck had now incorporated into his everyday wardrobe. It seems apparent that the example of Russell Day, with his willingness to astonish through his appearance, had rubbed off, supplementing Chuck's existing predisposition. This was a young man who was determined to be noticed.

His confidence grew from semester to semester. Balancing skills and deficits was no longer problematic because Chuck had no further need to mask academic deficiencies, in fact he found himself comfortably able to handle the academic workload, making up grades in the process. Reading for its own sake was still not a favorite activity, but an exception was made for any book or periodical related to art.

Attending Everett Junior College was a transformative experience for Chuck, and for other members of his graduating class. The school's impact on these young lives is strikingly expressed by Mike Monahan as he remembers the aftermath of a final meeting, at Rus and Marjorie Day's exquisite house, where Day, along with Don Tompkins and Larry Bakke, gave a last critique, evaluating portfolios produced over the previous two years.

> The memories of what we said that night are now forgotten. What remains vivid is the emotion I experienced. After a lengthy evening of food, drink, and discussion [several of us] left in one vehicle. As we were leaving the driveway, I was overcome by the feeling of great loss. The passion I now had for the making of great art and the possible spreading of the word was due directly to the motivation of the three men we were now leaving. The emotion from this awareness manifested itself in a gasping shortness of breath. I WAS SOBBING. My three friends laughed nervously, unsure of how to respond to a grown man's tears. After all, I was a baseball player and we all knew, as Tom Hanks later expressed in *A League of their Own*, "There's no crying in baseball." Perhaps I had been given a gift by [these three teachers] that was greater than baseball.[6]

Chapter 6

Bicoastal Adventures

Chuck Close now had an Associate of Arts degree and the grades to transfer to the University of Washington, where he arrived highly touted by the Everett faculty. Of the old EJC crowd, Donn Trethewey—whose primary interest was three-dimensional design—moved to Southern California, enrolling at Art Center College of Design in Pasadena, but others, including Larry Stair, Mike Monahan, and Joe Aiken, joined Chuck as art majors on the Seattle campus.

By comparison with Everett, Seattle was the big city, but Chuck remembers it as having been, in the very early sixties, a cultural backwater, self-involved and self-satisfied. There was an art community there, but it was not one that was in any way oriented towards New York to which Chuck already looked for inspiration. Collectors tended to specialize in areas such as Japanese art or Native American art of the Pacific Northwest, which also provided the focus of art history courses at the university. As already noted, the local heroes were Mark Tobey and Morris Graves, both of whom had been greatly influenced by Asian art, and especially by Zen painting and calligraphy. This set the tone for the Seattle art scene.

Luckily for Chuck, there were some exceptions among the faculty of the University of Washington art department. Spencer Moseley, for example—though very involved in promoting the art of the Northwest (he established an Index of Northwestern Artists)—had studied in Paris with Fernand Léger and worked in a style that derived from Léger's interpretation of Cubism. Close has positive memories of Moseley as a painting instructor but singles out the art history course that Moseley taught—"Painting since Cézanne"—as being especially important to him.

Chuck Close at Yale University's Summer School of Music and Art, Norfolk, Connecticut, 1961

"I was hungry for knowledge about what it meant to be a real painter. Moseley was a practicing artist—also a writer, not an academic—and he taught art history from the point of view of the processes involved, not the iconography. He gave the viewpoint of the creator, not the critic."

Another faculty member Close recalls with affection was Fred Anderson.

"Fred was neurotic. When everyone submitted paintings for some juried show, his would be five years old because he hadn't done anything since then—and the reason he hadn't been painting was because he was always building the perfect studio. Just as he was about to finish it, he would sell the house and start all over. The paintings he did manage to get done were biomorphic—part Miró, part Arshile Gorky—and often there was something inappropriate about the scale. They should have been bigger. They were what we used to call station-wagon art—there were these guys who never made anything that was too big to fit into the back of the station wagon. That meant that gesture was limited to what you could do with wrist and fingers."

Close recalls Anderson's generosity with gratitude.

"I was always running out of canvases, and he would try to give me old paintings of his to work on. I'd tell him, 'I can't do that, Fred. This is a good painting.' So he'd paint over the painting himself, with gesso, and then give it to me."

But Chuck's most important teacher during this period was Alden Mason, who at that time was painting in a style strongly inflected with the gestural characteristics of Abstract Expressionism. Mason had been Larry Bakke's mentor, and now he became something of a father figure to Close. Born in Everett in 1919, Mason, like Close, had lost his father at an early age, had grown up with an overprotective mother, had poor eyesight, and was un-athletic. Neither was aware of all these parallels, but they perhaps help to explain how empathy could develop between them.

In a 1984 interview, Mason described his initial impressions of Chuck Close.

"He used to knock on the door of the office about ten times a day for a while. At that time he chewed his fingernails down short and he was very nervous—and he painted kind of big gesture, abstract sort of expressionist things which I was doing at the time . . . and which he liked very much. He in a sense was emulating what I was doing, and he did it really very well. But he'd come in and ask, 'What'll I do with this painting, Alden? What'll I do?' He was always so nervous and upset and, you know, wanted some kind of confirmation [that] what he was doing was okay."[7]

The nervousness remembered by Mason—the chewed fingernails are a telling detail—is certainly in sharp contrast with the impression Chuck made on his contemporaries, who almost universally were struck by his self-confidence. Close acknowledges those frequent visits to Mason's office and explains them by saying, "I was doing so much work. Sometimes I would finish several paintings in a day and I would want to get Alden's reaction, because he was the person there whose opinion I respected."

Whatever insecurities he may have experienced, Chuck clearly made a strong and favorable impression on the faculty. As with any academic body, there were political divisions within the art department, but Chuck seems to have managed to get along well with all factions, partly, he claims, because—despite his continued bias towards the New York School—he was prepared to try his hand at any idiom. It was all grist for the mill, part of the process of acquiring knowledge about making art. (He is fond of saying that he has learned as much from bad art as from good.)

The move to the University of Washington was significant too in that Chuck and his old Everett friends were now living away from home for the first time. For several months, Chuck and four others—including another old crony, Don Campbell, from Everett Junior College—squeezed into a one-bedroom apartment in a new building hanging from a cliff overlooking the city. Later, Chuck and half a dozen others—including EJC alumni Larry Stair, Mike Monahan, and Joe Aiken—moved into a large, dilapidated frame house near the university that would become another place in which to paint—much needed, because by then Chuck was making very large paintings, some ten and twelve feet wide—and also the focus for much *Animal House*-style revelry. The police became regular visitors, usually called out because the neighbors felt that one of the many parties held there was getting out of hand.

"We had the greatest party house on campus," says Stair. "The police were so used to being called to our house that they made it a weekend thing . . . slowly driving by around eleven o'clock. . . . They would shine the spotlight slowly across the length of our porch that went the width of the whole house. . . . One Friday I got home around 10:30 and as I came through the door there was the gang. . . . Chuck handed me a straw hat and a cane. A few minutes of practice, and when the cops came by with their scanning light, in perfect timing we did a Bing Crosby/Bob Hope hat and cane line dance with the cop spotlight on us right to the end of the porch. Even the cops were laughing."

Another denizen of the house was Seth Greenwald—known in those days as Al—who is now director of the Orthopaedic Research and Education Center at the Cleveland Clinic in Ohio. Back in the early sixties he was a young engineer at Boeing, recently arrived in Seattle with his brother and looking for somewhere to live. He does not remember how he met Chuck and the other EJC alumni, but he had no problem fitting in with their bohemian lifestyle.

"The artists accepted us," he says, "because we were pretty easygoing and could afford to pay rent. Anyone who could pay rent was welcome, plus there was a guy called Roger who lived rent-free because he cooked, and a couple of girls who cleaned. Seattle was a great place for girls and partying, and we were in the thick of it."

Making music in their rented house in Seattle, c. 1962;
from left: Larry Stair, Alan Seth Greenwald, Harvey Greenwald,
Lee Dalton, Mike Monahan, Ira Silver, and Chuck Close

He remembers Chuck as someone who was always at the center of things.

"He was a character—the leader of the band. I wouldn't say he was aggressive, but he wasn't afraid to let you know what he wanted. He was in on all the decisions—when we redecorated the place with orange crates, he was behind that. As soon as you met him, you knew he knew where he was headed. He wanted to be someone, and luckily he had the talent to do it. . . . I got the sense that he figured things out ahead of everyone else. Sometimes he seemed a little crazed, but there was always method to his madness. He was a great self-promoter, but at the same time he was one of the boys. We had a band, and he was a big part of that. We had a softball team too. . . . I don't remember him playing much, but he came to the games."

Greenwald recalls how, in August 1962, the entire gang drove down to a rock 'n' roll party in Seaside, Oregon, that got completely out of control and escalated into a full-scale confrontation with the authorities. It started with hundreds of kids sleeping out on the beach and lighting bonfires to stay warm. Local "Louie Louie" bands laid on entertainment but, as more partygoers arrived from out of town, tipped off that this was the place to be, the townsfolk began to panic and the next thing anyone knew the governor had called out the State Patrol and the National Guard. The main drag was sealed off with barriers and police cruisers and a state of siege was maintained for hours. There was a lot of milling about and yelling, but violence was avoided—which did not prevent the incident becoming known in the media as the Seaside Riots.

Back in Seattle, Chuck made everyone customized tee-shirts celebrating the episode. Greenwald, who is not tall, still has his, emblazoned "The Shortest Seaside Rioter."

By his own admission, Chuck walked around in costume all the time during this period. His mother had sewn him ruffled shirts and lavender paisley vests which he wore with the derby he had been favoring since his Everett Junior College days. Add to this his beard, which still inspired shouts of "beaver," and there was little danger of him not being noticed.

The Seattle art world may have been provincial, but there was a thriving music scene. Chuck and his friends were regulars at jazz clubs and folk venues, as well as at performances by black R&B artists. In movies, this was the era of Bergman, Antonioni, and the French New Wave, and the art majors made a point of seeing any foreign film that was shown, not only those by Goddard and Truffaut, but also features like *Monsieur Hulot's Holiday*.

There were frequent trips to San Francisco, then on the cusp of its Beat Generation heyday. Sometimes Chuck would drive down with a largish group all jammed into a single car. On other occasions he would go there with his old high school pal, Lee Dalton, who was by then a science major at the University of Washington. Sometimes they would camp out on the roof of the California School of Fine Arts (which around that time became the San Francisco Art Institute). The Bay Area art scene had far more to offer than anything that Seattle could provide. Clyfford Still and Mark Rothko had spent time there in the forties, and their influence had played an important role in making the region a breeding ground for major West Coast artists like Richard Diebenkorn, Elmer Bischoff, and David Park. During the period when Chuck Close and his friends would camp out on the roof of the California School of Fine Arts, students enrolled there included gifted young artists such as William T. Wiley and Joan Brown, who, like Chuck, were coming to terms with the legacy of Abstract Expressionism.

Chuck has said that he and his fellow Seattle students would think nothing of making the 1,000-mile round trip just to see a play. He remembers listening to a lot of jazz in San Francisco, and hanging out at North Beach spots like the Purple Onion, and the legendary hungry i, where he saw performances by Lenny Bruce, Shelley Berman, and other politically inclined comedians. Folk music and Beat poetry readings were also on the agenda, and he remembers being at the West Coast premiere of *Pull My Daisy*, the Beat film by Robert Frank and Alfred Leslie, featuring Jack Kerouac's voice-over and appearances by Allen Ginsberg, Gregory Corso, and Larry Rivers.

These trips to San Francisco were eye-opening, but they were nothing compared to the extended summer expedition that rounded off Chuck Close's junior year at the University of Washington. The art department was able to nominate one student to attend Yale Summer School in Norfolk, Connecticut, on a fellowship grant. Chuck was chosen—not, according to him, because he was the most talented but because he was a compromise candidate whom all members of the faculty could agree on without having to bend to the political agenda of another faction.

"Because I was a transfer student," he says, "I hadn't been around long enough to make enemies."

This may have been a factor in his selection, but it's difficult to imagine that talent did not play a larger role, and Chuck acknowledges that he worked harder and was hungrier than his fellow students, qualities that seldom go unnoticed. Even so, he tends to play down his selection for the Norfolk program, on one occasion at least dismissing it as an example of the truth of a favorite adage of his, "It's better to be lucky than gifted."

Being elected to attend Yale Summer School carried considerable prestige and would provide the opportunity for Chuck to study with artists of national and international stature who until then had been just names in books and magazines. This was an exciting prospect, but perhaps even more exciting was the fact that it brought with it the opportunity—weeks before his twenty-first birthday—to pay a maiden visit to his artistic Camelot, New York City, where he stayed for a thrilling week packed with the kind of experiences he had craved since his horizons had been expanded during his years at Everett Junior College.

He in fact traveled by way of Boston because at the last minute a friend of his mother's, a radio disc jockey whose own mother was seriously ill in Massachusetts, offered him a ride. They drove cross-country in two-and-a-half days—barely stopping to eat—each taking eight-hour shifts at the wheel. From Boston, Chuck took a train down to Manhattan.

He may have been fixated on New York, but says that he had absolutely no preconception of what the physical reality of the city would be.

He describes himself as being a total hick. "I'd fallen off the turnip truck. I didn't read, so I hadn't looked at a guidebook. I knew the Empire State Building and the Brooklyn Bridge, but that was about it. I'd heard the title *A Tree Grows in Brooklyn*, and I took that literally—one tree in the entire city! When I saw whole avenues lined with trees, I was astonished."

On arrival at Grand Central, he found a taxi and threw himself on the driver's mercy, telling him he needed to find a cheap hotel, preferably near the museums. The driver took him to the Ansonia, a monumental, Belle Époque–style structure containing 2,500 rooms, with a facade that fills the west side of Broadway from Seventy-third to Seventy-fourth Street. Famous for having been the first air-conditioned building in New York, the Ansonia had at one time or another been home to Babe Ruth, Florenz Ziegfeld, Arturo Toscanini, Igor Stravinsky, Enrico Caruso, and many other celebrities. (It was especially popular with musicians because of its thick, soundproof walls.) The last word in luxury when it opened in 1904, the hotel was going through a down-at-the-heels period in the early sixties, and Chuck was just about able to afford a gloomy cell that provided barely enough space to park his suitcase. He didn't care, because he would not be spending much time there other than to sleep.

On Broadway he saw Zero Mostel in Eugene Ionesco's *Rhinoceros*. At the Five

Spot Café he heard Charles Mingus and other jazz greats. The biggest attraction, however, was Manhattan's museums and galleries. The cabbie who took Chuck to the Ansonia may have had the Museum of Natural History—just a few blocks away—in mind when he dropped him off. Chuck's interests lay elsewhere, but still the Ansonia was not a bad location. A walk across Central Park (more New York trees) would bring him to the Metropolitan Museum, the Frick, and Frank Lloyd Wright's new Guggenheim Museum, open for just two years. A short subway ride, or a leisurely stroll downtown, brought him to the Whitney Museum, then in its old digs on West Fifty-fourth Street, and the Museum of Modern Art, where the big show that summer was a survey of Futurism. Chuck was more interested in familiarizing himself with the permanent collection—gallery after gallery packed with masterpieces by Picasso and Matisse, Mondrian and Giacometti, Pollock and de Kooning. This was his first opportunity to take in the entire sweep of modernism, up to Abstract Expressionism and beyond.

MoMA had acquired work by Jasper Johns, Robert Rauschenberg, and other younger figures in the fifties. By 1961, the museum had purchased work by Frank Stella—just three years Chuck's senior—who had made his mark at MoMA's 1959–60 *Sixteen Americans* exhibition. Stella's precocious success would influence Chuck's sense of the impact that young artists could have on the rapidly evolving New York art scene. It was just one short step to imagining his own work hanging on the hallowed walls.

Since this was summer, many commercial galleries were closed, but Chuck made the most of those that were not, quite struck by the friendliness with which he was received.

"I'd go into a Fifty-seventh Street gallery and tell the guy behind the desk I'd like to see something by, say, Hans Hofmann. No one could mistake me for a collector. There was no way anyone could think I was going to buy something—but they'd take me into the back room and pull things out of the racks. They seemed happy that I was interested."

New York did not disappoint, and the eight weeks that followed at Yale Summer School proved equally satisfying. In most ways, the Norfolk campus was a total contrast to Manhattan, being idyllically located on a spectacular country estate near Litchfield, Connecticut. The faculty that summer included Bernard Chaet, who ran the program, Elmer Bischoff, Philip Guston, Richard Lydel (who had been included with Frank Stella in MoMA's *Sixteen Americans* exhibition), and the great photographer Walker Evans. In addition there were visits from New

York–based painters and sculptors, and artists from other disciplines—Morton Feldman lecturing on musical composition and John Ciardi on poetry. The campus was also home to a summer music program and festival, and that year the band shell hosted concerts by the Guarneri Quartet, among others.

In the case of the fine art program, all this was for the benefit of some thirty-five undergraduates from all over the country, each of whom, in Chuck's words, was accustomed to being a big duck in a small pond. Three who went on to build major reputations were Brice Marden, down from Boston University; David Novros, from the University of Southern California; and Vija Celmins, from Indianapolis. As might be imagined, competition was intense, and when painting was done for the day and critiques had been completed, fierce arguments would break out, passions running high.

Vija Celmins (left) and Brice Marden (right), 1961

"It was as though," Chuck says, "everyone had arrived with a completely different point of view about what art was supposed to be."

Heated dialectic, however, was balanced by moments of hilarity. Chuck remembers in particular a "happening" that was staged, at Chaet's suggestion, to greet the wealthy aunt of one of the students, who had decided to visit for reasons that the young woman could not quite fathom. One student, Allen Blagden, owned an old sedan with a limousine-style body but no backseat. With Blagden dressed in a chauffeur's uniform, several sizes too small, this was sent to pick up the unsuspecting woman, her niece also riding in the car, dressed in paint-caked overalls, along with a well-to-do student from Wesleyan dressed in polo gear. The visiting aunt was bundled unceremoniously into the back of the decrepit limousine, where, throughout the ride back to Norfolk, her niece and the polo player plied her with a stream of art-historical gibberish. Arriving at the estate, the car drove up to the big house—a mansion filled with Hudson River School paintings—where the visitor was greeted by someone in a tree playing a banjo, a voluptuous young woman from Mississippi smoking a cigar, a member of the faculty casting a fishing line and reeling in imaginary fish, along with many other distractions including Chuck, in his everyday costume of ruffled shirt and derby, spouting endless platitudes about Greek art and archaeology. This event probably lacked the incoherent coherence of happenings by people like Claes Oldenburg and Jim Dine, but it was certainly a bonding experience, and incidentally it delighted the visiting aunt who, it turned out, had once been in the theater.

Between the arguments and the hijinks, Chuck fitted in classes in photography, painting, drawing, and printmaking. If he had ever had any second thoughts about his need to find a way to move to the East Coast, they were dispelled by that summer in Norfolk.

Back in Seattle, Chuck embarked on his senior year, which would entail making-up credits in a number of academic subjects, though he still found time to produce a prodigious quantity of paintings. He also drew a good deal of attention to himself when one of these provoked a flurry of political controversy. At this point in his student career, he saw himself as a radical, both culturally and socially, identifying strongly with the Ban the Bomb movement and other antiestablishment groups. Soon after enrolling at the University of Washington, he had begun painting American flags. He acknowledges that he'd probably seen Jasper Johns' flags, at least in reproduction, but Chuck's were quite different in intention and spirit from Johns' ultra cool encaustics, which were implicit statements about the demise of Abstract Expressionism. Close's flags were passionate tributes *to* Abstract Expressionism, fiercely gestural acts of filial devotion.

The example that became notorious was titled *Betsy Ross Revisited*, which he had begun work on in December 1960, just before Christmas. As mentioned, Chuck often painted several canvases a day, but this ambitious work fell into a different category. It was assembled and painted rather slowly and was not completed until some time in the spring of 1961, at about the time of the Kennedy

Betsy Ross Revisited, c. 1961.
Mixed mediums on canvas, 86 x 111 in. (218.4 x 281.9 cm).
Private collection, New York

administration's attempted invasion of Cuba, which history knows as the Bay of Pigs fiasco, an event that doubtless gave the painting additional resonance.

Betsy Ross Revisited—a work almost ten feet long by a little over seven feet high—was made from a large American flag, bought in a thrift store, extensively cut up and restitched, then stretched in reverse (so that the stars are in the upper right corner, except for two rows assigned an entirely new role at the base of the image) then painted on, with splashy verve, so that Old Glory comes to resemble a mushroom cloud in Technicolor. At the upper left, Chuck scrawled the words "E Pluribus Unum."

After returning from Yale Summer School, he entered this work in the Northwest Annuals, a juried exhibition held at the Seattle Art Museum. He was competing for a place in this show with faculty members and other senior Northwestern artists (including his former teacher, Larry Bakke). Not only was *Betsy Ross Revisited* selected by the jury, it was awarded third prize, which Chuck recalls as coming with a $1,000 stipend. That, however, was just the beginning of the story. In the conservative climate that prevailed in Seattle in those days, the painting could not fail to offend, which of course is precisely what he had intended. One member of the jury, Nathan Oliveira—a prominent representative of the San Francisco Bay Area figurative group—walked out and insisted that his name be removed from the roster. Dr. Richard Fuller, cofounder and de facto director of the museum, banished the painting from the exhibition.

This was widely reported in the local press, and proved to be just the beginning of the painting's notoriety. A few months later, *Betsy Ross Revisited* was included in an exhibition at the Puyallup Fair (the Western Washington State Fair) held annually at fairgrounds south of Seattle, once the location of a World War II Japanese-American internment camp. *Betsy Ross*'s iconography aroused ire at the local American Legion post to the extent that a group of angry veterans chopped down the door of the building in which the exhibition was housed, with the vociferously stated intent of destroying the painting. They were prevented from doing so by Don Scott—a friend of Chuck's who was one of the show's organizers—and a group of supporters who put their bodies on the line, standing in front of the painting to defend it. After this episode, the media frenzy was even more intense.

Chuck admits that he found provoking such a violent reaction to be very exciting at the time, though in retrospect he describes it as sophomoric, adding that, in any case, back then it was all too easy to stir up controversy in places like Puyallup.

Betsy Ross had one more adventure in store, which unfolded after Chuck had left town. When he and his friends gave up their lease on the big frame house near the U, the painting was left in a storage space in a kind of semi-basement (the house being built on a slope so that there was an extra floor at the rear). A Seattle art dealer expressed an interest in showing the painting, and he and Mike Monahan went to the house to retrieve it. They discovered that the new tenants were two young women who Monahan suspects were probably hookers. The dealer explained that they had come to pick up the painting, which provoked little interest until he told the women that he was planning to exhibit it. Hearing this, their attitude changed. They had picked up the scent of money and now did everything they could to prevent the dealer from removing *Betsy* from the house, claiming it as their property and eventually scaring the men off.

Later, Chuck's mother decided that she wanted the painting and, being made of sterner stuff, soon had it hanging in her home.

During Chuck's senior year, the Seattle World's Fair brought another opportunity to get a close look at work by some of the artists he had come to admire, and a few he hadn't encountered before. This came in the form of the exhibition *Art Since 1950*, curated by Sam Hunter, a prominent figure in the New York art world, who had selected 100 works, half by Americans and half from abroad. The show presented Abstract Expressionism in some depth, but also included work by younger artists like Johns, Rauschenberg, and Stella, as well as examples of European postwar modernism by the likes of Joan Miró, Jean Dubuffet, Fritz Hundertwasser, Antoni Tàpies, and Francis Bacon.

Chuck's final semester was so taken up with makeup work on academic subjects that he failed to attend one particular painting class until the final session, at which he was required to present seven works to be critiqued. Mike Monahan and Larry Stair arrived that day to find a handwritten sign outside the studio— "Artist at Work." Inside they found Chuck painting seven canvases, each set up on its own easel.

"Each one was in a different style," says Stair, "and they were all pretty good."

Chuck Close graduated magna cum laude. Surprisingly, he had not thought seriously about going to graduate school, his plan having been to find a job locally and make enough money to move to New York and paint. Until that time, he had not paid much attention to the possibility of being drafted either, assuming that his neuromuscular problems would be enough to keep him from military service. Following the Bay of Pigs episode, however, with Cuba's potential as a platform for Soviet missiles becoming apparent, the geopolitical climate had changed and Chuck began to fear that his physical impairments might not be sufficient to guarantee his exclusion. At his initial draft board interview, he wore his most outrageous clothes, hoping that these might help create an unfavorable impression. Still, he was far from certain that he would be safe. To be accepted into graduate school, on the other hand, would be a secure insurance policy against the draft. The problem was that he was too late to apply to schools in the conventional way.

Chuck contacted Bernard Chaet, head of the Yale Summer School program, with whom he had forged a strong rapport. Was there any possibility, he inquired, of getting into the Yale MFA program at that late hour? Chaet responded that all places had been assigned, but he talked to the faculty and Chuck was placed at the top of the waiting list. If anyone dropped out, he could enroll. At the last moment, one young woman did withdraw from the program, and—at three days' notice—Chuck found himself headed once more for New Haven, this time for an extended stay.

On the surface, Mildred Close was immensely proud of her son's achievement—his being accepted by such an illustrious school. At the same time, she had to struggle with many misgivings about him moving so far from home, possibly never to return. Even his sojourn in Seattle had provoked a certain strain, which Millie had responded to in interesting ways. For one thing, she promptly enrolled in the exact same courses that Chuck had taken at Everett Junior College, and for two years she assiduously attended Rus Day's design classes and took life drawing with Larry Bakke. Later she would say that she had attended these courses so that she could keep up with the latest trends in the art world, and therefore better understand Chuck's progress.

(Recently, someone tried to sell Chuck a sketchbook from that period, identified as belonging to "Close." It was his mother's.)

Millie also began to seek out surrogate sons, befriending young men—one was an art major at EJC—and sometimes housing and feeding them. At this time, she was living in a run-down millworker's cottage on a hillside in Lowell, having sold the Cady Road house to finance a comfortable home she was building for herself—often with Chuck's help—in Lake Stevens, a resort community a few miles from Everett. Having earned her real estate license, she bought first an MG sports car, and then an Austin-Healey roadster in which, the Washington climate permitting, she drove around Everett with the top down. When Chuck was her passenger, she would sometimes embarrass him by suggesting that anyone seeing them together would assume they were out on a date since, she insisted, they must appear about the same age. Once again, in this kind of a situation she showed herself to be emotionally tone-deaf.

"My mom," says Chuck, "was the kind of mother every guy thinks he would like to have. She was determined to be hipper than thou. When we started smoking pot, she smoked pot, but that wasn't enough—she had to grow it too. She would bake hash brownies for my friends. Naturally they loved her. 'Millie's so great! She's so cool! You're so lucky!' But having the kind of mother everyone *thinks* they would like to have isn't really so great. It's extremely *annoying* to have a mother who thinks she's one of the boys—who wants to be included in everything you do. I'll always be grateful for everything my mother did for me—she was an amazing woman—but I didn't have to think twice about getting out of there."

Perhaps surprisingly, in view of this, Chuck has often spoken enthusiastically about the advantages of growing up as an only child. Given his dyslexia and other early problems, it's undoubtedly true that he benefitted from having a fierce advocate to take up his cause. Clearly, too, he basked in that undivided attention, until it went too far and the advocacy turned toxic.

It is important, though, not to overlook the point of view of Mildred, herself an only child. She saw her son respond to the determination with which she championed him—and to the challenges she set—then experienced the perceived rejection that inevitably came as his world expanded so that she lost the central role she had played in his life. This is not an unusual story, but it's one that has a special poignancy in this case because of the intensity of Mildred's hunger to share in Chuck's success, her own frustrated ambitions, and the cruel reality of her widowhood. Mildred Close was a woman who had more than her share of demons to fight, and she battled them with gusto.

"If you ran into my mother during the day," says Chuck, "she'd always have a big, fixed smile on her face—a fierce smile. That was her public persona. If you ever saw her asleep, it was as if the smile had been flipped over. Her mouth came down at the corners—turned into a scowl. The contrast was like those theatrical masks of comedy and tragedy, and maybe that sums up who my mother was."

Chapter 7

New Haven

Chuck Close has said many times that backing into the Yale MFA program was the best thing that ever happened to him.

"When I finished up at the University of Washington, I thought I was ready to move to New York and make paintings. In Seattle, I'd been a big shot. I'd won prizes. I'd attracted attention. The truth is, if I'd taken any of those paintings to a New York gallery, I would have been humiliated. I was nowhere near ready. But Yale gave me access to the New York art world, and in New Haven I found myself part of another golden generation. This was the right place for me and the right time. The two years I spent there were the most important of my life."

The golden generation Chuck refers to included Brice Marden, Richard Serra, Nancy Graves, Robert Mangold, Janet Fish, Jennifer Bartlett, Rackstraw Downes, Don Nice, Kent Floeter, Steven Posen, Harriet Shore, and Newton Harrison. They did not all enter the department at the same time as Chuck, and some—like him—were on two-year programs while others were on three-year programs, but all overlapped with him for at least one year.

He had not lost his flair for being noticed. His proto-hippie style of dress guaranteed that, but some of his classmates—Richard Serra for one—first became aware of him when, for reasons Chuck does not recall, he was crawling across a rooftop and fell through a skylight into a life-drawing class, terrifying the model as shards of glass flew in all directions.

Chuck Close in his studio at Yale University, 1963

The Yale painting faculty during this period included abstractionists like Al Held and realists such as Alex Katz and Philip Pearlstein, all three at the time relatively unproven artists still in their thirties. Held, who joined the Yale faculty in 1962, had started out his career in the thrall of the Abstract Expressionists and had recently switched to a more hard-edged and considered form of nonfiguration. Katz's portraits and landscapes at the time were showing the influence of Pop art, while Pearlstein—a former classmate and roommate of Andy Warhol—had recently embarked on a series of very direct figure paintings which suggested that a radical approach to representational art remained possible. Each, in a different way, anticipated aspects of Chuck Close's mature work. There were also art history courses with distinguished teachers such as Jules Proun and Egbert Haverkamp-Begemann, and Close recalls with enthusiasm the legendary, packed house lectures of the architectural historian Vincent Scully. Chuck claims that he thinks every day, moving around the city, about one of Scully's talks—"The History of the Cornice—The Way Buildings Meet the Sky"—a lecture rich in meaning for anyone living in Manhattan with its fretted skyline of water towers, setbacks, and skyscrapers.

In his 1987 Smithsonian interview, Chuck compared the way the Yale faculty operated to the way skilled psychologists conduct group therapy sessions, not intruding too much but rather allowing the group members to develop a dialogue among themselves. Since the graduate students were an opinionated bunch, the dialogue—or dialogues—that evolved often became heated and sometimes threatened to explode into violence. As at the summer school session Chuck had attended, this was a collection of aspiring artists who mostly had been first magnitude stars in the provincial academic firmaments from which they had recently been plucked. (Chuck notes that admission to the Yale MFA program was unusual in that it depended more upon a student's intellectual qualities than on his or her portfolio. These were young men and women who not only made art, they thought about it day and night.)

One group of students, including Marden, Serra, Floeter, Downes, Graves, Posen, and Chuck, were housed in an old studio building on Crown Street. Asked why they were isolated from the rest of the MFA community, Chuck replies, "We were the troublemakers." Later he amends this by explaining that they were the students looked on by the faculty as being "less teachable"—more determined to find their own way even if it meant the occasional bloody nose. "Group therapy" in the Crown Street building was a sometimes wild, 24/7 kind of an activity.

Close attributes the success of this unstructured but stimulating system to the arrival of Jack Tworkov as faculty head at the beginning of the 1963–64 academic year. Prior to Tworkov's arrival, the dominant influence at Yale for more than a decade had been the teachings of Joseph Albers, who had headed the Depart-

ment of Design from 1950 until his retirement in 1958. At Yale, he had continued
to promote the academic philosophy he had evolved at the Bauhaus, and later
refined at Black Mountain College, introducing his famous color theory course
in which students were encouraged to discover an internal logic in the interaction of colors. (Simultaneously, he was working on his own celebrated *Homage
to the Square* series of paintings.) Although Albers had been gone for four years
by the time Chuck arrived in New Haven, his teachings were still current there
under the stewardship of Sewell Sillman. Chuck managed to avoid Sillman's
classes entirely, feeling that the course had become stale, in addition to which,
it might be noted, he had in fact already absorbed much of the post-Bauhaus
legacy embodied by Albers in the design courses taught by Rus Day at Everett
Junior College.

On the roof of Yale's Art and
Architecture Building, c. 1963-64

Tworkov, a Polish immigrant, brought a breath of fresh air to the department.
Well known as an Abstract Expressionist—a close associate of Willem de Kooning, Franz Kline, Mark Rothko, Jackson Pollock, and other founding members
of the New York School—he was nonetheless very open to the work of painters
of the generation that had emerged in the wake of Abstract Expressionism, and
enjoyed a reputation for actively supporting younger artists.

"Jack was far more adventurous in his tastes than the students were," Chuck
reports, "which was also true of some other faculty members like Al Held. Several
times a semester, artists would come up from New York to look at our work and
give crits. The students requested people like Isabel Bishop and Edwin Dickin-
son! We were incredibly conservative. Reactionary! It was the faculty, and Jack
Tworkov in particular, that invited Bob Rauschenberg and Frank Stella—and
we were suspicious as hell of those guys. When Stella gave a talk, Richard Serra

stood up in the middle of the slide show and called him a fraud then walked out on him."

Robert Rauschenberg's visit was marked by an incident of which Chuck was an instigator. Rauschenberg was notorious at the time for the examples of the taxidermist's art that he had incorporated into his combines. One of these– *Odalisk* (1955–58)–featured a stuffed rooster. On the day Rauschenberg was due in New Haven, Chuck and his roommate, Bill Hockhausen, went to a poultry store and purchased a live chicken which they installed under a paper bag, on a pedestal, in the sculpture studio where the critique was scheduled to take place. Rauschenberg duly arrived and stirred things up from the outset by announcing, "This place reeks of Matisse." When Rauschenberg started his crit, Hockhausen removed the bag from the pedestal, revealing the startled bird that until then had apparently managed to sleep through the whole thing. Rauschenberg immediately entered into the spirit of the joke, laughing and launching into a mock-serious critique of the chicken, which responded by sending a projectile stream of excrement across the room, as if in rebuttal.

Afterward, Chuck and Hockhausen returned the chicken to the poultry store, explaining that they had grown too fond of it to eat it. The store owner offered to kill it and pluck it for them, but they demurred.

"We went down to New York all the time," Chuck says, "and saw all the shows–which doesn't mean we *got* them, but we looked at everything. I was probably more open-minded than most. I was quite taken with Pop, which was very new at the time. Some of my contemporaries at Yale really hated it, thought that it was meretricious, phony, commercial–all those things that critics like Hilton Kramer and John Canaday were saying about it at the time. I went to the Castelli Gallery one day and bought a Roy Lichtenstein screenprint for ten bucks–I think that's what I paid for it–a signed image of a weeping woman. I took it back to Yale and I was mocked–vilified."

Chuck goes on to describe how it would be impossible to guess the identity of now-famous artists from their student work. Richard Serra, for example, was painting rather than making three-dimensional objects and had periods when he was heavily influenced by Matisse, Soutine, and Hans Hofmann. Rackstraw Downes, now a rigorously disciplined realist, made geometrical nonfigurative paintings. People who became sculptors were making paintings, people who are now known as painters were working in three dimensions.

Untitled painting (approximately 9 x 7 feet), c. 1963–64,
no longer extant, created by Close while in graduate school at Yale

Chuck himself did not change his style a great deal during these Yale years, continuing to paint large canvases in a latter-day Abstract Expressionist idiom. They became more accomplished, certainly, but essentially the influences remained the same, with de Kooning dominant.

Chuck remembers as a defining moment a critique given by the painter Philip Guston—a high school classmate of Jackson Pollock and himself a pioneer Abstract Expressionist—who was in a belligerent mood and tore everyone's work to shreds, until he came to Chuck's. His canvas had been buried at the bottom of a pile, so it was the last thing Guston came across, and he praised it to the skies, saying that finally here was someone who understood what art was about.

"I took him very seriously," says Chuck. "I mean, Philip Guston was someone whose work I really respected, and he's telling me I'm doing everything right. The result was I found myself trying to paint that same painting over and over again. I think it might have set me back a year or more because it delayed me from trying to kick the de Kooning habit and figure out my own thing. I reminded Guston about that crit years later, and told him it would have been much better if he'd ripped my work apart."

Close also recalls a memorable afternoon with Guston and Tworkov during this period. These two old cronies, veterans of the downtown Manhattan art scene, were going to lunch at Old Heidelberg—a famously seedy New Haven institution fondly remembered by generations of Yalies—and Chuck was invited to join them. He found himself in a deep, gloomy booth, beneath the Ballantine Ale signs and crew memorabilia that hung from the flyspecked walls, watching two of his heroes down one boilermaker after another, hour after hour, becoming drunk and very sorry for themselves.

"I haven't sold a painting in two years," Guston complained.

"That's nothing," countered Tworkov. "I haven't sold one in three."

For Chuck, it was a sobering experience. Here were two men whose work he had admired since first seeing it in the form of black-and-white reproductions in the library at Everett Junior College, and they were crying into their drinks and talking like a pair of hopeless failures. Both were represented by top galleries and had had retrospectives at the Whitney Museum, but nobody was buying their work. If these demigods found themselves in that position, how was Chuck going to get by in New York? It scared him to think about it, but in retrospect he sees that afternoon as the beginning of a learning process. The art world is cyclical. A few years later, Guston would turn from abstraction to a cartoonish figurative idiom and enjoy enormous success, becoming a major influence on younger artists in the process.

This was a lunch Chuck would never forget.

Chuck took Egbert Haverkamp-Begemann's course on the history of printmaking, a subject that might have seemed dry if it had not been for the fact that Haverkamp-Begemann encouraged the students to handle actual proofs of prints by masters like Rembrandt and Piranesi, so that they could see how the imagery evolved through a succession of "states" as the artist modified, almost by trial and error, the marks engraved or etched into his plate. This emphasis on the importance of process as a means to an end would have profound reverberations in Close's mature work.

He also gained valuable practical experience of printmaking as the assistant to Gabor Petardi, a Hungarian printmaker who had worked with the English virtuoso Stanley William Hayter at the latter's Atelier 17 in Paris prior to World War II. (Atelier 17 was a studio much favored by Picasso and the Surrealists.) Chuck recalls that Petardi once told him he was the worst assistant he had ever had. This had nothing to do with the quality of Close's work, but rather with his inability to maintain the sense of order that is essential in a print shop. Chuck remembers him as a nice guy who spoke his mind and was given to occasional acts of generosity that went beyond the usual relationship between students and faculty. He once handed Chuck a hundred dollars and said, "Here, kid—go to New York and get laid."

Along with looking at art, hoping to get laid was a regular component of trips to the city. There were women like Janet Fish and Jennifer Bartlett in the graduate program at the School of Art and Architecture—and they were a force to be reckoned with, ready to go head to head with the men—but essentially Yale was still an all-male school in those days, with no female undergraduates. Chuck recalls that the gender imbalance put a crimp in his style, at least so far as forming any kind of serious relationship was concerned.

"You were supposed to be married to have sex," he says, and in fact a number of his Yale contemporaries, like Brice Marden and Kent Floeter, were already married, while others like Richard Serra and Nancy Graves soon followed their lead.

For Chuck, on the other hand, this was a time for acquiring sexual experience without commitment. He remembers, for example, sleeping with a life model he had recognized—from drawings he had seen—as having been a favorite of the highly regarded California artist Richard Diebenkorn.

A faculty member with practical advice to offer was Al Held. Chuck had problems with Held as a teacher, because he tended to be overly free with suggestions as to how a painting should be resolved, sometimes to the extent of wanting to repaint it himself. Chuck recalls becoming so enraged at this interference that he once locked Held out of his studio. When it came to the nitty-gritty of functioning in the real world, however, Held was worth listening to. It was he who told the aspiring artists what it was going to take to survive in New York. Raised in Brooklyn, Held knew what he was talking about.

His father had run a coffee stand on Prince Street, in what would become SoHo. Young Al had put in his time delivering coffee and bagels to sweatshops in neighborhood loft buildings. By the sixties, when Chuck met him, those sweatshops were being turned into artists' studios. Held's advice to his students was that they should go to New York and be prepared to work hard in unglamorous trades to support their painting habits—slapping up sheetrock, sanding floors, ripping out tin ceilings, making frames, or stretching canvases for other people, maybe driving a taxi or a truck.

"This may not sound like fun," he would tell them, "but it's infinitely preferable to the living death of teaching untalented students in some provincial art department."

Chuck was not totally convinced by this advice. He was more than a little afraid of New York, not because it was a big, intimidating city but because it was the place where he would have to put up or shut up. He loved to go there, to feel that he knew his way around the galleries and the museums, but the idea of actually moving into a loft and putting his ambitions and work to the test was daunting. Giving him further pause was the knowledge that the Yale School of Art and Architecture had a reputation for being able to place its best students in plum teaching jobs in colleges not too far from New York—places where you could pull down a decent salary and find time to paint while still being able to get into Manhattan to see the big museum shows and stay in touch with what was happening in the galleries on Madison Avenue and Fifty-seventh Street.

The big decision was still a way off, however, and meanwhile New Haven was a great place to procrastinate.

When Close signed up for Jules Proun's "History of American Art" course, he presumed that it would provide insights into the worlds of the Abstract Expressionists and other modernists, and was a little taken aback to find that it was concerned with such topics as early American architecture and furniture. He enjoyed the course, however, and it provided the occasion for perhaps the most spectacular of all his nonverbal papers. This took the form of a comparison between a Hepplewhite-style chest, and a Federal Period villa, which Close achieved by superimposing an image of the former over the latter—the chest inverted so that its legs corresponded with the villa's chimneys—a device that permitted similarities of structure and ornament to become immediately apparent. For years Proun used this as an example of how an outstanding paper could be produced without using any words.

During his Yale sojourn, Chuck made a couple of trips back to Washington, one in the summer of 1963, during which he helped his mother build her new house at Lake Stevens, and one a Christmas visit for which he took advantage of a Greyhound bus deal which offered up to ninety-nine days of travel anywhere in the United States for $99. Traveling across the northern states as winter tightened its grip made for tedious journeys, the outbound trip taking seven days and the return trip eight. Chuck occupied himself by working on the assignment set by Proun. Most of his fellow passengers were servicemen headed home on leave, or returning to base. It would be a year or two before the word "hippie" came into common usage, but these young soldiers and marines saw Chuck, with his beard and unkempt hair, as some kind of freak and made their opinion clear. Always gregarious and willing to join in the often scatological singsongs that helped keep boredom at bay, Chuck won them over, which proved critical on at least one occasion.

During a Nebraska blizzard—not far from his mother's birthplace—the bus pulled into the parking lot of an old-fashioned diner converted from a railroad car. The seats at one end of the diner were occupied by a group of raucous townies. The servicemen, most dressed in civilian clothes, sat at the other end of the car. Chuck sat between the two groups and ate quietly till one of the townies, offended by his appearance, put salt in his coffee. Chuck called the waiter/owner and asked for another coffee, which was duly brought to the table. The townie had just gotten started, however, and now he escalated his torment, pouring hot sauce and other unwanted condiments onto Chuck's food until finally Chuck blew up and cursed the man.

This gave the entire group of townies license to rise to their feet and strike menacing poses. Chuck began to wonder if he would ever see New Haven again. His fellow passengers had taken note of all this, however, and—perhaps relishing the opportunity to relieve the tedium of the journey—rushed to his defense. The fight that ensued was like something out of a vintage Western with townies being thrown over the diner's counter where bottles were sent flying and dishes smashed to the floor, with splashed ketchup adding appropriate color to the scene. The driver—a veteran of such situations—took all the bills he had in his wallet and threw them at the frantic owner, then shepherded his fired-up passengers back onto the bus which took off into the driving snow just as two police cruisers with flashing lights appeared out of the darkness. As the bus headed through the blizzard, the passengers passed around a hat into which bills were thrown to recompense the driver and thank him for his quick-witted actions.

A couple of years later, many of these young servicemen might have been bound for Vietnam and Chuck might have been more conflicted about thinking of them as comrades. Yale, during his time there, was not yet the hotbed of political radicalism it would become later in the sixties, but causes such as the antinuclear movement and civil liberties were already the subjects of intense campus debate. The Reverend William Sloane Coffin, Jr.—the inspiration for much of Yale's radicalization—had been appointed chaplain of the university and promptly upset many of the people who had selected him by demonstrating his fierce dedication to the civil rights movement, which in 1961 had led to his being jailed during a "freedom ride" through Alabama and Georgia. Chuck was of course sympathetic to such causes, and his political awareness grew by leaps and bounds during this New Haven period. He recalls in particular one memorable chance encounter that contributed to this.

He was on York Street, near the edge of the campus, when he spotted a small crowd gathered on a corner listening to a fiery speaker who turned out to be Malcolm X. Chuck stopped to listen and at the end of the speech, which was more of a harangue, he went up to Malcolm and said, "What can someone like me do to help?" Malcolm looked at him witheringly and said, "There's nothing someone like you can do to help. Just get out of the way."

(Thirty years later, watching Spike Lee's movie *Malcolm X*, Chuck was amused to see an almost identical incident on screen, though the student in the film is female.)

One source of informal political education was the folk music movement, which Chuck had followed since his Seattle days and his trips to North Beach in San Francisco, and which had a strong presence on the Yale campus. Brice Marden was married at the time to Pauline Baez, sister of the popular folk singer Joan Baez. Through the circle around the Mardens, Chuck came into contact with antinuclear activists, labor organizers, and politically inflected performers such as Joan Baez, Mimi Farina (the third Baez sister), and Bob Dylan. On at least one occasion he went backstage at a Dylan performance. This was at the Forest Hills tennis stadium in Queens. After the show, Chuck returned with the Dylan entourage to a nearby hotel, which was quickly surrounded by a mob of fans, some of whom attempted to climb the ivy-covered walls to reach Dylan's suite. A photographer for *Look* magazine had been covering the event, and as it happened he had frizzy hair that resembled Dylan's. This photographer was taken down to the basement parking lot and put into the limo provided for Dylan by the promoters. The limo's departure successfully distracted the crowd. Meanwhile, Dylan took refuge in the most unlikely vehicle available, which happened to be Chuck's tiny three-cylinder DKW sedan, a car so decrepit the driver's side door had to be held shut with baling wire. Without attracting unwanted attention, Chuck drove Dylan into Manhattan, leaving him outside his Greenwich Village apartment.

Chuck Close had been too young to vote in the 1960 presidential election (and would have preferred Adlai Stevenson as the Democratic candidate), but he welcomed John F. Kennedy's victory, and—the Bay of Pigs debacle notwithstanding—had for the most part found himself in tune with the mood of optimism and youthful energy generated by an administration that was perceived as having turned the White House into a modern Camelot and that seemed to be ushering in a new, more liberal and—not incidentally—more creative America, a country where young artists would be able to find a place for themselves and thrive. It was, of course, the First Lady, Jacqueline Kennedy, who placed a special emphasis on the arts, and Chuck experienced her enthusiasm first hand when, along with Nancy Graves, he was selected to conduct Mrs. Kennedy on a tour of the almost-completed Paul Rudolph Building that would become the new home of the Art & Architecture School.

Chuck had several jobs to help pay his way through Yale. Early on the afternoon of November 22, 1963, he was leaving the Economic Growth Center Building on Hillhouse Avenue—the location of one of these—on his way to the Law School where he worked in the kitchens and dining room. In the parking lot, he heard that President Kennedy had been shot. He jumped into his car to listen to news coverage, sitting there for a long time until he realized that he was late for his shift at the Law School. Hurrying there on foot, he let himself in by a back entrance, partly as a shortcut to the dining room and partly because this route would take him through the students' smoking room where he knew there was a television set. Gathered there was a group of students, many of them in the uber-Wasp Law School uniform of the period—blazers, J. Press shirts with frayed collars, loafers held together with adhesive tape. As Chuck arrived, they were raucously toasting Kennedy's death as the best thing to have happened to American politics in decades. Shocked, Chuck screamed at them and, in a rare display of physical aggression, took a swing at one.

Then he went to the kitchens and began his shift washing dishes, but the bitter memory of that occasion reinforced his existing political convictions and nourished his determination to lend his support to liberal and sometimes radical causes, both as an activist and as a proselytizer.

Chapter 8

Transitions

At the end of his first year at Yale, Chuck was awarded a BFA with the highest honors, and the following year, 1964, he received his MFA, once again with the highest honors. Simultaneously, he was awarded a Fulbright scholarship to spend a year in Europe, selecting Vienna as the city where he would be based, nominally so that he could study the works of Gustav Klimt and Egon Schiele but in reality because he thought it would provide a central location from which to make expeditions to the continent's great museums and galleries, both west and east of the iron curtain. In Vienna, he familiarized himself with the great collections of the Kunsthistorisches Museum and the Albertina, painted at a studio near the Sudbahnhof providing easy access to the trains, and acquired an Austrian girlfriend, Karin. It was the travel outside Austria, however, that defined his time in Europe.

His expeditions could be planned, in part at least, around visits to fellow Yale alumni who were also on scholarships to Europe at the time. Richard Serra and Nancy Graves were in Paris, and while visiting them, Chuck got to know their friend the musician Philip Glass, who would come to have a special significance for Chuck in his future career. Steven Posen was in Florence, and Kent Floeter was in Barcelona. In addition, an old University of Washington friend had been awarded the Prix de Rome. At the end of each month's explorations, Chuck returned to Vienna and the Akademie der Bildenden Künste, where he was enrolled, in order to receive his Fulbright stipend. With money in hand, there were more cities and museums to be visited, and plenty of floors, sofas, and park benches on which to sleep.

At Donatello's tomb in Florence, Italy, 1965.
From left: Nancy Graves, Chuck Close,
Richard Serra, and Steven Posen

He had already had considerable exposure to the great European masters at institutions such as the Metropolitan Museum of Art and the Yale University Art Gallery, but walking streets where Velázquez or Veronese had walked and sitting in cafés that Picasso and Matisse had patronized not so many years earlier transformed his sense of their achievements and made them more concrete. Cumulatively, his European experiences were overwhelming. He saw so much in such a short time he could not take everything in, but it shocked him out of his complacency. He knew now he could not just continue doing de Kooning knockoffs. He had to find something of his own, though he had no idea what that might turn out to be.

As this year of travel wound down, he found himself confronted once again with another major decision, one that he had managed to postpone since completing his bachelor's degree at the University of Washington. Where was he going to put down roots, and how was he going to support himself?

He remembers being on a beach on the Costa Brava with Kent Floeter and the pair of them becoming paranoid as they talked about their futures. Floeter had a wife and two children to support, making him even more nervous than Chuck. The result was a long-distance call to Bernard Chaet urgently seeking advice and assistance. Luckily for them, Yale MFAs were in demand and Floeter was quickly offered a job as chairman of the art department at Ithaca College, while Chuck found himself signing up for a teaching position at the University of Massachusetts, Amherst.

By the time the ship bringing him back from Europe tied up at its pier on the Hudson River, a number of Chuck's old Yale friends were already established in Manhattan lofts. Brice Marden, for example, was only months away from having his first New York show. Chuck was envious of them, but after staying briefly with Bill Hockhausen, he was on his way to New England.

The reality was that he was still intimidated by New York. When he talked to contemporaries who had made the move, they urged him to do the same, assuring him that a work space would cost next to nothing and he would find some way to get by. He knew it was true, but something was still holding him back. A teaching job in Massachusetts seemed like a workable compromise. It would be almost like an extension of Yale, he told himself. He would be close enough to New York to make regular visits. He would be able to see all his old friends. He would stay in touch with what was happening in the galleries and museums. He would have time to paint—and somebody would be paying him.

He visualized himself, in effect, as the artist equivalent of a gentleman farmer, but it did not take him long to find out that he had made a horrible mistake.

"I soon discovered the truth of what Al Held had said about the deadening effect of provincial teaching jobs. My first year in Amherst, I was a painter who also taught. At the end of the second year, I was a teacher who used to paint."

Chuck was miserable in Amherst. He bought a used Mercedes 220 to try to make himself feel better and drove down to New York to visit Marden who was living on the Lower East Side. He remembers opening the trunk to take out a nice bottle of wine he'd brought, and seeing the skeptical look on Marden's face.

"He thought I'd sold out, and at that moment I felt like a total bourgeois pig. I'd sold my soul for a pre-owned Mercedes!"

Amherst had been a mistake, but it seems probable that Chuck would have been going through a crisis regarding his artistic identity no matter where he was. His over-indulgence in the manifold pleasures of the great museums of Europe had been like an endless series of binge drinking sessions that had left him groggy, hungover, exhausted, and confused. The avalanche of masterpieces of all periods suggested all too many possible routes out of his cul-de-sac of Abstract Expressionist clichés and mannerisms. He knew that, once and for all, he had to exorcise the ghost of his surrogate father de Kooning, but those painterly gestures he had borrowed and practiced for years had become so ingrained they had become a kind of addiction. To kick the habit, he would have to go cold turkey.

The fact that, of all the Abstract Expressionists, de Kooning had been his idol meant that Close had stayed in touch with figuration, spellbound by the master's ability to transform a nude into a maze of abstract fields of color, yet retain a sensuality and a feeling of sheer fleshiness that was worthy of Rubens or Boucher. All those old masters he had seen in Europe, however, had caused Chuck to reconsider figuration from many different points of view. He was well prepared for this, having, after all, had his introduction to art, and the magic of illusion, by way of the great American illustrators of the mid-century period who had employed techniques that derived directly from Van Eyck and Vermeer; Giorgione and Jordaens; Brueghel and Bronzino; David, Delacroix, and Degas. When Chuck Close peered through his corrective lenses, studying a panel by Hans Memling, his nose a few inches from its crystalline surface—probably arousing the nervous attention of museum guards in the process, this exotically dressed, oversized young American with the long hair and aggressive beard—he was in fact continuing a practice inaugurated in his grandmother's living room back in

Everett, Washington. He was figuring out, through rigorous examination, how this fifteenth-century master had achieved his effects. Finding answers to the question "How was it done?" had become a lifelong obsession.

During his time in Amherst, however, that question was not entirely relevant since he did not know what it was that he wanted to do, but he began from the position that he was going to introduce imagery into his work, unadulterated by gesture or modernist distortion. One way to achieve this was to incorporate photography into his imagery (and by this time he was, of course, very familiar with the work of artists like Rauschenberg and Warhol who had already made extensive use of photographic imagery).

Chuck started modestly by incorporating, into a painting, photographs taken at a friend's wedding. The results failed to excite him, but the break had been made.

At U Mass, Close taught three classes, each made up of forty students. It can be imagined that this presented something of a challenge to someone suffering from prosopagnosia. Since there were students he could not recognize from one class to the next, he hit on the device of making little drawings of each of their paintings in a notebook and writing the artist's name alongside. As he went from easel to easel, he could greet people as if the face was familiar when it fact it was the work he recognized. He claims he can look at these more than forty-year-old notebooks and recall each painting in detail, not just as they were when finished but as they looked at every stage. It's been a godsend, he says, when ex-students have asked for references.

The crisis in his own work continued, and increasingly he moved back towards explicit figuration, returning again and again to photographic imagery as source material, borrowing pictorial elements from magazines and record album sleeves. In some cases, this Pop-inflected imagery was incorporated into three-dimensional constructions that utilized real objects, Plexiglas panels and vacuum-shaped plastic forms. Little has survived from this period, somewhat to Chuck's relief since these pieces apparently displayed an awkward eclecticism indicative of his continuing struggle to find an authentic idiom. In 1967, however—towards the end of his second year at the school—a selection of works from this period of abortive transition was hung in the Student Union Building, provoking a scandal comparable with the one stirred up by *Betsy Ross Revisited*. This time official ire was sparked by the perception of obscenity arising from the inclusion of full-frontal male nudity in some works, and the unfathomable conclusion on the part of someone in authority that a patch of yellow paint in one painting represented urine. Campus police raided the show, and it was shut down despite the fact that the entire faculty of the art department backed Chuck's position. The show was then rehung in a local gallery where it became the focus of protests against the school administration. With the aid of the American Civil

Teaching at the University of Massachusetts, Amherst, c. 1966

Liberties Union, Close brought a suit against the college. The case was initially decided in his favor, but that decision was overturned on appeal. In retrospect, Chuck regrets having taken matters this far because he feels it placed an unnecessary burden on the faculty members who had supported him—forcing them to jeopardize their own positions with the administration—over a matter that was not really important given that this was a period when B-52s were bombing North Vietnam and the U.S. military buildup in the South was approaching the 500,000 mark.

Chuck Close in his studio, Northampton, Mass., 1966

The practical outcome was that his career at the University of Massachusetts was at an end. He had learned Al Held's lesson the hard way.

By far the most ambitious work Chuck embarked on during this period was a mural-scaled nude, 21 feet long, based on photographs he had taken of a young woman who was a secretary at the school. This was to be an entirely realistic painting, its impact dependent upon scale and fidelity to the photographic source. The impetus behind the painting was the desire to make a complete break with his past. He had had plenty of experience with working on a large scale, and at Amherst he had been flirting with photography as source material. Combining the two was logical, but now the intent was radical. The project would prove prophetic of the direction in which Chuck's work would evolve, but in this original form it did not get very far. The photographs were black-and-white but his intention was to make the painting in full color. Looking back, he cannot imagine what he was thinking. In any case, it quickly became apparent that flesh tones could not be improvised to his satisfaction, and additionally he found that conventional brush on canvas technique was not giving him the look he had hoped for. When that became evident, the painting was abandoned—a single foot was all that had been completed—but the project would be revived not long after, with some important differences.

While at Amherst, Chuck did form some real friendships, including those with faculty members Keith Hollingworth and John Roy, both of whom would become the subject of major Close portraits. Early in his U Mass career Chuck struck up another friendship with a graduate student by the name of Michael Burns who, like him, was from the Pacific Northwest. Burns was in a drawing class taught by Chuck in which another student was a talented and very attractive freshman from Long Island, Leslie Rose, who was attending U Mass almost by chance because of a family connection. One day during Leslie's first semester, she answered a phone call to find both Michael Burns and Chuck Close at the other end of the line. Jointly they invited her to a poetry reading.

Leslie says that her first impression of Chuck was extremely negative. More than once he had showed up late to teach his drawing class, appearing disheveled and obviously drunk. (Close is more succinct, saying, "She hated me.") Nonetheless she consented to accompany the two young men to the reading, and at the agreed-upon time they arrived to pick her up. Chuck's pre-owned Mercedes was parked outside the dormitory and, without knowing who the driver was, Leslie got into the back of the car. According to her, her dates appeared to interpret this as a significant choice on her part, though she does not remember that as having been the case. They went to the reading, then on to a party, and the upshot of the evening was that Leslie found herself in a relationship with Michael Burns. Chuck did not vanish from the picture, however. Rather, the three of them became a social unit, going everywhere together, sometimes with Chuck bringing another girl along, this being a period when serial relationships between students and junior faculty members were not actively discouraged but rather were overlooked or taken for granted. (Another female student who attended the school shortly after Leslie reports that what would now be considered sexual harassment on the part of faculty was commonplace.)

"There was a pizza place in town," says Chuck, "where we would hang out till two in the morning, eating and drinking—not just us, there would be other teachers there, other students. And the three of us would go to movies together, things like that. Sometimes Leslie and Michael would sleep over in my studio. I would set up a curtain for privacy—if you can call it that."

At Thanksgiving, Leslie took both young men home to East Meadow, a bedroom community forty minutes from New York City by Long Island Railroad. This was very much a family affair, with Leslie's three younger siblings—David, Debbie, and John—on hand. Predictably, Leslie's parents, Nat and Shirley Rose, did not warm to Michael Burns—the unmistakably gentile person she was involved with—but did take to Chuck who at this time was not perceived as a threat to their daughter's honor. The social threesome continued for several months until it emerged that Burns had been in contact all along with another girlfriend back in the state of Washington—a long-term relationship that dated back to high school and that now was reignited, much to Leslie's dismay. To make things all the more painful, she received the news immediately after attending her grandfather's funeral. Needing a shoulder to cry on, it was inevitable that she would turn to Chuck.

"I think he saw me as a bit exotic," says Leslie. "A New York Jewish girl—nothing like the girls he had grown up with."

Chuck acknowledges that there's a good deal of truth to this. There had been a small Jewish community in Everett, and one Orthodox temple, but with his solidly Baptist background Chuck had had little contact with Jews till he moved east. Leslie's conjecture is further borne out by Donn Trethewey, who agrees that she did indeed seem exotic, and enchanting, when he and other Everett friends first met her a couple of years later.

"As you might imagine, Everett's Jewish community was miniscule. Lutheran, Catholic, Episcopal, and so on, were represented in great numbers. . . . I remember meeting Leslie at a party at [Joe] Aiken's house. She was, in a whisper, Jewish. Who knew? Who cared? She could have been from Neptune. We all just liked her, as simple as that. We still do."

Larry Stair recalls meeting Leslie on what must have been the same occasion.

"I liked Leslie from day one. I first met her at Joe Aiken's house where, during a humorous conversation, she autographed my ankle with an indelible Sharpie. Spunky enough for Chuck, I thought."

Everett was in fact a typical Scandinavian-American town where, according to Close, it was understood that nobody talked about anything personal, anything psychological; a place where feelings were kept under wraps until it was too late

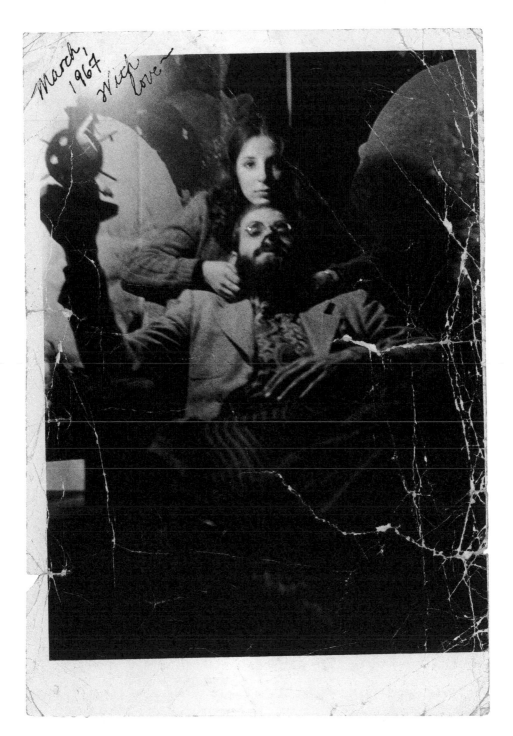

Chuck Close and Leslie Rose, 1967

to control them—a world that would have seemed familiar to Ibsen and Ingmar Bergman. Chuck was drawn to Leslie because she embodied a temperament that was the opposite of the repressive values he had grown up with. She spoke her mind without hesitation and tackled real issues without embarrassment. She was not slow to let her emotions show, or to let him know what was bothering her. She could be volatile, had a sharp and sometimes sarcastic sense of humor, and was not shy about expressing her anger.

He found this refreshing. It also intimidated him.

Back in Amherst, Chuck and Leslie were now a twosome. This was a classic rebound situation in which the physical attraction that Chuck had suppressed during Leslie's affair with Michael Burns was let loose. If Chuck saw Leslie as exotic, she seems to have seen him as an antiestablishmentarian bad boy—the kind your mother warns you against, hence irresistible, or at least intriguing. Yet from the outset Leslie seems to have detected a vulnerability about Chuck. She was swept up by his skill and ambition and his youthful arrogance, but she quickly grasped how dissatisfied—to the point of desperation—he was with the work he was making (a dissatisfaction that he did nothing to hide). She saw that he was obsessed with the fact that so many of his Yale friends were already established in New York, living the life that he wanted for himself—in some cases on the verge of professional success—while he was stuck in the boonies. Leslie was happy enough in Amherst, and enjoyed the community there, but it became increasingly obvious that if she was going to stay with Chuck then a move to the Big Apple was inevitable.

When Leslie first met him, Chuck had been renting in the small town of Leverett just north of Amherst, a place he describes as consisting of a gas station, a post office, and a few houses. By the time they got together, however, he had moved to a loft in a seedy section of Northampton, Amherst's neighbor across the Connecticut River.

"It was above a beauty parlor," Leslie recalls. "The whole place was permeated with that sickly smell of the chemicals they used to give perms in those days. And Chuck lived in squalor. He'd have a party and weeks later there'd still be paper cups and pizza boxes and empty wine bottles all over the floor."

This disregard for the niceties of living was one expression of Chuck's frustration with what he now perceived as his own cowardice in not taking on the New

York art scene. He was also drinking too much, running up debts and sometimes driving so recklessly that passengers in the Mercedes were terrified. Looking back on that period, Close credits Leslie for getting him to clean up his act. It was not just that she helped to get his life more organized. For the most part, her largely successful attempt to get him to shape up was by pointedly and persistently expressing her disapproval. The message she broadcast loud and clear was, "Straighten up or we're through."

At some point in the spring of 1967, Chuck asked Leslie to marry him, and she accepted his proposal.

New York could not be put off any longer. The fiasco resulting from the charges of obscenity being leveled at his work had brought things to a head, and Chuck eagerly accepted the offer of a part-time teaching job at the School of Visual Arts instigated by his former Yale classmate Don Nice. Appropriately, given the way his work would evolve, he was hired to teach painting and drawing in the photography department.

Surprisingly, perhaps, Chuck was retained by U Mass to teach summer school. (The circumstances were that he had faculty support, his lawsuit was ongoing, and the administration was probably just relieved that he would not be coming back in September.) Leslie meanwhile moved to Manhattan ahead of him, having been accepted as a transfer student in the art department of Hunter College for the coming fall. In the meantime, she doubled up with a friend in a small apartment in Yorkville and worked at the Barnes & Noble bookstore at Eighteenth Street and Fifth Avenue. Chuck joined her when summer school was over, and they began to hunt for a studio/living space downtown.

"I went along with the move to New York," she says now, "partly because at that age–I was just a sophomore–I didn't have enough sense of myself to question it. I would have been content to stay at Amherst, but on the other hand, I felt pretty comfortable about going to the city. I'd grown up in Queens and on Long Island so New York wasn't threatening to me, and there was something romantic about the idea of becoming part of that downtown world."

She acknowledges too that at that time, she was in fact in revolt against her parents' values.

Chuck's U Mass contemporary Keith Hollingworth had made the move to the city earlier in the summer and was the first to find a studio. As he settled in, he heard of another loft that was available and tipped Chuck off. In September, 1967, Chuck and Leslie moved into a raw space at 27 Greene Street. They kept this information from her parents, who would not have countenanced the idea of cohabitation before marriage, with Leslie maintaining the fiction of staying with a family member who was prepared to go along with the deception.

On December 24 of that same year, Chuck Close and Leslie Rose were married at a country club in Roslyn, Long Island, not far from her parents' home. The ceremony was performed by a rabbi, the only one who could be found who would marry them without Chuck converting to Judaism. Because of the Christmas holidays, very few of Chuck's friends attended the ceremony. His mother flew out from Washington, staying with him on Greene Street. Both she and Chuck were hurt by the inexplicable fact that Millie was not invited to a number of prenuptial parties thrown on Long Island. Eventually Chuck would form close bonds with Nat and Shirley Rose, just as his father had formed close bonds with his in-laws, the Wagners. At the time, however, it was apparent that this was not seen by Leslie's family as a marriage made in heaven.

Weddings are probably not the best time to make the acquaintance of a daughter-in-law or a mother-in-law. Decorum was maintained, but Leslie did not take to Millie, and Millie did not take to Leslie. We can only speculate as to how Millie felt about her late husband's name having been usurped by this young bride, barely out of her teens.

Part II

Chapter 9

Rags and Rats

On a fine Saturday afternoon in the twenty-first century, emerging from the subway station at Prince Street and Broadway, you will find yourself swept along by a tsunami of tourists, there to imbibe a potent cocktail of history and commerce at a nodal point where the monsters of retail culture have cannibalized Art in the ecumenical spirit of Andy Warhol, whose image is ubiquitous—on tee-shirts and shopping bags, and on postcards and in gallery windows—so that he seems to have assumed the position that the Dalai Lama or the Virgin Mary might occupy in an older civilization.

Had you climbed the same subway station steps on a weekend in 1967, you would have found yourself in a wilderness of empty streets abandoned even by the sweatshop workers and truckers who brought a hint of bustle to the area from Monday to Friday. At dusk you could sometimes walk from Prince Street to Canal without seeing a soul, though if you were lucky you might have caught a glimpse of the real Andy Warhol, who sometimes ventured to these parts from his Midtown headquarters. You would have sought in vain for Prada or Dean & Deluca; even the galleries that preceded the chic boutiques and eateries had not yet put in an appearance.

East side of Greene Street, looking north from the approximate location of Chuck and Leslie Close's loft, c. 1970

The area was not even called SoHo—that moniker was a half-dozen years away—in fact, it didn't have a proper name of any kind, though reverential city historians referred to it as the Cast-Iron District in deference to its architectural heritage, and a few old-timers called it The Valley, a reference to the fact that it was located between the high-rise buildings of the Wall Street area and those that had sprung up to the north around the Flatiron Building. The artists who began to move in during the sixties generally called it the loft district and left

New in town: Chuck and Leslie Close on the New York City subway, c. 1967

it at that. New York City's firemen had a more sinister name for the neighbor-hood, "Hell's Hundred Acres"–World War II slang for a concentrated but deadly combat zone. A series of blazes in the late fifties and early sixties had resulted in department fatalities. When these ornate cast-iron loft buildings caught fire, the wood floors burned like tinder and the metal framework softened in the intense heat so that the structure quickly collapsed under its own weight. As long as the area remained an industrial enclave, deserted at night, Fire Department policy had been to fight loft blazes from the street and not risk men's lives by asking them to enter unstable buildings. The arrival of artists as illegal residents in the neighborhood changed all that, since there was no telling where a painter with his highly flammable materials or a sculptor with his acetylene tank, welding tools, and blowtorch might be hiding out behind shutters to escape the notice of city inspectors. Buildings could no longer be allowed to burn to the ground with minimal intervention, so the men in fire stations and ladder companies around Lower Manhattan had to be put in harm's way.

The new loft dwellers were surrounded by reminders of immigrant New York. Italian street festivals invaded adjacent thoroughfares, while Chinese New Year was celebrated nearby with firecrackers and heaving block-long dragons. Homing pigeons still took wing from coops atop tenements on Thompson and Sullivan Streets, flocks circling above the wooden water towers that were the defining feature of the SoHo roofscape. To take up residence in the loft district was to embed oneself in the historical and cultural infrastructure of Lower Manhattan.

Bounded by Houston and Canal Streets to the north and south, and by Crosby Street and Sixth Avenue to the east and west, much of the area had once been owned by the old buccaneer capitalist John Jacob Astor. In the mid-nineteenth century it had been the city's most fashionable retail and entertainment district, home to stores like Lord & Taylor and Tiffany & Co. as well as oyster palaces, casinos, theaters, minstrel halls, and opulent brothels, the latter concentrated on Greene Street, where one spectacular example, at the corner of Canal Street, featured seven orchestras, one for every floor, each playing in a different style.

As the theaters and department stores migrated uptown, SoHo was inherited by small manufacturing and warehouse companies, mostly owned and staffed by immigrants, many of them Jewish. Leases were reasonable, the location was conveniently central, and the layout of the cast-iron buildings, with open, well-lit floors, was ideally suited to the needs of sweatshop operators. You could fit a lot of sewing machines into one of those lofts, and it was easy for a supervisor to keep an eye on the underpaid employees.

For more than half a century prior to the arrival of the artists, these buildings had been pretty much fully occupied by commercial tenants. That situation was coming to an end partly because the lofts did not lend themselves to modernization, and also because the neighborhood was becoming a transportation nightmare. On top of that there was the Robert Moses factor. For forty years, as head of a dozen state and city authorities, Moses had transformed New York—sometimes for better, sometimes for worse—building spectacular bridges and providing modern, landscaped highways to give access to well-maintained parks and public beaches but simultaneously destroying neighborhoods to accommodate his megalomaniac vision of a metropolis bent to the needs of the automobile. One of the last of his grandiose schemes was a plan to construct a superhighway across Lower Manhattan, smack through the heart of what would become SoHo. A major reason for businesses quitting the loft district in the sixties was the likelihood that before long it might cease to exist.

This worked to the short-term advantage of artists because it meant still more empty spaces owned by landlords who were eager to cut a deal, turning a blind eye to the fact that many of those who signed leases were intending to live in buildings zoned for strictly nonresidential use. Every early settler has stories to tell of covert acts. It was not unheard of, for example, for a SoHo inhabitant to light his studio and provide juice for his power tools by tapping directly into the Consolidated Edison mains. This worked just fine until some eagle-eyed Con Ed inspector found reason to suspect foul play. One West Broadway resident, a sculptor, spent paranoid days drinking coffee and smoking cigarettes in a workman's café across the street from his loft, certain that the Con Ed man was about to arrive with a summons that very morning. At night, the sculptor worked behind World War II–style blackout curtains.

The artists were prepared to take their chances on living in firetraps, with ancient wiring and substandard sprinkler systems, in exchange for vast work spaces and rents that were so low they barely covered landlords' property taxes. They were following in a tradition that had taken root during the Depression when pioneering downtown painters like Arshile Gorky and Willem de Kooning had rented raw space in Chelsea and on the outskirts of Greenwich Village.

The Closes established their initial toehold at 27 Greene Street, a run-down industrial building next door to a brush factory. Five days a week, the block was clogged with commercial vehicles laden with bales of brightly-colored rags and shredded paper that were the most cheerful things around since the Victorian buildings, though architecturally remarkable, were coated with decades of grime and the sidewalks were littered with industrial detritus. Street life was largely limited to the loading and unloading of trucks, sometimes under the bleary gaze of stragglers from the Bowery clutching pints of Ripple or Thunderbird. By night, Greene Street, like all of its immediate neighbors, became an urban wasteland with rodents frolicking in the gutters.

"Rags and rats, rats and rags," is the way Chuck Close remembers the neighborhood.

If you were the kind of person who chose to live south of Houston Street, however, those vermin-infested blocks possessed a unique kind of beauty, like something that might have resulted from a perverse collaboration between Edward Hopper and Weegee—the Rembrandt of crime photography who had snapped some of his most picturesque corpses in neighboring alleys. On the other hand, prospective collectors were hesitant to visit artists' studios after dark because the district seemed scary—a muggers' paradise. On one occasion a cab driver refused to let Leslie Close out of his taxi outside her own home, saying he would not be held responsible for what might happen to her. In reality, leaders of the Italian communities that flanked the future Soho to the east and west made sure that the area remained largely crime free, at least so far as random violence perpetrated by unaffiliated outsiders was concerned (though cars parked on the street overnight were apt to be trashed). Greene Street was home, however, to private sanitation companies rumored to have mob connections, and it was hinted that the victims of gangland hits—or their dispersed body parts—routinely found their way there to be mingled with the refuse from pizza joints and construction sites, which was then tossed aboard trucks that ferried the garbage to various New Jersey landfills. During the Closes' tenure on Greene Street, a turf war between rival sanitation companies gave the Fire Department something to think about besides artists in unsafe buildings, as parked garbage trucks mysteriously burst into flame on moonless nights.

The Closes' Greene Street loft—which they occupied until 1970, and for which they paid a rent of $150 a month (considered outrageously high by some other loft dwellers)—was typical of these early downtown studios in its utter lack of creature comforts. Unbearably hot during the summer doldrums, it was often intolerably cold in the winter. Some loft buildings were heated during business hours, but that was not the case with 27 Greene Street. At first the only heat came from one small space heater. When they could afford to, the Closes supplemented this with electric stoves which they would huddle over for warmth, but on cold nights they continued to sleep fully clothed under an electric blanket. When the weather was really frigid, coffee left overnight would freeze in its mug. On such nights, the Closes would sleep at Don Nice's heated studio which he generously made available. They also went to Nice's studio to take showers since the Greene Street space had only the most primitive toiletry arrangements. (Ten years older than Chuck, Nice was a family man with an apartment in Brooklyn Heights.) To make 27 Greene Street marginally habitable, everything had to be fitted from scratch, even the plumbing—heavy duty to avoid burst pipes—which was installed by Philip Glass, who, while establishing himself as a musical presence on the downtown scene, performed the same service for many pioneer loft dwellers, often using scrap piping that he found on scavenging trips to Canal Street.

As for Leslie, there were times when she may have found the living conditions oppressive, but like her husband she was fleeing from a suburban past—just a couple of years and a short train ride away in her case—and relished the freedom from convention, at least for the time being. One thing she recalls dreading was her parents' first visit. When the day finally arrived, Chuck had to lift Leslie's mother onto the loading dock because there were no steps. Leslie and Chuck tried to hide from her parents the fact that the loft was unheated. They were not successful, and for the next fifteen years, wherever they lived, her mother kept her coat on when she came to visit.

By 1967, artist residents of the loft district had begun to develop a strong sense of identity with the scruffy yet scrappy neighborhood. Certainly that was true for the Closes. For them, it was an easy place to network since so many friends had already established themselves there. While there were very real, practical reasons for living in a loft, the romantic aspects of downtown life should not be overlooked. Wherever he had found himself since leaving home—from the big house he shared with fellow students in Seattle to the space over the beauty store in Northampton—Chuck had adopted a bohemian lifestyle. In the late sixties, the Ur-SoHo was the ultimate bohemian destination, as far removed from mainstream America as you could get and dripping with opportunities for self-imposed deprivation.

For New York artists of that generation, SoHo was Montmartre and Montparnasse rolled into one, every colonized loft building (and they were still rarities) an American reincarnation of the Bateau Lavoir, the Paris tenement building that was once home to Picasso, Modigliani, and other impoverished painters. If the area's immediate attractions were low rents and space in which to work, its industrial character proved to be of considerable importance to at least some of the newcomers. This was a period when many younger artists—including Chuck and several of his Yale MFA contemporaries—were experimenting with a systemic approach to art that depended upon faith in process rather than inspiration. The loft district was the perfect place to observe and absorb the liturgy of industrial process on a scale that was consistent with the technology available to these impoverished young artists. Those bales of rags and paper, for example, could be seen as sculptural objects created by the processes of shredding, shaping, and binding.

Process Art was one of the key ideas of the sixties, and it remains the concept that has determined the character of Close's work throughout his entire career. To fully appreciate his art, it's important to understand what it was that he and his contemporaries understood by "process." Most of them had been inspired by the example of Abstract Expressionist painters like de Kooning and Jackson Pollock, who had gambled on the possibilities inherent in the idea that the character of a painting could be determined by the actual process of painting—the manner and intent with which paint was applied—rather than by preconceived notions about pictorial content. In de Kooning's case, process had been inseparable from bold, painterly gesture, resulting in the idiom that Chuck had found so seductive in his student years. Pollock had taken process still further, capturing the public's imagination with the utterly radical way in which his paintings were produced—the act of splashing loops and swirls of paint onto the canvas without any intervention from the bristles of a brush.

Perhaps surprisingly, none of Pollock's important contemporaries adopted his exact methods, though his work gave them the license to employ more extravagant gestures and make use of unconventional tools. The impact of the *imagery* that resulted from Pollock's process—the matted skeins of flung pigment—was to make the drip itself a powerful symbol of modernism, soon exploited with a healthy dollop of irony by artists like Robert Rauschenberg and Jim Dine.

By the late sixties, younger artists had turned away from Abstract Expressionism as an idiom, but the generative potential of process derived from Pollock's work remained a rich area for exploration. By persistently, even monotonously, applying a particular procedure to a particular material, or combination of materials, an artist could create entities that were original and informed by a consistent logic. Richard Serra (often assisted by Chuck and Phil Glass) experimented with ideas such as creating forms by hurling molten lead into a corner so that the junction of floor and masonry walls served as a kind of open-faced mold and the velocity of the impact determined the end result. That particular example, with its emphasis on the way a given material behaved when subjected to a specific process, derived rather directly from Pollock. Other artists, though, applied process in a different way. A dozen years older than Chuck and Serra, Sol LeWitt had devised a process for creating impersonal yet dynamic modular sculptures (he preferred the term "structures") and by 1968 was devising large-scale wall drawings that could be made by other people who were required to follow his directions. Many of LeWitt's early wall drawings took the form of grids (and the "structures" were, in fact, three-dimensional grids). Chuck was aware of these and, in time, the grid would come to serve as the matrix of almost his entire output.

What made Chuck different from other process artists was the fact that he was not finished with representational art, though his attitude towards it had become far from traditional.

With all its drawbacks 27 Greene Street was a good place to work and Chuck wasted no time in devising his most ambitious project to date, a very large nude based on the same photographs he had used for the earlier monumental nude started in Amherst and abandoned. This is a clear example of the kind of persistence that Chuck has displayed throughout his career and that has roots in his early life. He had survived dyslexia and neuromuscular problems by setting himself specific goals and then meeting them one by one—sometimes doggedly, sometimes with flair. He had systematically mastered the skills of creating illusions with a paintbrush just as he had mastered the sleight of hand illusions of a conjurer. In Amherst, he had conceived of this enormous nude as a way of finally breaking through his filial piety towards de Kooning. Unwilling to accept failure, he started over in New York.

This time, though, the painting would be made in black and white. In part this was because attempting to translate the black and white photo into color had already proved such a fiasco, and in part, Chuck believes, because he had been impressed by a large painting of grapes made by Don Nice in 1967. That painting, which now belongs to the Walker Art Center in Minneapolis, was not strictly in black and white but the color was keyed so low as to give a monochromatic effect.

The canvas on which the nude would be painted was almost ten feet tall and more than twenty-one feet long.

Chuck was far from being alone among his contemporaries in his interest in the possibilities of large-scale painting, which had come to be seen as one of the chief legacies of the new American art. The Abstract Expressionists had made scale an issue. They belonged to the WPA generation that had learned much about size from Mexican muralists such as Diego Rivera and José Clemente Orozco. The whole point of Abstract Expressionism in its mature form was the sheer breadth of the painterly gestures involved—a generosity of body language as a way of making marks that could not be adequately accommodated on smaller canvases. This was most evident in the case of Jackson Pollock, and the public became aware of it through the widely seen photographs and movie footage of Pollock at work on his drip paintings, in which it's quite clear that he is painting with his entire physical being, carving out space for himself like a fighter or a dancer.

For the generation that followed, the sense of scale found in Abstract Expressionism fit in well with other concerns, such as an interest in the sheer size of the pictorial content encountered in such archetypically American forms of expression as Times Square billboards and CinemaScope movies. It's often noted that James Rosenquist had experience as a billboard painter before emerging in the early sixties as one of the pioneers of Pop Art. His feeling for large-scale imagery led to numerous billboard-sized canvases and allowed him to tackle paintings as big as *F-111* (1964–65)—a fragmented blend of pop and military/industrial iconography—which is 86 feet long. Few in the sixties tackled work on quite that scale, but the interest in near-billboard size was commonplace, affecting both figurative artists like Rosenquist, Roy Lichtenstein, Andy Warhol, and Alex Katz, and nonfigurative painters ranging from Frank Stella and Al Held to Larry Poons and Jules Olitski.

Even in that context, 21-foot long nudes, especially painted in black-and-white, were not commonplace. Chuck's reasons for painting the nude on that scale, and with that limited palette, were several.

Historically, if a painter or sculptor produced figures that were significantly larger than life size, they were almost always intended to be seen from a distance, such as those in Michelangelo's Sistine Chapel frescoes (or for that matter those seen on Times Square billboards). In painting a hugely enlarged figure, Chuck had something different in mind. He had no objection to the canvas being seen from afar, where the image's proportions could be understood in a conventional way, but he was much more interested in the impact that it would have at close range, where the information would take on very different connotations.[8]

It might be said that Chuck was inviting the viewer to look at a female nude as if at a landscape seen through a panoramic window. Shoulders and breasts become mountains, a surgical scar a crevasse. Or one might compare the experience to watching a widescreen movie from the front row of the theater, trying to adapt to the disturbing fact that the giant bodies on screen diminish in perspective as they move away laterally, while expanses of flesh close to the eye are experienced in embarrassing detail, every pore revealed. (In fact, Chuck has sometimes referred to this painting as his "CinemaScope nude.")

In a real sense, this monumental increase in scale tends to make that most figurative of figurative subjects, the human likeness, less representational and more abstract. From even a few feet away, it is impossible to take in the whole of *Big Nude* at once, and so the eye scans it, isolates elements, and begins to search for relationships between them. Part of the brain tries to use the magnified information to piece together what we know the naked female body to be. Another part takes elements that have been isolated and reads them in a wholly new way so that a suntan line might take on a significance equivalent to a slashing paint stroke in one of de Kooning's nudes.

Chuck Close's studio with *Frank* and *Big Nude*, 1968

The fact that Chuck's *Big Nude* is rendered in black-and-white is important in that it helps emphasize the photographic source of the image. This is not a painting of a reclining nude but rather a painting of a *photographic likeness* of a reclining nude. That simple fact is crucial to understanding all of Chuck's work from this point in his career forward.

A live model is three-dimensional, and artists have traditionally found ways to use foreshortening, lighting, virtuoso draftsmanship, and bravura brushwork to reproduce that three-dimensionality and bring the subject to life. A painting made from a photograph is very different. The camera lens has already done the work of reducing three dimensions to a flat representation, producing an illusory likeness that is mechanical yet extremely convincing to the human eye. When an artist reproduces that likeness in paint on canvas, the result is a two-dimensional translation of the preexisting two-dimensional image. In theory, it is possible to reproduce *exactly* the photograph of a nude model in the form of a painting. A painter working from a live model, on the other hand, can only approximate, however skillfully, the likeness of what he sees in front of him.

When he painted *Big Nude*, Chuck was creating a handmade reproduction of something that had been mechanically produced, reversing the more familiar practice of the camera being used to create a reproduction of something hand-made, such as a painting.

Despite the heroic scale and the considerable ambition involved, there is a deliberate banality about the whole enterprise. The model is attractive enough, yet the way in which she has been photographed is far from idealized, or even flattering. In this regard she can be seen in a direct line of descent from the frank but un-prettified nudes that go back at least to Manet's *Olympia* a century earlier. Even the title emphasizes the work's deliberate ordinariness. Another artist might have been tempted to call it *Great Nude* or something similar in order to conflate monumentality with intimations of grandeur, but that too would have been contrary to Chuck's purposes.

In short, *Big Nude* is both ordinary and extraordinary at the same time, and this places it firmly in the long tradition that takes the mundane and raises it to aesthetic heights through the application of an original vision and painterly skill. Artists such as Vermeer, Chardin, Degas, and Picasso come to mind, and Chuck's level of ambition in creating *Big Nude* makes such comparisons appropriate even though the painting fell short of the Olympian goals the artist had set for himself.

The primary element lacking in *Big Nude* is a fully conceptualized and consistent approach to the process of making a painting of this sort on this scale. As earnestly as Chuck tried to approximate the mechanical character of the image, there is something vestigially improvised about the way the painting was made, a makeshift quality that prevents it from being entirely successful.

The primed canvas had been squared into a grid to ensure accuracy of copying from the proportionately squared-off photographs, a traditional technique Chuck would continue to use in future work. The way of handling pigment, however, varied in ways that he would soon abandon. For the moment, he employed brushes, sponges, rags, and an airbrush, among other methods, to lay down the paint in thin, transparent layers that would allow the image to retain luminosity. (Because of the cold, he often worked wearing gloves with the fingertips cut off.) He used various kinds of blades and an electric eraser—actually a pencil eraser fitted into a power drill—to scrape paint off in order to reveal more of the white ground underneath. The level of technical achievement was impressive, yet the different elements did not quite gel.

Chuck says that he was aiming for an "allover" effect—in which every square inch of the canvas is assigned equal importance, a patch of background carrying the same significance as the features of the subjects' face. The allover concept had been made familiar by Pollock, whose drip paintings abolished the idea of a painting being composed of figure and ground, so that they had more in common with woven fabrics than with conventional imagery. That did not happen with *Big Nude*, however, because a representation of a naked person might be seen as the definition of figure and ground, and because the viewer's eye settled, by reflex, too easily on "hot spots" in the painting, such as the breasts and pubic area.

In retrospect, it's apparent that the nude as a genre did not lend itself to the allover ideal. The naked body is so charged with erotic meaning that it's difficult to see it with total objectivity. Another problem was that Chuck had not yet hit upon a consistent process that would permit him to bring the exact same level of concentration to every square inch of the painting. To do so, he would have to embrace the unglamorous idea of transforming himself into a production line worker.

Chuck Close at the School of Visual Arts, c. 1967–68

Chapter 10

Grand Unions

As he worked on *Big Nude*—which he recalls completing in about ten weeks—Chuck eased into a routine that was typical of the young downtown artists of the sixties, in his case earning his bread and butter by teaching at the School of Visual Arts (SVA) on East Twenty-third Street, while Leslie was studying with well-known artists like Robert Morris and Ralph Humphrey at Hunter College.

SVA was founded in 1947 by Silas Rhodes and Burne Hogarth as The Cartoonists and Illustrators School, but over the next decade it expanded into areas such as fine arts, photography, and filmmaking with the present name adopted in 1956. By the late 1960s, SVA boasted a faculty made up largely of artists who, though unknowns at the time, later became eminent in their fields, among them Richard Serra, Joseph Kosuth, Sol LeWitt, Robert Israel, Malcolm Morley, Barry Le Va, and Joe Zucker, the core members of the faculty being only a few years older than the students. It was a place where strongly held ideas and fierce passions intersected, sometimes explosively, spilling over from the classrooms into neighboring bars and delicatessens. Politics—predominantly in the form of anger at America's role in the Vietnam War—was on everybody's mind, and neo-Marxist tendencies were in the air, but for a while it was art itself that was the chief source of passion. Richard Serra has recalled how people would argue all night, scream, and sometimes come to blows about such burning issues as whether one of Carl Andre's floor pieces was "about a line or the relevancy of materiality being a brick."

Lest it seem that the loft crowd was wholly Nietzschean in its concerns and single-mindedness, it's worth remembering that these were the glory days of New York sporting greats like Joe Namath, Willis Read, and Tom Seaver, and in SoHo as elsewhere much time was spent following the fortunes of the Jets, the Knicks, and the Miracle Mets, with the then-hapless New York Rangers attracting a particularly headstrong contingent of admirers. In the miracle year of 1969, many expeditions from SoHo to Shea Stadium were mounted, and the Mets' World Series victory brought studio activity to a temporary halt. (Chuck Close, however, was and remains a devout Yankees fan.)

To an outsider, downtown might have seemed like an urban desert, but settlers soon learned where to find those places where intellectual and aesthetic energy was exchanged. The first uptown dealer to establish a SoHo outpost was Richard Feigen, who bought a building on Greene Street just south of Houston, which he used primarily for storage but occasionally opened to the public for exhibitions. Far more significant was the Paula Cooper Gallery, which was established in 1968 in a second-floor loft on Prince Street. Its first show, featuring artists such as Carl Andre, Dan Flavin, Donald Judd, Robert Ryman, Robert Mangold, and Sol LeWitt, was a benefit for the Student Mobilization Committee to End the War in Vietnam. Other early arrivals on the SoHo scene were Ivan Karp's OK Harris Gallery, the first to open on West Broadway, and the Reece Paley Gallery, which was easy to locate because the owner's white Rolls Royce—an uncommon sight for the SoHo of that era—was usually parked outside.

Chuck recalls that he and Leslie would attend some performance or other almost every night of the week—typically something on the order of a dance work in progress at somebody's loft, where the furniture had been moved to one side to provide floor space. Many such events were organized by women, including Joan Jonas, Yvonne Rainer, Judy Padow, and Trisha Brown, early proponents of a shift in gender politics that would have a profound effect on the art world. Leslie Close sometimes participated in these events as a dancer. Growing up, she had trained as one and—although she displayed considerable talent as a visual artist—was in fact probably more drawn at that point to the emerging dance and performance forms. (That said, when he needed an opinion on his painting in these early years, Chuck relied heavily on Leslie's eye, saying, "She was my best critic.") Some of the more ambitious venues where this kind of activity was nourished eventually evolved into organized cultural entities, a notable example being the influential White Columns Gallery—founded by Gordon Matta-Clark and Jeffrey Lew—which began life as a loft space called 112 Workshop for its Greene Street address.

Then there were the parties. Almost every Saturday night there was a loft party, or more often several, and these had a character all their own in part because of the scale of the setting. A gathering in a 2,500-square-foot open-floor industrial space was very different from a gathering in a Greenwich Village brownstone or a Riverside Drive apartment, however commodious. For one thing, it meant that there was plenty of room for dancing, and this was the era of dance crazes like The Frug, The Jerk, and the Watusi. Around midnight, you would arrive at a building on Grand Street or West Broadway, climb five steep flights of narrow stairs towards the sound of the Supremes or James Brown blaring at full volume, enter a crowded loft perfumed with tobacco, cannabis, and spilled alcohol to find a heaving mass of dimly lit bodies. The bulk of the dancers would be artists and their girlfriends, aficionados of the downtown music and performance scenes, and hip younger curators and dealers, along with smart young women with jobs in the publicity departments of MoMA and Parke-Bernet and Bennington girls down for the weekend, hoping to attract the attention of Clement Greenberg protégés. The atmosphere was Dionysian, and familiar art world figures were transformed beyond recognition. Critics and scholars better known for their closely argued essays on the antecedents of stain painting, or the relevance of Wittgenstein's *Tractatus* to analytical cubism, abandoned themselves to The Mashed Potato. The newly converted would practice all week in front of a mirror in order to perfect their moves in anticipation of one of these Saturday shindigs.

New York had long been known for bohemian parties, but these loft affairs were something very new—representing an embrace of popular culture with an enthusiasm that had not been seen before. It had been one thing for artists to listen appreciatively to Miles Davis at the Vanguard or Thelonious Monk at the Five Spot, but abandoning themselves to the irresistible energy of sixties' rock 'n' roll and soul music was as much of a breakthrough, in its way, as Jackson Pollock's action painting revolution, to which it was related in its embrace of full-body gesture and rejection of decorum.

Saturnalias at Andy Warhol's Forty-seventh Street headquarters, The Factory, were prototypical of these loft parties, and in the mid-sixties Warhol imported some of that spirit to La Dom (locally called *the* Dom), a venerable Polish social club in the East Village that for a while became host to the Exploding Plastic Inevitable, Andy's peripatetic multimedia experiment in extreme entertainment. The Inevitable owed something to the psychedelic shows that had begun in San Francisco a little earlier, but it had a perverse over-the-top New York edge to it that had little to do with the love beads philosophy of the flower children. It was, rather, pure Warhol.

If Andy and his extensive entourage showed up at your shindig, it was considered an unqualified success, especially if he chose it as the occasion for one of his offhand Duchampian gestures. On one occasion he arrived at a party with a tiny transistor radio in his mouth, tuned to a talk show. He was thus relieved of the burden of making conversation, which in those days he chose to find odious.

In retrospect, loft pioneers often joke, or even boast, about how difficult it was to find food, prepared or otherwise, in Ur-SoHo. When listening to these stories, the fact that Chinatown, Bleecker Street, and Little Italy were short strolls away should provide grounds for skepticism, and there was a Grand Union supermarket just a block north of Houston Street that was such a staple of SoHo life that Yvonne Rainer named her first dance company for it. If you were adventurous, you could find within a few blocks of the future SoHo three stores—one kosher, one Italian, one Chinese—that sold live chickens.

On the southern border of Hell's Hundred Acres, very handy for 27 Greene Street, was the Canal Luncheonette, a favorite of the Closes, who, on those rare occasions when they were flush, went there for egg creams and lime rickies, one of Chuck's favorites. Still, there was not much on offer between Houston Street and Canal, the two iconic exceptions being Fanelli's Café at Prince and Mercer and the little grocery store known simply as The Bodega at Prince and West Broadway.

The Bodega was run by an amiable Puerto Rican who would extend credit to regular customers and was said to be well informed about upcoming cockfights. Open from early in the morning until late at night, it was the kind of place where you went to buy beer, cigarettes, baked beans, and canned enchiladas, or to nurse a scalding coffee when your loft became unbearably cold. It was also a place where you were likely to run into friends who had information about a teaching job that was about to open up at Parson's, or who would alert you to the fact that Steve Reich would be performing in Alan Saret's studio later that evening.

Now a magnet for tourists, Fanelli's was then an unpretentious pub—already in existence for more than a century under various names—the domain of a diminutive ex-boxer, Mike Fanelli, who had bought the place during Prohibition, operating it as a speakeasy (though the fact that the 1925 city directory openly listed the establishment as a saloon suggests that Mike was not subject to undue harassment by the Feds).

In the late 1960s, Fanelli's daytime patrons were a comfortable mix of artists and the local blue-collar workers who had sustained the place prior to the artists' arrival. Occasionally a visit from some Hall of Fame prizefighter like Rocky Graziano would add a touch of glamour, and on one occasion Mike was ready to throw out "da bum" who had fallen asleep in the back room till other patrons informed him that "da bum" was Bob Dylan, a name unknown to Mike. Until the Spring Street Bar opened in the early seventies, Fanelli's was the only saloon in SoHo proper that stayed open past about 6 p.m., and in the early evening after the blue-collar crowd headed for home, the café turned into an artists' bar. Since it was almost next door to Paula Cooper's gallery, it was also a place to hang out before and after readings or performances, though this was subject to Mike's unpredictable whims regarding closing time.

Chuck Close was a Fanelli's regular for several years until—as SoHo changed, and the tavern began to attract a different crowd—its long-time regulars abandoned it, cruelly dubbing it "the losers lounge."

The most important meeting place for the loft dwellers was not in SoHo at all, though it was only a dozen or so blocks away. Located at 213 Park Avenue South, just north of Union Square, max's kansas city (the logo eschewed capital letters) had opened in December of 1965, the brainchild of Mickey Ruskin. After a brief law career, Ruskin had come to the restaurant business by way of owning and operating a couple of downtown coffee shops that featured poetry readings. In 1962, he and a partner opened a Greenwich Village bar, the Ninth Circle, which soon began to attract downtown artists like John Chamberlain and Neil Williams. After a couple of years, Ruskin was bought out by his partner and, after some time off in Europe and North Africa, began to look around for somewhere to start anew. A place called the Southern Restaurant was for sale. It was cheap and a stone's throw from the Village. He bought it and set about transforming it into max's kansas city.

There have been plenty of legendary downtown bars, clubs, and eateries, but Max's was destined to become something extra special, a place that occupies a unique position in the history of New York social and cultural life, arguably the pivotal institution in the transformation of downtown Manhattan from a loose assemblage of largely run-down neighborhoods into the trendiest part of the city. There was some luck involved—Max's happened to be the right place at the right time—but much of the credit should go to Ruskin because he was smart enough to see what he had and to make all the right moves. With his beak of a nose, his dark, lank hair, and his gaunt, bemused expression, Ruskin was an archetypal urban cowboy, as quirky as any of his patrons. The later entrepreneurs who have made fortunes from Tribeca lofts, SoHo boutiques, and NoHo bistros should erect a monument to him. He was the man who paved their way.

Paul Morrissey, Andy Warhol, Janis Joplin, Tim Buckley,
at max's kansas city, NYC, 1968. © Elliott Landy / Magnum

Max's eventually became known as a focal point for New York rock music, especially the punk wing, but at the outset it was an artists' hangout, a sixties successor to the nearby Cedar Tavern where the Abstract Expressionists had downed their Rheingolds and fought the good fight, sometimes with bare knuckles. The original core group of Max's patrons—mostly of the two-fisted, hard-drinking variety—was made up of former Ninth Circle regulars. Along with Chamberlain and Williams, you would find Larry Poons, Larry Zox, Dan Christiansen, Donald Judd, Frosty Myers, and a handful of poets and writers including Joel Oppenheimer. For about six months, business was fairly slow, then Andy Warhol started coming in, bringing the many and marvelous denizens of the Factory with him. They took up residence in Max's back room, which became the precursor to the balcony at Studio 54 with erotic exhibitionism a staple of the evening's entertainment. Once Andy was installed—or at least a frequent presence—a whole new clientele was attracted, ranging from slumming members of the Park Avenue crew to rock stars to politicos like Jacob Javits and Ed Koch to visiting Hollywood filmmakers and stars to curators from all over the world. By the time Max's was a year old, you were likely to encounter celebrities ranging from John Lennon to the Duke and Duchess of Windsor, and from Warren Beatty to Joe Namath, squeezed together at tiny tables, sampling the $2.95 steaks (eventually they went up to $5.95) and hoping for a glimpse of downtown drag superstars like Holly Woodlawn and Candy Darling.

The astonishing fact is that—if you were art world hip and thought of yourself as cutting edge—there was nowhere else to go in those days, with the partial exception of Elaine's, way uptown, which shared some qualities and patrons with Max's but was smaller, more intimate, quieter, far more literary, and exclusive in an altogether snobbier way.

However much Max's clientele grew, Ruskin was careful to maintain the atmosphere—dimly lit and noisy, Bob Dylan (a regular customer) or Jimi Hendrix (another Max's devotee) on the jukebox, black-painted walls, peanut shells on the floor. To get to the tables in the middle section of Max's you had to fight your way through the mob of artists around the bar. Ruskin realized that this was a big part of the appeal of the place and made sure he maintained the artists' patronage by accepting work in exchange for food and bar bills so that the place was full of art, ranging from the Dan Flavin neon piece in the back room, which lent Warhol and his acolytes a suitably ghastly pallor, to the big Chamberlain crushed steel sculpture near the entrance, which in the winter served as a coatrack. Ruskin also provided free bar food in the early evening so that anyone who had not yet made it could come in and eat dinner for the cost of a beer. If you were known to the staff, even that nominal purchase could be deferred.

Chuck Close has often spoken of the important role that Max's played in his early New York years. Ruskin's generous policy towards young artists permitted regular visits, even when times were tough. In a 1997 interview with Robert Storr, then a curator at New York's Museum of Modern Art, Chuck recalled how, "[At Max's] you defined your allegiance by what part of the bar you sat in and who you wanted to spar with."[9] Usually he could be found in one of the booths near the Chamberlain and just past the Donald Judd wall piece, often joining in passionate arguments with people like Robert Smithson, Mel Bochner, Richard Serra, and Dorothea Rockburne, a highly verbal and combative group, rarely at a loss for strong opinions. Occasionally Leslie accompanied him to these disputatious encounters, though more often not since she felt intimidated in those situations and only a very few women such as Rockburne and the formidable Nancy Graves were accepted as equals. Leslie was smart and savvy, but as a fresh-faced Hunter College coed she did not stand much chance of being taken seriously in this company. There were other evenings, however, when there were a few spare dollars in the bank and Chuck and Leslie would go to Max's to enjoy relatively quiet dinners with friends.

Hanging out at Max's—and you could do so till 4 a.m. if you were still standing—provided a strong sense of community. Beyond that, its importance for younger artists was that it was a powerful symbol of the fact that art had arrived in a big way. People went there to enjoy the art world as theater and to try to channel some of its energy and creativity. The Abstract Expressionists had dissipated America's indifference to homegrown art, while artists like Robert Rauschenberg and Jasper Johns had proved that Pollock, de Kooning, and Co. were not flashes in the pan. Andy Warhol and the other Pop artists had captured the public's imagination, and excited media attention as well. The scene had become international: artists, dealers, curators, critics, and collectors—not to mention actors, musicians, and filmmakers—arriving from London, Frankfurt, or Tokyo made Max's their first stop. New art—and the men and women who made it, sold it, and collected it—had begun to generate the alluring scent of serious money. Whereas someone as extravagantly gifted as de Kooning had not been able to make a living from his work until he was well into middle age, it was suddenly almost commonplace for artists in their twenties to be signed by a gallery and to find patrons. Most still depended on their teaching jobs, or loft-restoration work—some, like Brice Marden, Sol LeWitt, Robert Ryman, and Joel Shapiro were employed at various times as museum guards or in museum bookstores—but they did not feel that there was anything to prevent them from becoming artists, and uncompromising ones at that.

By 1969, Max's had become Celebrity Central. If Mick Jagger, Dennis Hopper, David Bowie, or Jane Fonda was in town, you knew you would find them there. Sometime that year, Ruskin started handing out cards to Max's regulars, explaining that these provided membership to an upstairs disco. Upstairs at Max's had never been much patronized—it was so quiet that future mayor Ed Koch once accepted Ruskin's offer to use it as his headquarters for a congressional campaign— so it made sense to try something new up there. At first there was dancing to canned music, then, in the summer of 1970, live music was inaugurated with a season by the Velvet Underground. Suddenly Max's became a major force on the New York rock scene, the place you went to hear Bruce Springsteen or the New York Dolls (and occasionally a country & western act like Waylon Jennings that reflected Mickey's own taste). The artists still came, but gradually the emphasis at Max's shifted towards music, making it the immediate precursor of CBGB, which opened on the Bowery in 1973. By then, new art world venues like Remington's, near Washington Square, and St. Adrian's, in the Broadway Central Hotel, had begun to siphon off the SoHo crowd. The original Max's closed in 1974. Under new ownership, it reopened the following year, and finally went out of business in 1981.

Before his death in 1983, Ruskin went on to run other *boites*, but it is max's kansas city that he will be remembered for.

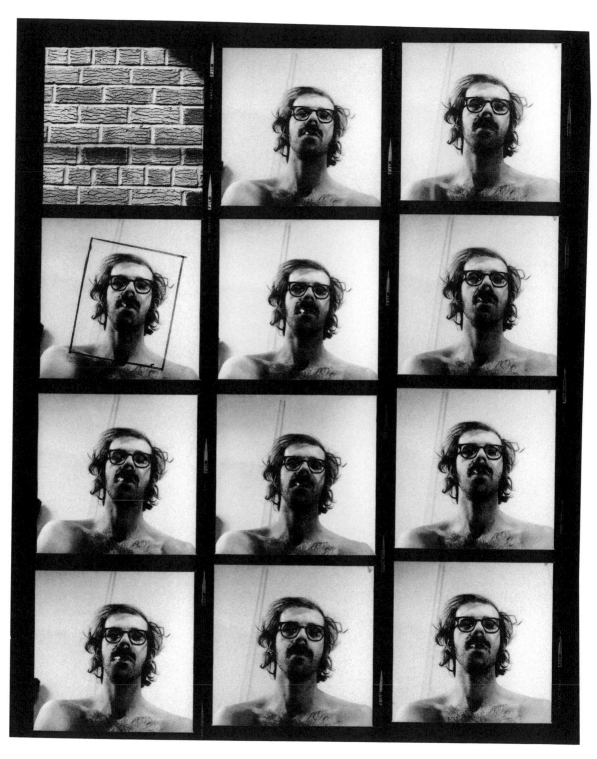

Proof sheet for *Big Self-Portrait*, 1967

Chapter 11

Heads

Chuck Close was never reticent about acknowledging a firm belief in his own ability. In the fall of 1968, he had not yet sold a painting, yet he was comfortable telling me, on my first visit to his Greene Street studio, that he had no interest in producing work for private collectors. The paintings he was planning to make were meant to be hung in museums and seen by large numbers of people. He was quite firm about it.

I recall too how, during one of those long nights of intense dialectic at Max's, Chuck threw out the remark, "An artist's style is what he happens to be doing when he is discovered." Like all good aphorisms, this one contains more than a few grains of truth. In Chuck's own case, however, chance played a minor role. Once he had made the break with gestural painting, it took him a relatively short time to focus in on his initial goal. *Big Nude* was an important first step towards achieving it, and one more stride would be all it would take to get him the rest of the way. As he contemplated that final step, his aim more than ever was to achieve—within the parameters of representational art (and that part was the challenge)—an allover, frontal, two-dimensional effect such as he found in Pollock's drip paintings, but also in certain very different, less overtly emotional works, such as Ad Reinhardt's monochrome canvases of the late fifties and early sixties, and the early sixties work of Frank Stella.

Born in 1913, Reinhardt was an almost exact contemporary of Pollock. Trained as an art historian as well as a painter, he brought an intellectual rigor to making art that was the opposite of Pollock's angst-ridden and intuitively physical approach. In reaction to the calligraphic drama of Abstract Expressionism, Reinhardt produced flat, single-color, nonrepresentational paintings that culminated in a series of black-on-black canvases. The ascetic coolness of Reinhardt's approach appealed to Chuck at this stage in his development and helped give him the resolve to break with his surrogate father figure, de Kooning.

Chuck was even more taken with Reinhardt's writings than with his paintings. Reinhardt was given to coining koan-like statements such as "Art is Art. Everything else is everything else." An "artist-as-artist" he would insist, has nothing to say and must say it over and over again. The products of an "artist-as-artist" would have nothing to do with utility, nor would they strive for meaning. Above all, an "artist-as-artist" would reject servility in any form, and especially in relation to the marketplace.

Reinhardt's disdain for "selling out" was very appealing to a young artist who had flagellated himself for accepting a comfortable teaching job in the provinces rather than seeking fame in the city at whatever cost. Nor did Chuck see the refusal to sell out as being at odds with that sexy aroma of art world money that was drawing the rich and famous to max's kansas city. It was okay to enjoy financial success as long as it did not involve compromise. (Chuck has always maintained that he has enjoyed such success precisely *because* he did not care about money.)

An important quality of Reinhardt's paintings is that they presented an archetypal instance of art that could not be photographed or reproduced satisfactorily; thus, it was vital for his paintings to be seen in the original. (This might be compared to John Cage's insistence that the full musical experience cannot be captured by a recording.) By the late sixties, other artists too—Robert Irwin, for one—were consciously making "non-reproducible" art. (Irwin is reported to have become incensed when *Artforum* placed a photograph of one of his "unphotographable" wall-mounted, illuminated discs on its cover.) What would prove novel about the way in which Chuck tackled this challenge was that he would make paintings so blatantly photographic that a reproduction of the painting would *exactly* resemble a reproduction of the photograph on which the painting was based, making it impossible to tell which was which. Even today, when his work is well-known, it's impossible to gauge the size of his portraits from reproductions unless there is supplemental imagery to lend scale.

As for Frank Stella, born in 1936, his example was especially potent for young artists in the sixties because he was one of them but had already arrived on the scene in a big way. His early paintings are still highly prized, but unless you were there at the time, it's difficult to grasp the explosive impact they had. The name "Frank Stella" was spoken with a certain awe. He was the wunderkind of the decade, and the quality of his work justified any hype to which his career had been subjected.

Stella was only marginally Chuck's senior, but his art had already been in the public eye for several years, since 1960 in fact, when not long after he had graduated from Princeton University a group of his so-called pinstripe paintings was exhibited at the Museum of Modern Art (making him an early example of a very young artist enjoying acclaim straight out of college). Painted in black enamel and barred with thin stripes of raw canvas as regular as the lines on a legal pad, these works challenged the viewer with the blatancy of their symmetry and their uncompromising flatness. A great European abstractionist such as Piet Mondrian had organized geometrical shapes on canvas in a manner that was not so different from the way that someone might place furniture in a room, looking for interesting ways to articulate space, and for satisfying ways to create a sense of balance between different elements. Stella, by contrast, composed paintings rather as you might apply shingles to the walls of a Cape Cod saltbox cottage. In a Mondrian, the geometrical shapes set up a figure-and-ground relationship in which some shapes seem to jump forward from the background every bit as much as in a conventional still life or landscape. In Stella's pinstripe canvases, figure and ground were to all intents and purposes one and the same. At first glance, it was difficult to tell if the lighter stripes were on top of a black ground or vice versa.

Chuck speaks of being shocked by the first Stella painting he saw, which would have been in the early sixties.

"I was affronted by it, much in the way I'd been affronted by my first Pollock."

It didn't take him long to grasp what Stella was about, however, and by 1967 he was ready to attempt paintings that were as flat and frontal and non-relational as Stella's abstractions, and as "allover" in composition, but that differed radically in being representational by way of photography. *Big Nude* had told him that the human body, with all its limbs and appendages and associations, was difficult to treat in this way. It now occurred to him—perhaps through intuition rather than intellect—that the head alone, and specifically the face, would be much better suited to his purpose. The shape of the head—seen in full-face portrait format, cropped at the collarbones—fills a conventionally proportioned vertical rectangle rather completely, making an allover approach more feasible. The familiar layout of the face—the distribution of eyes, nose, mouth, ears, and so on—provides a fixed set of references that cannot be altered and that therefore constitute a kind of grid.

By concentrating on the head, Chuck would also be able to place an even greater emphasis on the scale of the image (and this may have been the decisive factor in his thinking). Painted on canvases nine feet high, the portraits he was about to embark on would be seven or eight times as large, by area, as the head of *Big Nude*, thus calling for far more detail.

Since this was the crucial moment that determined his subject matter for the remainder of his career, it's appropriate to recall Chuck Close's prosopagnosia, the "face blindness" which still caused him problems. He gives the example of an incident on a subway train soon after he and Leslie moved to New York.

"There was a young woman sitting opposite us, and she seemed to be looking at me. She was vaguely familiar, but that was all, and I forgot about her until the train pulled into a station and–as she left the train–she surreptitiously slipped me a note. It was my old girlfriend from Vienna–Karin–my roommate three years earlier. She'd seen I was with another woman and must have assumed that was why I'd ignored her. In fact I simply hadn't recognized her. I mean, she was the last person I would have expected to see on the New York subway so the context didn't give me a clue. I tried to follow her onto the platform, but it was too late, she was gone. I felt terrible."

It would be foolish to suggest that face blindness was Chuck's sole reason for choosing portraiture as his subject matter, but it seems likely that a predisposition existed, as the artist himself believes, and it may be that the condition gave him the intensity of interest and the degree of patience to deal with the human face in a particular way.

Whatever its size, the portrait comes loaded with art-historical baggage. Chuck has said that in part he was drawn to the subject in ornery reaction to Clement Greenberg's assertion that portraiture was the one subject that could no longer be plausibly tackled by artists who made any claim to being modernist. Greenberg was the autocratic spokesman of the Abstract Expressionist generation, but by the late sixties many younger artists and critics were vociferously rejecting his teachings–a phenomenon dubbed "Clembashing"–just as they were turning away from the example of the painters he had championed. This was very much a case of the sons trying to shake off parental authority, but Greenberg's admittedly dogmatic philosophy in fact had a great deal of relevance for the artists of Chuck's generation. In particular, Greenberg's emphasis on the essential flatness of painting—his rejection of illusion—remained a key concept for many younger artists. Traditional portraiture is rooted in illusion, hence Greenberg's assertion that it was antithetical to modernism. As will be seen, however, Chuck in his portraits would embrace the idea of flatness as fully as any Abstract Expressionist or color field painter, so that, while he was in one sense thumbing his nose at Greenberg, these portraits actually would not contradict Greenberg's dogma, though certainly they would demonstrate that there was more to the conflict between flatness and illusion than had previously been suspected.

Historically, portraitists have employed carefully selected angles and dramatic lighting to achieve their effects. Chuck was not interested in exploiting such devices. He wished to take advantage of the near symmetries existing in the face by working from aesthetically neutral, frontal photographs—"mug shots," such as those that adorn passports and the FBI's "most wanted" posters; his intention was to present the face as being as structurally predetermined as the facades of those SoHo buildings.

That said, a stroll through SoHo provides ample evidence that a great deal of variety is possible within the conventions of the cast-iron idiom. So, of course, do human faces differ enormously despite the fact that everyone possesses a similar underlying armature of bone, muscle, and cartilage. No matter how rigorously objective one might be in setting down someone's features as they appeared in a photographed likeness, it would be impossible to ignore the matter of identity and the underlying sense of a complex being beneath the nexus of visual information. This dichotomy—the need to create a precise likeness while aiming for an aesthetic ideal that was virtually a form of abstraction—would produce a powerful dynamic tension (to borrow a term from the pioneer bodybuilder Charles Atlas, a Close namesake who also understood the significance of size) within the artist's work. Chuck confronted the challenge boldly by making the first of these paintings a self-portrait. He would even title it *Big Self-Portrait*, though at the time he habitually referred to it and the paintings that followed not as "portraits" but as "heads."

According to Chuck's telling of the story, the first of these "heads" was a self-portrait quite simply because he was the only person around at the moment he initiated the series. The source of this first self-portrait was a black-and-white photograph made when he was alone in the studio one day, using a borrowed camera equipped with a cable release. There was an element of trial and error about the shoot. His recollection is that he stripped to the waist because he was still involved with the idea of the nude, and thought of the head as a detail of a nude rather than as an independent subject. (This notion carried over to his second large portrait, *Nancy*. The sitter, Nancy Graves, was actually wearing a peasant blouse when she was photographed, but Chuck painted it out so that she is represented with bare shoulders.) The fact that he was alone—had no assistant or stand-in available—meant that he had to estimate focus and angle as best he could. He came up with the idea of focusing on a brick wall, then improvising a ruler out of cardboard, measuring the distance from the lens to the wall. He then posed himself in front of a different wall—one that was plastered, providing a light-colored neutral background—and used the improvised ruler to measure how far from the lens his face should be in order to make the most of a deliberately shallow depth of field. He selected a fairly low angle, so that the camera seems to have been looking up his nose. There are eleven portrait exposures on the contact sheet in addition to a photograph of the brick wall. The image he selected to work with displays very explicit shifts in focus—the frames of his glasses being sharp, for example, while his nose is not—the consequence of that shallow depth of field.

To create this first self-portrait, Chuck worked from two "maquettes"—each an enlargement of the photograph squared off for copying into a grid consisting of 546 squares, and in the case of the smaller one attached with masking tape to a sheet of cardboard measuring 18 5/8 by 13 3/8 inches. The other, almost twice as large, was assembled from four different prints because Chuck did not have access to an enlarger that would produce a big enough image. The smaller of these maquettes was printed slightly dark, so that he could more accurately read the lighter detail, the other slightly light, so that he could more accurately read the darker detail.

(The term "maquette" is used by sculptors to describe a model made as a study for a larger sculpture. Close has appropriated the word to refer to the photographs that serve as the source for his paintings. Originally he thought of them merely as a means to an end, but they have taken on a life of their own and are now eagerly sought after by collectors.)

Curiously, given Chuck's intention of working from images that were not overly charged with subjective information, this first self-portrait photograph, seen in retrospect, is very much of its period and is characterized by what ap-

Detail of proof sheet for *Big Self-Portrait*, 1967

pears to be a "fuck you" truculence. The artist's hair is long and unkempt, his moustache and unshaven cheeks managing to contribute to an antiestablishment feeling, as does the half-smoked cigarette projecting from his lips. The lighting is brutally dramatic, in a *noir*-ish kind of way, so that the frames of his glasses cast shadows around the eyes, and the low angle adds to the mood of the image, which is challenging, verging on the threatening. A few strands of chest hair curl into view at the bottom of the image, a fact that somehow contributes to the faint sense of menace.

As in the case of *Big Nude, utilizing* black and white was part of the strategy, emphasizing the photographic origins of the image. A canvas of very fine weave was stretched on a frame nine feet tall and seven feet wide, then carefully prepared with a dozen coats of gesso, each sanded down before the next was applied.

He was now ready to begin painting, and the lessons he had learned from *Big Nude*, along with the thought he had put into the theory of process art, were about to pay off.

Chuck's challenge was to match the idea of process to the needs of the highly refined concept of representation with which he had chosen to work. He understood that this meant getting away from what he has called the "erratic anthology of styles and techniques" that had gone into producing *Big Nude*. On many occasions, he has spoken of his need to escape from virtuosity, stating that if you understand what art is about, and you know how to make the appropriate marks on canvas, then it's easy to approximate any style. The act of making such paintings can be fun, he says, but when they are finished, the results are unsatisfying. In the 1967–68 self-portrait, he intended to reverse this by adopting a system of working that might be arduous and repetitive but that would produce wholly satisfying results.

The first step was to transfer a lightly rendered pencil drawing of the photograph to the canvas, making use of a faint and erasable charcoal grid to ensure accuracy. That established, he took an airbrush loaded with diluted acrylic and employed it to begin delineating the upper sections of the image, where features were most sharply focused. He then continued to the remainder of the image, employing the same diluted mix of paint and water, slowly increasing the density of the pigment as he built up the darker tones. Highlights were established by removing paint—much as when painting the nude—using various tools such as razor blades and his improvised electric eraser, so that the white gesso ground could show through.

If this sounds somewhat like the method used by some commercial illustrators and billboard artists, that is superficially true, but in this first monumental head Chuck made no concession to slickness of any kind and refused to indulge in effects that might read well from the sidewalks of Times Square but that would seem rather cursory when viewed from up close. Nor did he indulge himself by giving in to any hint of emphasis on what would normally be thought of as the principal features of the face. The rendering of a mole received the same degree of attention as the rendering of an eye. *Big Self-Portrait* was designed to be seen from close range, and if the head itself was approximately fifty times life size, by area, so was every detail—every eyelash, every pore. Thus magnified, each minute scrap of information took on fresh meaning, much in the way that the wings of an insect take on new meaning when viewed under a microscope. If

Big Self-Portrait, 1967–68. Acrylic on canvas, 107 1/2 x 83 1/2 in. (273 x 212.1 cm)

the viewer stepped back from the canvas, however, the photographic derivation of the image was very clear, emphasized by the out-of-focus look of some parts, the ears, for example, and much of the hair. Paradoxically, this draws attention to the essential flatness of the painting.

This fidelity to camera-derived illusion would lead to him being considered a leading exponent of the so-called Photorealist movement, pioneering members of which, such as Robert Cottingham, Robert Bechtle, Richard Estes, and Ralph Goings, began to attract attention a couple of years later. What these artists had in common with Chuck was that they used photography to gather information that was then transferred to canvas or paper. The parallels did not go much beyond that. Typical Photorealist paintings were designed to be looked at like ordinary realist paintings, seen as a whole from a normal viewing distance. Popular subject matter included such items as street scenes, cars and motorcycles, supermarket parking lots, and commercial signage. The appeal was to the viewer's sense of everyday contemporaneousness, with everything presented in sharp focus and Kodachrome color. For the most part—Bechtle is something of an exception—these artists were not much interested in representing people, which in itself is enough to distinguish their work from Chuck's.

"I have a lot of admiration," Chuck explains, "for Cottingham and Bechtle, and Goings, and Estes, and some of the others, but I felt that what they were doing was quite distinct from what I was doing. I didn't want to be seen as a member of any group. I wanted to be judged as an individual, which is why I eventually signed with a gallery that was known for showing nonrepresentational work."

Typical Photorealist canvases sought to satisfy by directness of representation, co-opting the look of the snapshot to create a new genre of popular realism that to some extent took its impetus from Pop Art. (Cottingham is a partial exception in that his images are cropped in such a way as to have a strong abstract quality.) Chuck, on the other hand, borrowed from photography in very different ways, making paintings that are complex, indirect statements about the way in which photography has influenced our way of seeing the world, exploring, for instance, how focal length can be used to enhance, and at the same time question, illusion. Above all, most Photorealists had no philosophical engagement with the idea of process as a way of creating art. Chuck's dedication to that idea meant that he had much more in common with New York (and Yale) contemporaries like Richard Serra and Brice Marden, whose work was entirely nonrepresentational. The proof of the pudding is to be found in Chuck's later paintings and multiples in which he transformed his original camera-based imagery into idioms that remain rooted in photography but that have been radically transfigured by extreme variations in the application of process. Photorealism as a school has shown no such evolution.

A few New York painters were in fact using photographic source imagery in ways that Chuck found interesting. The example of James Rosenquist has already been noted, and, starting in the mid-sixties Joseph Raffael (then spelling his name Raffaele) produced a series of works that, like some of Rosenquist's paintings, resembled hand-painted photomontages. The artists Chuck could most usefully be compared with were Malcolm Morley and Andy Warhol. Morley, who taught with Chuck at the School of Visual Arts, was a Manhattan-based British-born artist who, starting around 1965, had made paintings based on commercial reproductions of photographic images such as postcards and brochure illustrations for cruise ships. This subject matter might seem to link him with the Photorealists, but his imagery was loaded with an irony that theirs generally lacked and his work methods were rigorous in somewhat the same way as Chuck's. (He used squared-off grids and made his paintings upside down in order to distance himself from any emotional attachment to the imagery.) Chuck and Morley maintained a relationship that was superficially friendly, laced with respect and a generous shot of mutual suspicion.

As for Warhol, his working methods differed radically from Chuck's, and the fact that he frequently dealt with celebrity icons gave his work a paparazzi-tinged aura of borrowed glamour that was alien to Chuck; yet there were some similarities between Chuck's heads and Warhol's portraits. Both artists worked with photographic imagery; many of Warhol's subjects were cropped at the collarbone like Chuck's. Earlier in the sixties, Warhol had confronted much the same kinds of concerns that Chuck did later, searching for ways to combine figuration with post-Pollock American modernism. Warhol's solution to the challenge of process was to use silk-screening, a mechanical procedure that in his hands (or those of his assistants) still left room for gestural touches. (Chuck talks of Warhol reducing gesture to a single squeegee stroke.) His solution to the problem of composition was often to organize multiple near-identical images into a grid so that an allover effect was achieved.

The Warhol works that most nearly anticipated Chuck's early portraits were the *Thirteen Most Wanted Men* images installed on the outside of Philip Johnson's New York State Pavilion at the 1964 New York World's Fair. These were silk-screened blowups of actual "wanted" photographs issued by the New York Police Department. Objections were raised by the governor's office because so many of the criminals portrayed were of Italian extraction. This caused a political stir, and eventually the panels were obliterated with silver paint. In their original state they very literally embodied the mug shot ideal that Chuck spoke of later in reference to his own paintings, but they differed from his work both in the way in which they were manufactured and in that they were essentially photographic readymades.

Half a century earlier, Marcel Duchamp had invented the idea of the readymade, putting forward the notion than anything could be designated as art—even a mass-produced bottle rack, or a porcelain urinal signed R. Mutt and impudently titled *Fountain*. Warhol inherited this idea and carried it to previously unimagined levels. Repeated silk-screened images of dollar bills or soup cans, and facsimiles of Brillo boxes, could become art if Andy said so. (It was a sign of his incipient celebrity that everyone called him Andy, whether they had met him or not.) He could turn brutal photographs of car accidents into instant masterpieces. He could film the Empire State Building from a fixed camera, from dusk to dawn, and create an instant cinematic classic, the significance of which had nothing to do with whether anyone actually sat through the entire eight hours' running time or even watched a single frame. Warhol seemed to have the magic touch. It did not matter if the work was made by him or manufactured by Factory assistants or farmed-out to a commercial printer. Technical imperfections were inconsequential, or better still were perceived as part of the Warhol aesthetic. It was enough that the work was unquestionably relevant to the moment.

If you were an ambitious young artist in the sixties—whatever your inclinations—Warhol's example was impossible to ignore, if only because he seemed to have unlocked so many possibilities. The entire Warhol phenomenon was swathed in enigma. Was Andy smart or merely shrewd or perhaps a new kind of urban naive possessed of intuition preternaturally attuned to the zeitgeist? Was he shallow or perversely profound? Was he some novel kind of idiot savant or an old-fashioned genius? Nobody was sure, but at that time it seemed that he could do no wrong, and his impact was all-pervasive. His example was impossible to follow, since no one fully understood where he was coming from or where he was going, but it quickly sank in that after Warhol's arrival on the scene the art world could never be quite the same again, and younger artists like Chuck Close were obliged to rise to the challenge this presented.

In advanced circles, Warhol was so well established by 1967 that Chuck was careful not to be perceived as borrowing from him, and in any case his taste was inherently very different from the maestro of Camp. Still he made no bones about his admiration for Warhol, and Leslie Close recalls the afternoon in 1968 when her husband brought home a silk-screened *Marilyn* he had bought for the seemingly outrageous price of $350. This led to a fierce row since they were living hand to mouth and $350 represented more than two months' rent. Making such a reckless purchase during that time of hardship hints at the pervasiveness of Andy Warhol's perceived authority and Chuck Close's response to it.

Almost twenty years later, Chuck and Andy were seated next to one another on a flight from New York to Virginia. During the course of that flight, Warhol said that they should do each other's portrait. Chuck of course agreed, but before anything could come of the plan Warhol was dead.

It had taken Chuck three months of slow, meticulous work to paint the first self-portrait, the strict discipline he had imposed on himself—progress measured in terms of a few square inches a day—finally yielding up something astonishing. As the now iconic image approached completion, word began to spread in places like Max's, Fanelli's, and the School of Visual Arts. Soon friends began to stop by at 27 Greene Street to take a look at this tour de force. Not perhaps quite as refined as some of the half-dozen heads that would follow, the self-portrait was nonetheless astonishingly accomplished, and it had that un-fakeable look of an authentic breakthrough painting, a masterpiece in the medieval guild sense of the word: a painting by which a young artist proves himself to be a master. Also, in this case, it was an innovation because Chuck had produced a painting that was not only spectacular but also a totally original synthesis of challenging, iconoclastic ideas that only the boldest of his generation would dare to take on.

One of those who came to see the painting was the future stage designer Robert Israel, who visited Chuck's studio at the suggestion of Don Nice and was blown away by what he saw. That evening Bob called me in Minneapolis, where I was then an associate curator at the Walker Art Center, to tell me about this amazing work. He began to describe it but then said, "You have to see it for yourself." I was in New York shortly after and called Chuck to make an appointment. I was staying with friends on Greene Street, so one evening I walked the short distance to number 27, climbed onto its battered loading dock, and rang the bell. The door was answered by a denim-clad man about my own age—well over six feet tall, friendly, with thinning hair worn long and a recently regrown beard.

Chuck greeted me and led me up to the third floor where I was ushered into an unprepossessing, sparsely furnished space with an ancient pressed tin ceiling of the sort found in many loft buildings. There I was confronted by *Big Nude* and *Big Self-Portrait*, an extraordinary conjunction of images to come upon without prior warning. Although it was the smaller of the two, it was *Big Self-Portrait* that commanded my attention. I like to flatter myself that I sensed immediately that I was in the presence of something authentic and special, but, at the same time, I was struck by the dislocation between the sneering, punk image and its amiable, smart, and personable creator. My first conscious conclusion was that this unknown artist had somehow managed to translate into figurative terms the vision of minimalist artists such as Donald Judd and Carl Andre—Frank Stella too. Recently arrived from the UK, I saw the painting as very American—something that no one in London would have conceived of at that time. In any case, Chuck was not slow to articulate the goals he had set for himself, and we embarked on the first of numberless conversations about art, and his work in particular. A serial consumer of art magazines, he had encountered examples of my writing, which helped lubricate the dialogue. Probably, though, he saw me as primarily a curator and was emphatic in pitching the idea that his work belonged in public collections. I took very little persuading, having already decided that, if I had anything to do with it, the Walker would acquire this painting.

I returned to Minneapolis with an eight-by-ten glossy of *Big Self-Portrait*, which of course looked exactly like a photograph of a truculent young man looking down his nose at lesser mortals. When I showed it to Martin Friedman, the museum's director, and other staff members, they looked at me askance as if I had jumped the rails. I recall telling Martin, "You have to imagine that when you're standing next to this picture you barely come up to the nostrils." His response was along the lines of "That's not a pleasant thought."

I insisted that the Walker ought to buy the painting and begged Martin to have it sent out so that he could get a proper look at it. Bob Israel was making the same case by telephone and during visits to Minneapolis to work on sets and costumes for the Minnesota Opera Company. Initially, Martin balked on the grounds that it would be expensive to crate, ship, and insure a painting that size and difficult to justify the cost since it was by an unknown artist. On a future trip to New York, however, he visited Chuck's studio accompanied by Bob. After seeing *Big Self-Portrait* in the original, he authorized the shipping of the canvas to Minneapolis. This gave board members and other interested parties a chance to get a firsthand look at the painting, and Martin offered me the opportunity to make a presentation to the acquisitions committee. The purchase was agreed to for the asking price of $1,300, which was paid in two installments of $650 so that it was two years before Chuck received full payment.

Years later he told me he had thought long and hard about how he should price this and other early black-and-white paintings. He does not recall quite how he arrived at that precise sum—extremely low even by sixties standards—but his policy was to keep it as reasonable as possible so that the paintings would be affordable to public institutions. One way in which this paid off was that *Big Self-Portrait* was seen by other Minnesota art world figures with the result that, not long after the Walker's acquisition, another of the black-and-white heads, *Frank* (1968), was acquired by the Minneapolis Institute of Art, and a third was bought by local art dealers and collectors Gordon Locksley and George Shea.

Chuck was thus able to launch his professional career in exactly the way he had envisioned, by making a sale to a major public institution. By the time he had received the final $650 from the Walker, he had painted a remarkable series of black-and-white heads that included likenesses of New York art world friends Nancy Graves, Richard Serra, Joe Zucker, Bob Israel, Philip Glass, Keith Hollingworth, and one of his SVA photography students, Frank James. When exhibited, these sitters would be identified only by their first names, a practice that Chuck continues to this day.

In photographing these subjects, Chuck inaugurated what would become his normal procedure for photo shoots of this kind—those that utilized cameras loaded with conventional film—working with a professional photographer who would serve, to borrow from movie terminology, as the camera operator while the artist himself filled the role of director of photography, making the decisions that determine pose, lighting, exposure, depth of field, and so on. He explains that a major reason for this is that, although he had received a thorough training in the technology of photography, he never wanted to be stuck with owning cameras and expensive photographic equipment or handling the darkroom chores.

"That's not what it's about for me."

When directing these early shoots, Chuck aimed to achieve the mug shot look, though when seen today not all the images quite match FBI standards of full frontal aesthetic nudity. While Serra manages to live up to expectations by

Joe, 1969. Acrylic on canvas, 108 x 84 in. (274.3 x 213.4 cm)

coming across as someone wanted for questioning in connection with knocking over gas stations and 7-Elevens, Nancy Graves, to whom Serra was married at the time, is presented in a way that now seems almost romantic. Viewed–like the initial Close self-portrait–from a relatively low angle, her eyes raised skyward, she is caught in a pose that evokes the Pre-Raphaelites.

Joe Zucker, as painted, might pass for a Depression-era confidence man. (Chuck remembers him saying he tried to look like a Midwestern car salesman.) This image bears no resemblance to the Joe Zucker who could have been encountered almost any evening at Fanelli's. The everyday Zucker sported a kind of Harpo Marx–like, dirty-blond, Jewish Afro and habitually wore Chicago Blackhawks away jerseys. The Zucker of the portrait has his hair plastered down, not entirely successfully, and is dressed in a white button-down shirt and a tie. The explanation is that he entered into a tacit conspiracy with Chuck that would ensure that this was not a conventional portraitist's attempt to capture a sitter's "character." This was in fact an illusory Joe who existed only for the fraction of a second that the camera's shutter was open.

An important factor in the character of these black-and-white canvases was the closeness, in terms of friendship, between artist and sitter. With one partial and special exception, which will be discussed in a later chapter, Chuck has never accepted a commission to make a painting or drawing. It is crucial to him that the sitter is in some way integral to his life. Chuck Close, the only child, was building an extended family that would exist through his work.

Zucker was very much a part of that extended family–someone Chuck saw on an almost daily basis and with whom he had logged hundreds of hours of dialogue on many aspects of art, and the making of art–process art in particular–to the extent that Zucker felt that in some way he could actually participate in the conception of the work.

Throughout his career, Chuck has often returned to a given image again and again, rephrasing it in different idioms or different media. Of the photographs taken for the black-and-white portraits, the one that Chuck has gone back to most often has been *Phil*, the likeness of Philip Glass. (There have also been multiple versions of *Bob*, and especially *Keith*.) Taken on the same day as the Joe Zucker photograph, this is its opposite in that it shows the Phil Glass you might have run into on West Broadway almost any day in the late sixties. Like both Chuck

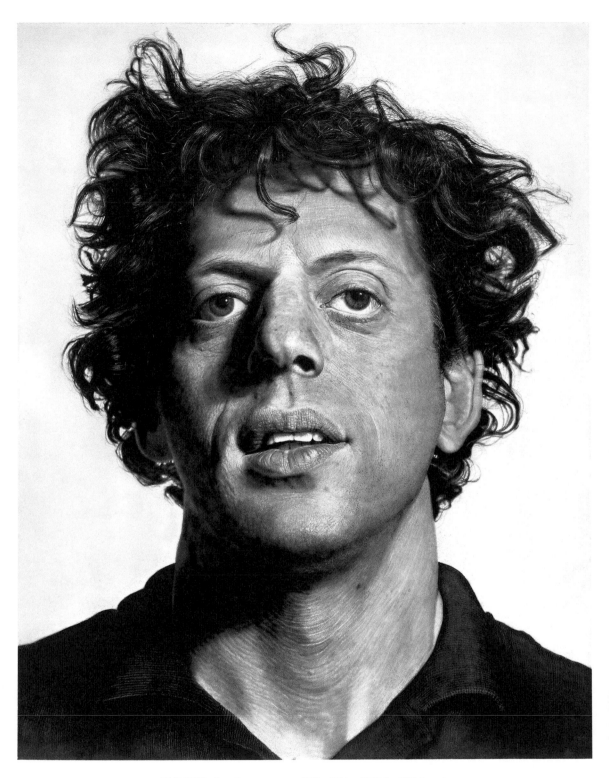

Phil, 1969. Acrylic on canvas, 108 x 84 in. (274.3 x 213.4 cm)

Chuck Close with *Phil* (on the left) and *Richard*, 1969

and Zucker, Glass was very much involved in process—in his case as a way of generating music—providing an intellectual bond in addition to friendship.

Chuck photographs many people for his paintings, but only a fraction of them turn out to be images he chooses to work with, and he reports that it is impossible to predict which ones they will be. *Phil* was an image that he became fascinated with because of "that Medusa hair, those hooded eyes, the lips." It became a challenge for him to take those visual elements and find different ways to represent them—to bring them alive with different kinds of marks.

This image can be taken as a prototype for the portraits Chuck would make in the future. The head is presented straight on, the depth of field very shallow which, when translated to a canvas nine feet tall, paradoxically produces an almost 3-D effect because the tip of the nose and some fronds of Glass's "Medusa" hair are out of focus (just barely, in the case of the nose), precipitating a strong sense of dimensional illusion—one that depends on our experience of having learned to read photographs rather than from being in the presence of an actual person. Combined with the hidden grid used to organize the information required to create an illusion, this shallow frontal format (which allows for a maximum payload of information) has provided the basic formula on which Chuck has built his career.

These first black-and-white portraits can be seen as unflattering in the extreme, emphasizing as they do personal flaws, from skin blemishes to poor eyesight. By translating the camera's mechanical objectivity into paint applied to canvas, however, Close invested his sitters with heroic dignity, not by portraying them as heroes but by including them in a heroic project.

Working on *Keith* in his studio at 27 Greene Street, 1970

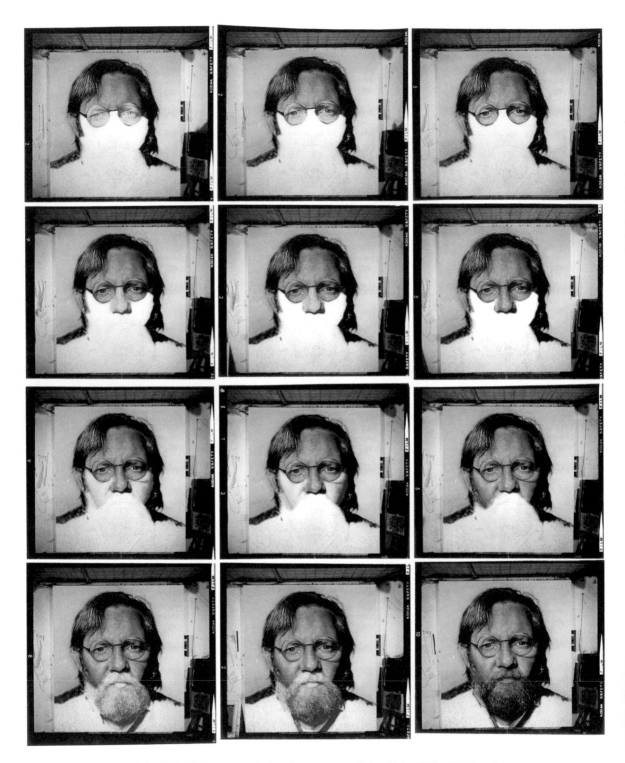

John, 1971–72 (in progress). Acrylic on canvas, 100 x 90 in. (254 x 228.6 cm)

Chapter 12

Recognition

As the sixties merged into the seventies, there were several important developments in Chuck Close's life and career. In 1969, his work was included in the Whitney Museum's Annual Exhibition, an important sign of recognition; at about the same time, he became associated with the Bykert Gallery, first showing there in a group exhibition that May. The following year, he had his first full-scale New York exhibition, at Bykert, and that summer the Closes were invited to join several other artists and their families in purchasing a loft building at 101 Prince Street, a few blocks north of the space they had been renting.

Backed by collector and Museum of Modern Art board member Jeff Byers, Bykert was directed by Klaus Kertess, who had studied art history at Yale during the period that Chuck was in the MFA program there, though they did not meet at that time and in fact Kertess says he had very little contact with the studio arts students. The gallery had opened in September of 1966 at 9 West Fifty-seventh Street, a space previously occupied by Richard Bellamy's Greene Gallery, an important venue that had served as a springboard for several major artists including Claes Oldenburg, James Rosenquist, and Mark di Suvero. In some ways, the Bykert came to enjoy the same kind of reputation that the Greene Gallery had had, a place where both director and artists were perceived as being at the forefront of current trends. There was a difference, however, in that while Bellamy's taste had been decidedly eclectic, taking in both Pop Art and the new wave of nonfigurative painting and sculpture, Kertess—initially, at least—showed only the pared-down paintings of nonrepresentational artists like Brice Marden, Ralph Humphrey, and David Novros, who were among the earliest members of his stable. Bykert was perceived as a venue for the most uncompromising wing of New York nonfigurative art, so that Chuck Close was far from an obvious candidate to exhibit there.

Chuck and Leslie Close at Tobey Pond,
Norfolk, Connecticut, 1971

Other dealers, including Bellamy and Ivan Karp, had preceded Kertess in visiting the Greene Street studio. (Bellamy had been disinterested. Karp–then associated with the Leo Castelli Gallery–had advised Chuck to paint machines, finding heads overly sentimental as subject matter.) Chuck was an admirer of Bykert's uncompromising exhibition program and was anxious to have Kertess see his work–he remembers tossing photographs onto Kertess's desk hoping for a favorable reaction. Kertess finally came to the studio on the strength of a recommendation from Marden. On that first visit, which occurred towards the end of 1968, Kertess was more impressed by Chuck's intelligence than by the paintings themselves, telling the artist later that his initial reaction had been, "This person is so smart and articulate, why is he making these weird paintings?" The overt strength of the work began to break down Kertess's resistance, however, and the artist's defense of his approach began to persuade him that this might be more than a one-shot *tour de force*, so he decided to include a Close painting in a group show to see how well one of these monumental heads would stand up to weeks of daily viewing.

By the time of this exhibition, Bykert had moved to a space on East Eighty-first Street, recently vacated by the Richard Feigen Gallery. Chuck's portrait *Frank*

Close's first art dealer, Klaus Kertess,
at Yale Summer School, Norfolk, Connecticut, c. 1971–72

shared a room with a poured latex floor piece by Lynda Benglis, a gifted and innovative artist who for a while had doubled as Kertess's part-time assistant. It was
a happy conjunction since the two works represented complementary extremes
of process art, the Benglis piece fluid and organically abstract, the portrait meticulous and iconographic.

Kertess found that not only did the Close painting hold up to prolonged viewing, it gained from it. Convinced now, he offered Chuck a one-man show which
opened in February of the following year, bringing together three of the black-
and-white heads and a film titled *Bob* in which the camera panned slowly across
the portrait of Bob Israel. Critic Cindy Nemser had reviewed Chuck's contribution to the group exhibition favorably in *Arts* magazine,[10] and now, on the occasion of the one-man show, she interviewed him for *Artforum*, the conversation
appearing in the issue dated January 1970, under the title "An Interview with
Chuck Close." Almost simultaneously, an article by Nemser titled "Presenting
Charles Close" appeared in *Art in America* so that suddenly a wider audience
became aware of Chuck's work, though anyone reading both magazines may
have ended up a little confused about his name.

It was as a result of the *Artforum* interview that the artist became known to the public as Chuck Close. Old friends like Donn Trethewey and Larry Stair report that they always knew him as Chuck, while in school yearbooks he appears as both Chuck and Charles. By his teens "Chuck" had become the normal usage in everyday social situations, but when it came to his professional aspirations, he continued well into his twenties to think of himself as Charles Close and it was under that name that his work was exhibited and reviewed on the occasion of the 1969 Bykert group show. The manuscript of the *Artforum* interview was handed in with the abbreviation CC used to indicate his responses to Nemser's questions. A photograph that was to accompany the interview arrived at the magazine's offices labeled "Chuck Close," the name by which the photographer knew him. The editors assumed that this was how he chose to be known and so "An Interview with Chuck Close" was the title under which the piece appeared. Given *Artforum's* prestige, it would have been counterproductive to attempt to revert to Charles, so the name Chuck Close stumbled into the annals of twentieth-century art. To this day, however, Chuck jokes that he might have enjoyed more respect had he been able to hold on to his given name.

By chance, Chuck's 1970 Bykert exhibition opened one day after the February 25 suicide of Mark Rothko. The funeral took place two days later at Frank. E. Campbell's Funeral Parlor on Madison Avenue, a few steps from Bykert, the painter's body having been placed on view the previous day. Among those who visited on February 26 were three of Rothko's contemporaries—Jack Tworkov, Philip Guston, and Al Held—who knew Chuck from his Yale days. After leaving Campbell's, they stopped by the Bykert to see his show, and Chuck thanked them for all the encouragement they had given him, saying something to the effect of, "I couldn't have done this without you."

Held was deeply offended, saying "You can't pin this shit on me!"

(Thirty-five years later, having developed a warm relationship with his former teacher in the interim, Chuck delivered one of the eulogies at Held's funeral.)

In the summer of 1970, Chuck taught at his alma mater, the University of Washington, where he met another faculty member, Mark Greenwold.

"I had read the *Artforum* interview," Greenwold recalls, "and had decided that I hated Chuck's paintings—which I'd seen only in reproduction, of course—and that I didn't much care what he had to say about them. I just didn't like the whole concept.

"There was a guy in the art department called Bruce Everett who was very excited about Chuck's work and the fact that he would be in Seattle for the summer. He arranged for a get-together in a bar, and I went along. I didn't like the way Chuck looked—the long hair and the New York hippie manner—or the way he presented himself, which seemed kind of cut-off and snobbish. I probably didn't open my mouth, and that would have been the end of it except that Alden Mason, who had been Chuck's mentor when he was at the University of Washington, had a party. At that party, Barbara—who I was married to at the time—hit it off with Leslie and they became instant friends. We started hanging out—two couples dating, spending a lot of time together. Often we were up all night and would end up having breakfast in some diner. I remember Chuck would order a big mess of eggs over-easy with bacon and hash browns and he would inhale the whole plateful before I had had my first nibble of toast. It was amazing. He also had a knack of being able to fall asleep in a chair. I envied that. Then he'd snap awake again and we'd talk about art—a lot of talk about art."

Greenwold was then working on a series of realist paintings utilizing photographic source material, which he describes as "Hockney-esque Mediterranean acrylics."

"I had always used photographs as source material, but what Chuck was talking about was something completely new to me. The idea that a photograph could become the basis for a painting in a philosophical way—that was something I could hardly grasp at the time."

Nonetheless, over the course of that summer Chuck and Greenwold developed a friendship that would become crucial to both of them. Superficially, they may seem to have little in common as artists—Greenwold became the author of small-scale, highly charged domestic psychodramas painted with a precision reminiscent of Flemish paintings of the fifteenth century (some of them feature Chuck in various guises)—yet the two men share an obsessive streak that drives each to lavish months of effort on a single work. The artistic and personal relationship they developed might reasonably be described as symbiotic, though the character of the symbiosis is difficult to define.

This interlude in Seattle inevitably involved spending time with Chuck's mother, which, for Leslie, was not the most welcome of experiences.

Earlier that year, Millie had married Art Sipprell, a widower she had known as a neighbor for many years. (As children, both his daughters had taken piano lessons with Millie, so Chuck knew his new stepsisters, Elizabeth and Barbara, quite well.) The Sipprells honeymooned in New York, staying with Chuck and Leslie on Greene Street, a not entirely comfortable arrangement given the space's primitive appointments and the fact that the newlyweds were bedded down on a mattress on the floor in close proximity to Chuck and Leslie's sleeping loft.

Mildred and Chuck Close, early 1970s

For Leslie, this proved to be something of a baptism by fire, which continued that summer. Any mother is apt to regard a son's new partner with a degree of caution, especially when that son is an only child. In Millie's case, it would probably be appropriate to substitute "suspicion" for "caution" and add that the position she adopted towards Leslie—though superficially welcoming—always had the potential of becoming adversarial.

Leslie believes that Millie perceived her rather blatantly as a rival for Chuck's affection and on some level held Leslie responsible for keeping him away from God's Own Country where he had had the good fortune to be raised. On top of that, Millie suspected Leslie of being phobic, which in her eyes was high crime indeed. She had spent years coaching her son to avoid girls who displayed any signs of phobia.

Peace reigned that summer, at least on the surface, but not without an undercurrent of distrust that would erupt later.

Returning from Seattle, the Closes were able to move into their new quarters, a loft space in a building that housed the studios and/or homes of other well-known or soon to be well-known artists including Ray Parker, Joe Zucker, Peter Dechar, Reeva Potoff, and Jack and Sandra Beal. Except for the Closes, all of them had been renting at 101 Prince prior to the formation of a cooperative to purchase the structure. The asking price for the entire building was $100,000 and, like everyone else in the co-op, the Closes were required to make a down payment of $5,000, which they did in order to acquire the empty top floor previously used as a studio by Sandy Beal. They borrowed the money from Leslie's parents, who were repaid almost immediately from the summer's earnings at the University of Washington.

Chuck's relationship with his in-laws was very different from Leslie's with Mildred, though he gained their full acceptance only after something of a false start.

"They liked him when I was with someone else," says Leslie, "but when we got together they weren't so sure—in fact they decided he was a no-good bum, probably because I had told them he was a slob who never turned up to class on time, and stuff like that."

There was perhaps a religious factor as well. The Roses had not anticipated their daughter marrying a moneyless, bearded gentile who would spirit her off to live in buildings formerly occupied by sweatshops. Leslie's grandmother, Fanny—later the subject of one of Chuck's greatest paintings—was especially suspicious of him. It took a while, but Chuck's friendliness and openness eventually won everybody over, Fanny included, as did his evident readiness to become part of the Rose family, willingly joining in Seders and other traditional festivities. Like his father, and his maternal grandfather Charlie Wagner before him, Chuck made every effort to make his wife's family his own. Any reservations that the Roses may have had soon vanished, and when Chuck's career began to flourish, they were as proud of him as they would have been of their own son.

The top floor at 101 Prince had been raw space at its rawest, with battered floors, peeling walls, and a sagging tin ceiling. Once again the Closes turned to the SoHo art community to find people to help with the necessary renovations. The task of removing the old ceiling and replacing it with plaster, for example, was contracted out to Tony Shafrazi, later infamous for defacing Picasso's *Guernica*, and later still prominent as a SoHo and Chelsea gallery owner associated with such artists as Keith Haring, Jean-Michel Basquiat, and Kenny Scharf, and with the estate of Francis Bacon. (Chuck still complains Shafrazi did a lousy job.)

The Closes had made the passage from hand-to-mouth garret-living—an essential stage in any self-respecting artist's curriculum vitae—to owning their own living space, but it would be a mistake to think that loft life in 1970 was in any sense comparable to what it would become just a few years later. They were still living on the edge in a decrepit building not zoned for residential use, located in an area that at night remained an urban desert. The asking price of $100,000 for a SoHo building might sound like an incredible bargain (and it certainly turned out to be a sound investment) but at the time it was a struggle for young artists, largely dependent on part-time teaching positions or casual labor, to come up with monthly mortgage payments, however modest, in addition to putting food on the table and keeping a studio supplied with expensive art materials.

The social and cultural tightness of the community helped compensate for this, however, and in the spring of 1970, an event hundreds of miles away provided the downtown artists with a common cause that united them as never before.

The great majority of downtown New York artists had long been politicized by both the battle for civil liberties and opposition to the Vietnam War. Feminism too was becoming a hot issue, and the 1969 Stonewall riot, just blocks from SoHo, helped make homosexuality another radical cause. (The Gay Activist Alliance Firehouse on Wooster Street in SoHo became a major cultural center and hosted some of the area's wildest dance parties.) New York artists traveled in convoy to Washington protest marches, and conversations about the future of art—did it in fact have a future?—were liberally laced with heady references to Marx and Mao. Above all, SoHo artists saw themselves as workers—the denim-shirted inheritors of the traditions of the former sweatshops that they had appropriated as studios.

When, on April 30, 1970, Richard Nixon announced the invasion of Cambodia, protests were launched on college campuses from coast to coast, and a bottle-throwing disturbance at Kent State, on May 1, led Ohio governor James A. Rhodes to call out the National Guard. Rhodes further inflamed the situation by calling the student protesters un-American—"worse than the brownshirts and the Communist element, and also the nightriders and the vigilantes." During a second protest at the school, on May 4, guardsmen attempting to disperse the crowd opened fire, killing four students and wounding nine.

Students on campuses across the country reacted to the news of the massacre with outrage, and none more so than those attached to the School of Visual Arts where Chuck was teaching. The SVA president, Silas Rhodes (no relation to the Ohio governor), had maintained a policy of giving out no failing grades in order to protect his students from the Vietnam-era draft. This had attracted to the East Twenty-third Street campus a significant number whose interest in art was minimal. The legitimate art students found themselves having to step over the bodies of druggie draft dodgers nodding off in the corridors, a situation that was not helped by the fact that, not so far away, the Lower East Side was then a major center for heroin distribution while even closer was a methadone clinic.

All components of the student body were united in their rage at the Kent State killings, however, and it was apparent to faculty members—who were equally enraged—that if they were to retain credibility they would have to demonstrate their solidarity. A brainstorming session was held in the president's office at which the question was posed, how could art be leveraged in order to achieve political currency? It seems to have been at this meeting that the idea was first posited that the only way you could make an effective statement through cultural artifacts was by withholding them from the public. At the same meeting, Chuck and Joe Zucker were elected to represent the SVA faculty in whatever proceedings might evolve, though nobody knew quite what these might be.

In fact, there was some precedent for SVA's involvement with collective action on the part of the art community, as the school had hosted, a year earlier, an "open hearing" sponsored by the Art Workers' Coalition, a group dedicated to the idea of pressuring New York museums into giving artists a greater say in the way that these institutions were run. The primary target was the Museum of Modern Art and among the concerns expressed by the coalition's members—who included well-known art world figures such as Carl Andre, Hans Haacke, Lucy Lippard, John Perreault, and Gregory Battcock—was the museum's perceived indifference to women artists and artists of color. Bates Lowery, then director of MoMA, had refused to allow the coalition to stage a debate at the museum so that the venue was switched to SVA and, on April 10, 1969, hundreds of members of the art community, including Chuck Close, showed up to discuss ways in which New York's museums could be reformed. Later debates sponsored by the coalition tackled subjects ranging from an artist's right to benefit from the resale of his or her work to ways of expressing opposition to the Vietnam War, and these debates often continued into the early hours as groups dispersed to bars like Remington's and St. Adrian's.

By the time of the Kent State shootings, the art community as a whole was primed to act, though first there were more meetings, formal and informal, held at locations ranging from the New York University Student Union Building to lofts all over downtown. At NYU, Chuck was among the artists, along with Robert Morris and the veteran politically engaged painter Leon Golub, who addressed a packed house. Those who attended on that occasion were gratified to see anonymous-looking men with telephoto-equipped cameras snapping arrivals.

An outcome of these meetings was a decision to create a confrontation at one of New York's museums, with the intention of closing it down or at least drawing media coverage. Given that this was instigated by living artists, the obvious target was the Museum of Modern Art, but, perhaps because of this, MoMA was bypassed. This apparently was perceived as a slight by its newly appointed director, the studiedly boyish John Hightower—a self-described reformer intent on sweeping away the cobwebs—who probably relished the possibilities inherent in such a confrontation. (Bates Lowery had been fired after ten months on the job. Hightower would last just twice as long.) Instead, the artist-protesters staged their mass rally on the imposing tiers of stone steps—the ultimate New York front stoop—leading to the main entrance of the Metropolitan Museum. Having been forewarned, the Met's administrators closed the great bronze doors but left a side entrance open for any non-*engagé* art lovers who sought to pay homage to Vermeer or Van Gogh. In a Martin Luther–like gesture, a manifesto was taped to the bronze doors by the protesters, while minimalist artist Carl Andre produced a broom with which he swept the steps, symbolically cleansing them of bourgeois contamination.

At about this point in the proceedings, a small door in the great Italianate portals swung open and the dapper figure of Metropolitan Museum board president Douglas Dillon—former U.S. Secretary of the Treasury and a leading Republican Party fund-raiser—appeared bearing a large tray of cookies which he offered to the assembled aesthete revolutionaries. The preposterousness of this calculated gesture reduced even the most radical factions to laughter, so that the affair of the Metropolitan Steps failed to achieve critical mass.

Following this episode, those who remained committed to the cause followed the example set earlier by the Art Workers' Coalition and split into committees and action groups, espousing a variety of positions ranging from the promotion of mildly socialistic incremental change to outright anarchy. Meanwhile, like schools across the United States, SVA remained on strike till the summer break, and artist/teachers with unexpected time on their hands found themselves de-voting more energy to debating the interface between art and politics than to making art. In some quarters, a degree of narcissism crept into the proceedings, or perhaps it would be fairer to ascribe the shift in emphasis to an instinct for survival since the very notion of the validity of art seemed to be challenged by the more extreme philosophical positions of the day. Probably it would have been denied at the time by most of the participants, but the focus began to drift from Cambodia and the Kent State shootings to the role, if any, of the artist in a radicalized society. The fact that this radicalized society might be something of a chimera did not seem to occur to many at the time, and did nothing to dilute the passions that were generated.

Having posited the idea that art could best be utilized on behalf of The Cause by being withheld from display, a month was designated during which no artist who did not wish to be considered a scab could show his or her work in a com-mercial gallery. This had little impact on artists who were between shows, or who

With Joe Zucker in his loft at 101 Prince Street, early 1970s

did not have galleries in the first place, but it was devastating for someone like Keith Hollingworth—the subject of one of Chuck's black-and-white heads—who was scheduled to have his first one-man exhibition at Paula Cooper. The show went ahead, but Hollingworth conformed with policy by covering his works with black cloth so that they remained invisible.

When Chuck and Leslie left for the University of Washington that June—part of the traditional hot weather exodus that saw SoHo residents heading for the shore or for teaching jobs at provincial colleges—they might well have supposed that the art world's political fervor would lose steam by the time they returned. What in fact happened during the dog days of 1970 was that the revolutionary spirit—festering in humid lofts where cannabis plants flourished under grow lights—had become feverish, verging on the hallucinatory, and nowhere was this more the case than in the building that the Closes moved into that September.

Politics aside, 101 Prince Street was a lively building even by SoHo standards, in part because it was at the epicenter of downtown social life. On the ground floor was a blue-collar café, Hector's, popular with artists because the food was cheap and came in large portions. Almost opposite was Fanelli's, as was the Paula Cooper Gallery where many evening events continued to be staged. If you were in the small clan that then constituted the New York art world, you would have seen many familiar faces passing through 101 Prince's metal-reinforced front door, ringing for the venerable industrial elevator. There was a great deal of socialization among the residents themselves, and the dialogue between Chuck Close and Joe Zucker was especially intense and undoubtedly contributed to the evolution of each artist's thought. Zucker was then working on paintings in which images were created, mosaic-like, from hundreds of cotton balls dipped in Rhoplex paint. Superficially, these images were as different from Chuck's as could be imagined. A work such as *Amy Hewes* (1976), in which Zucker's subject is a Mississippi riverboat—the product of a society that built its wealth on slavery and cotton—takes on political resonance precisely because it is made from balls of cotton. At the same time, though, the process of assembling those cotton balls was not that far removed from Chuck's way of breaking down imagery into tonal elements placed according to the strictures of a grid. The methodological relationship between Chuck's compositions and Zucker's cotton ball paintings is perhaps most apparent in the pulp paper works Chuck made during the following decade, but in fact the underlying structural principle is present in all Chuck's work, starting with the 1968 self-portrait.

In the fall of 1970, the cultural and aesthetic dialectic that was an everyday feature of life at 101 Prince Street became infiltrated with a malarial strain of revolutionary thought that had incubated over the summer months. Chuck and Joe

Zucker were generous in entertaining artists and acolytes who espoused many different viewpoints towards the proposed brave new world in which art would become the handmaiden of revolutionary politics (without, of course, giving up its hard-won independence).

Another resident of the building, Peter Dechar—a young painter from a well-to-do family, who had enjoyed some commercial success—went considerably further than anybody else. Making contact with radical elements outside the art world, he became the advocate of extreme notions such as removing all the "elitist" work from the Museum of Modern Art and throwing its galleries open to anyone who wanted to show there. Paintings by numbers and portraits of Elvis on velvet would be welcome. More provocatively, he invited members of the New York branch of the Young Lords—a Puerto Rican radical group modeled on the Black Panthers—to make themselves at home in his loft. They took him up on his offer, and for a period of months visitors to 101 Prince were apt to encounter menacing-looking young men in battle fatigues with berets perched on Che Guevara hairdos. Unsubstantiated rumors suggested that some of them were armed.

Felipe Luciano, their leader—though not without charm and charisma (later he became a television journalist)—was capable of hinting at dire consequences if any word of the group's activities got out. At the same time, he liked to socialize with the artists, taking the opportunity to expound on his philosophy and vision of the future.

"I really like you," Chuck recalls him saying. "You're a nice guy, and I appreciate you sharing your scotch with me, but when this is all over—comes the Revolution—there won't be any place for people like you."

It was while 101 Prince Street was under siege by these would-be revolutionaries that Chuck began work on a new and ambitious series of paintings, the first of which—ironically, given the event that had precipitated the ongoing political furor—would have the title *Kent*, a portrait of his Yale contemporary, Kent Floeter.

Chuck felt that he had done all he wanted to do with the black-and-white portraits, so for some time he had been thinking about what he should choose for an encore. He had considered the possibility of changing subject matter—to landscape, for example—but instead he settled on the idea of remaining with the same photo-based portrait subject matter, but changing the means by which

Study for Kent in Three Colored Pencils, 1970.
Colored pencils on paper, 45 x 38 1/2 in. (114.3 x 97.8 cm)

the image was realized, though without abandoning the fundamentals of his process-oriented approach. He wanted to add variety to what he did in the studio every day. His conclusion was that he would achieve that more satisfyingly if he altered the way he made the pictures, rather than if he simply changed the subject matter.

This led him to think about how to produce photo-imitative paintings, in full color, in a way that would be consistent with the process he had followed for the black-and-white heads. By then he was fully aware of the work of the Photorealists, who were making paintings derived from photographs in much the way that realist paintings had always been made in that colors were premixed on the palette before being applied. (In some cases, the use of airbrush meant that there was no actual palette but the principle of premixed colors still applied.) Chuck decided to take a radically different approach.

While still living at Greene Street, he had photographed Kent Floeter, by then a downtown neighbor. The resulting transparency was used as the basis for magenta, cyan, and yellow color separations, and these in turn were used to make five dye-transfer prints: (i) magenta alone; (ii) cyan alone; (iii) magenta plus cyan; (iv) yellow alone; (v) magenta plus cyan plus yellow. This last print was in full color since transparent magenta, cyan, and yellow dyes function as primary colors that, when superimposed upon one another against a white ground, evoke the entire spectrum. (The process is similar to that used in offset printing.)

In making the black-and-white heads Chuck used only transparent black acrylic paint—no white pigment—relying on light reflected from the white canvas to glow through the thin film of acrylic paint to provide highlights. His new plan was to make a series of portraits that would be built from three very thin and hence transparent layers of diluted acrylic color—magenta, cyan, and yellow—brought to life by means of the reflectivity of the white support. He was in short planning to reproduce the dye-transfer process by hand, on his already established grand scale, using the sequence of actual dye transfers as his guide. Put another way, his ambitious intention was to make three paintings—each as detailed as any of the black-and-white paintings—directly on top of one another. Instead of being mixed on the palette, the color would be mixed by the viewer's eye. (Chuck says that it never occurred to him at the time that these paintings would take three times as long to make.)

He took the dye transfers to Seattle that summer, and in the small office/studio the college provided for him, he made three studies on paper, two of them using colored pencils that approximated magenta, cyan, and yellow and one using watercolor. Each was made on a white sheet marked into relatively large squares, and in each case only a few of these squares were completed, since his intention was to see how well the system worked rather than to create a finished piece of art. Perhaps the most interesting is the watercolor study, in part because traditional watercolor technique—which builds forms and colors from superimposed transparent washes—has much in common with his proposed method. In this drawing, some squares support a single primary color, while others are layered with two and sometimes three colors, thus providing a useful preview of the process he would be employing. Below the imagery is a color chart comprised of the three hues in various combinations. (A similar chart appears on one of the colored pencil drawings.)

These studies were the first gestures towards the generation of a new series of portraits every bit as remarkable as the black-and-white heads, and even more labor-intensive. Settling into the Prince Street loft as summer ended, Chuck began work on the full scale *Kent*, a task that would occupy him well into the next year.

Seen today, when they impress as much as ever but astonish a little less, the black-and-white portraits have a kind of classical gravity to them, a quality that derives in part from the fact that we perceive them in the context of black-and-white photography, which has a long history. The impact of the full-color photo-imitative heads would prove to be somewhat different, largely because of our very different experience of color photography—a now familiar but still far more recent technology—in which the approximation of natural color produces quite different expectations.

A black-and-white photograph of a nude can transform the components of the body into an almost abstract dialogue between intersecting planes rendered in terms of light and shadow, as in the case of works by Edward Weston, for example. Photographed in color, however—and even if composed in the same way—a nude becomes a catalogue of pigmented information in which the flesh tones predominate, conveying sensuality in chromatic terms. In the case of portraits, the contrast is less obvious, because a likeness is always a prerequisite, but the difference between black and white and color remains significant.

As he began work on the first of the three-color portraits, it quickly became apparent that Chuck's scheme of imitating the dye-print process worked well. I was a frequent visitor to the studio at the time and had the opportunity to see how fully chromatic flesh tones began to appear on sections of Kent Floeter's face, as if by magic, though in fact the process could not have been more objective and lacking in reliance upon painterly sorcery. In a sense this was a return to Chuck Close's childhood infatuation with conjuring tricks. The conjurer appears to be performing magic, but in fact he is deceiving the eye by the application of a carefully thought-out mechanical process. To witness the portrait of Kent evolve over a period of months, seeing it a couple of times a week, was like watching a sleight of hand performed in slow motion.

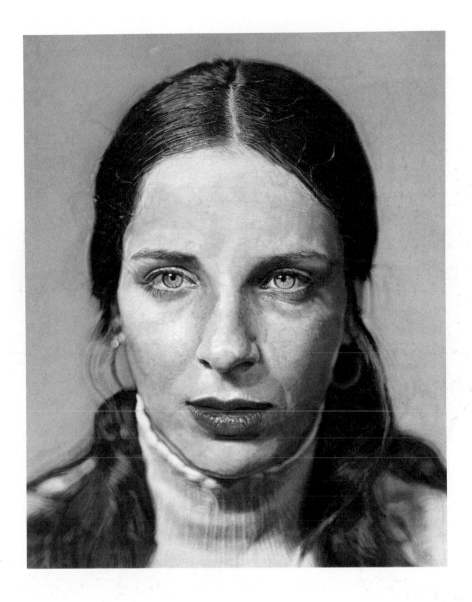

Leslie/Watercolor, 1972–73. Watercolor on paper
mounted on canvas, 72 1/2 x 57 in. (184.2 x 144.8 cm)

The color in this painting, and those that followed in the series, is entirely photographic in character. Looking at *Kent* (1970–71), *Susan* (1971), *John* (1971–72), *Nat* (1972), *Leslie* (1972–73), *Linda* (1975–76), and *Mark* (1978–79), one finds fully chromatic treatments of hair (and a beard too in the case of *John*) that are no less than spectacular. Its tone and texture, hue and gloss, gyre and tensile qualities become a complex narrative that seems to reveal secrets of the sitter's character and

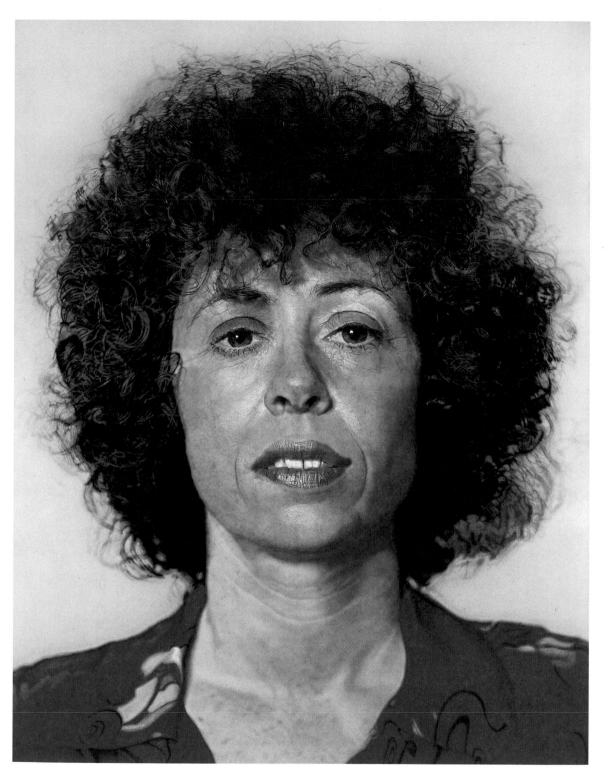

Linda, 1975–76. Acrylic on canvas, 108 x 84 in. (274.3 x 213.4 cm)

relationship to the gene pool. Standing in front of one of the paintings, you can lose yourself in the hair, or for that matter in the play of color in the iris of an eye.

Chuck himself is very clear about the differences between the black-and-white heads and the color portraits:

"The black-and-white heads are 'in your face.' They have no frames to insulate them from the world. They are hierarchical, and that's due to the figure on ground being so emphatic because of the white background. When you turn to the color portraits, the backgrounds are tinted—greenish-gray in some cases, a little warmer in others—which tends to emphasize the allover character of the paintings, because every square inch, even when there seems to be nothing there, is activated by the three layers of color. . . . If the black-and-white paintings are hierarchical, the color portraits are more wallpaper-ish. To put it another way, the black-and-white portraits seem to advance forward from the canvas, while the color portraits retreat into a 'window.'"

One cannot overstate how time-consuming and labor-intensive these continuous-tone color portraits proved to be, whether painted in acrylic or—as in the cases of *Nat* and *Leslie*—in watercolor. The main cycle, consisting of just half a dozen paintings, occupied the artist from the fall of 1970 until the second half of 1976—an average of about one a year, with *Linda*, whose hair proved a special challenge, requiring almost fourteen months of work. After a break of a couple of years, he then painted one last fully continuous-tone, full-color head, *Mark*—a portrait of Mark Greenwold.

The sheer painstaking slowness of the process itself is somehow embodied in the finished paintings, endowing them with a character that might be described as frozen obsession, a quality that they share with works ranging from Marcel Duchamp's *Big Glass* to the monuments at Mount Rushmore. (Chuck has compared the creation of his paintings to the way in which a book is built from daily increments of units of information. This is a useful comparison, but his paintings are like an epic narrative written entirely on a single oversize page.)

It's a measure of this deliberateness of pace that the years during which these few continuous-tone color portraits were made correspond to a period long enough to see major changes taking place in SoHo and on the New York art scene. The excesses of 1970's revolutionary zeal dissipated rather slowly—especially at 101 Prince Street, which for a couple of years remained a mecca for some of the more hotheaded elements—but the genuine outrage that had fueled the sometimes

farcical events of those early months had long-term consequences as artists now turned their attention to what seemed like achievable socioeconomic goals. Support was given to museum workers who sought to unionize, and plans were made to draw up innovative contracts that would allow artists to benefit financially from the resale of their work. SoHo's women, Leslie Close included, became especially active, forming support groups, staging performance pieces that challenged gender-based stereotypes, and lobbying aggressively for the greater visibility of female artists.

"In the end," says Chuck, "it was probably feminism that had the biggest impact. The way it changed the climate helped focus attention on artists like Nancy Graves and Lynda Benglis and Jennifer Bartlett, and it really had an effect on the population of our building. Guys left—or were thrown out—because their wives weren't taking shit any more. After a while, I was the only male still living there."

Downtown bars remained forums where a steady diet of new and not-so-new ideas, both aesthetic and political, were chewed over and occasionally digested. Many of the most heated discussions of the early seventies took place at St. Adrian's, located in the Broadway Central Hotel—formerly the Grand Central—just north of SoHo. This imposing edifice had once been the ultimate venue for Lower East Side Jewish weddings and bar mitzvahs, though by 1970 it had become a welfare hotel. In its art hangout phase St. Adrian's was filled with paintings and objects traded for food and drink, most prominently a large John Clem Clarke gloss on Manet's *Le déjeuner sur l'herbe* which hung behind the bar. One Friday in the summer of 1973, shortly before St. Adrian's was due to open, the front section of the hotel collapsed onto Broadway, burying the bar and its art beneath tons of masonry. Luckily no one was there at the time, though some residents of the hotel were killed.

As the seventies gathered momentum, SoHo proper acquired a new artists' hangout, the Spring Street Bar at Spring and West Broadway. By then the area had become a magnet for pioneering entrepreneurs as well as artists. An early arrival on Prince Street was Food, the first of the new wave SoHo restaurants, an inexpensive, scrubbed-wood cafeteria, the brainchild of Gordon Matta-Clark and Carol Gooden, which opened in 1971. Described as a "restaurant commune," Food served annoyingly healthy dishes (soup with their excellent bread was usually a good choice) and was at its best on Sundays when its kitchens were ceded to guest chefs—Robert Rauschenberg was one—who cooked potluck meals for friends and neighbors. Soon after the Closes' arrival at 101, their stretch of Prince Street also became home to The Cheese Store—the direct predecessor to Dean & DeLuca—a harbinger of the coming gentrification that at the time was utterly unsuspected.

Food and The Cheese Store were symptomatic of the fact that SoHo residents were beginning to feel more settled. They were no longer outlaw artists on the run from city housing inspectors and Con Ed investigators. The area had for some years had a real estate kingpin in the person of Jack Klein, who had begun his career by convincing commercial property owners that they could make money by renting to artists, before becoming a landlord himself. (Old-timers differ in their opinions of Klein, some describing him as a land shark, others remembering acts of kindness and generosity.) Now more and more residents were following the Closes' example by joining forces to buy buildings.

Finally, in 1971, the right to take up legal residence was granted (though with a number of irksome caveats); two years later, SoHo—at last known by that name—was designated a historic area. By then, the Closes had acquired a blue Volkswagen station wagon and a preternaturally smart black standard poodle, Ruby, to go along with their cat Sacha, who was later permanently loaned to The Cheese Store, which was in need of an experienced mouser. Ruby too had duties to perform. Along with the growth of SoHo's population had come an increase in crime—much of it drug related—including burglary. One gang, operated by a Fagin-like adult, employed kids who climbed onto fire escapes from the roof of a delivery van and broke into lofts by squeezing through the openings intended for air conditioners. This method was used once on 101 Prince, and it was not unknown for the Closes to hear people walking on their roof in the middle of the night. Ruby was no attack dog, but she learned to bark like a hungry mastiff whenever she heard a suspicious noise.

The Closes' plans for starting a family were inevitably tempered by practical considerations, but jobs such as a spell of teaching at New York University and a return to Yale Summer School, this time as a faculty member—supplemented by the now-steady sale of paintings, the majority to public collections, with the Whitney Museum acquiring the iconic *Phil* (1969)—began to provide a degree of security, and in the fall of 1972 Leslie became pregnant. On July 15, 1973, she gave birth to a daughter, Georgia Molly, marking the ending of what had been an adventurous half-dozen years during which the couple had become a fixture on the downtown scene and Chuck's career had been solidly launched.

Georgia and Chuck Close with the author and
his daughter, Chloe, summer 1976

Chapter 13

Downtown Domesticity

Georgia's birth ratified a shift towards a more domestic lifestyle for the Closes. Their social life was greatly constrained by a lack of babysitters—impossible to find south of Houston Street in those days—and even more so by the novel pleasures of parenthood. Not that the latter came without a cost. For a considerable period Georgia had problems sleeping, and one of Chuck's paternal chores was to rock her in her baby carriage, sometimes falling asleep himself on the floor, his hand still grasping some part of the vehicle's frame. On especially restless nights he would retrieve the VW from its West Broadway lot, next to the Bodega, and drive Georgia around nearly deserted downtown streets till she fell asleep, comforted by the motion of the car. As had always been his routine, he tried to put in a full day's work, though now it was often curtailed so that he could attend to domestic chores. If the early years in SoHo had been rather glamorous in a scruffy kind of way, the Closes' life in the mid-seventies took on a character that—despite the bohemian trappings of the setting—any new set of parents would recognize, a routine that had more to do with diapers and playdates than with dinners at the latest downtown bistros.

Very early in 1975, Chuck began work on a portrait of my wife, Linda Rosenkrantz—the last-but-one of the continuous-tone color paintings and the first of them to be done in his new West Third Street studio. Coincidentally, Linda was developing a project at the time that involved having friends keep detailed notes on a single typical day's activities. She would then tape participants as they verbally reconstructed their day. On January 9, 1975, Chuck took part in this experiment, detailing events a day or two later while they were fresh in his mind. A transcript of the tape presents a portrait of the artist as a young parent who is dedicated to producing a major painting by means of a technique as time-consuming as the handweaving of a Persian rug, while at the same time coming to terms with his responsibilities as a husband and father:

> At 5:00 Georgia cries and I remember my first groggy thoughts were whose day was it to get up and whether or not it mattered. I realized that it was Leslie's day . . . but I had to get up anyway. I can't remember why, and I felt I was cheated of my day to sleep in. I put Georgia back to sleep but I couldn't get back to sleep. I was worrying about how much money we had. This is the time when I do all my worrying. . . . And also the audit that's coming up, which somehow I manage never to worry about except in the middle of the night. . . .

At 7:30 the doorbell rings, waking Georgia again. Chuck goes down to the street to find a huge sanitation department police officer—"a guy who looks exactly like Rosey Grier"—"in full riot gear" and ready to write a ticket for the pile of trash left in front of the building, a result of the demolition work Joe Zucker was doing in his loft.

> I go back up. I get Georgia a bottle and a Pamper and try to get her set up for the morning. I'm very nervous and tired. . . . I try and take Georgia back to bed. I lay on the bed. . . . Fifteen minutes later, I finally just give up. I get dressed, make coffee, fry some bacon for Georgia and try to clean up the kitchen a little bit. I have to turn off the *Today Show* and turn on *Captain Kangaroo*, because Georgia's getting fussy. I really resent *Captain Kangaroo*.
>
> 8:00 to 8:30—I have to move the chest of drawers, move the bed and the bedding, take down the venetian blinds and move the filing cabinet and stuff out of the bedroom and make way for the carpenters who are supposed to arrive at nine o'clock.
>
> 8:45 to 9:00—I walk the dog, freeze my ass off and deliver the mail. I stop by Joe's to warn him the sanitation police are looking for him. . . . 9:00 the carpenters come and I talk to them about how I want things done, where can we cut back some corners. . . . I pack up my Con Ed bills and things to take to the studio. . . . At 9:15 I walk downstairs. I meet Joe in the street. He gives me a ride to the studio. . . . I buy milk from across the street [then] ride up and talk to Skippy, the elevator operator, about the elevator inspectors who had just required some other stuff be done. . . .

9:30 turn on TV and get to work. *Green Acres* is on. I love *Green Acres*. I think it's one of the best things on TV—very under-rated.... I'm into the seventh row, working from the top down and left to right, on the painting of you.... The seventh row and I'm still in the hair. I haven't got any face yet and I'm getting tired of it. Hair is very complex and I keep thinking I wish I'd waited till you got your hair cut....

When Chuck says he is into the seventh row of the painting, the row number refers to the underlying grid. As the following remarks make clear, he was actually working on the detailed pencil underdrawing—made directly onto the canvas—over which the layers of paint would be applied.

The drawing is going very slowly and I'm worried about it. I'm worried about the surface. I didn't realize how scratchy and rough it was. Maybe I haven't sanded it enough. The investment of time I will have to put in before I have any idea whether or not the surface is too bad is very scary. I could spend two weeks or more putting the drawing on then find that the surface wasn't good for painting and I'd have to start over. That just scares the shit out of me.

10:25 Skippy delivers the mail. Nothing interesting.... I go back to thinking about how the drawing is going. Last time the drawing was too light and when I started to paint the first few coats of paint totally obliterated the drawing, and this time I think I overcompensated. I don't want the drawing to show through because the paint is very thin. If I did overcompensate, I'm gonna be in big trouble because there's no way to paint out—to cover up the drawing....

I watch *Gambit*. Elaine [Stewart] is just unbelievable. [*Gambit* was a playing card–based game show hosted by Wink Martindale. Elaine Stewart was his pulchritudinous co-host.] She's wearing a snowflake outfit. I eat Oreos and drink some milk.... I'm worried that the drawing is too cartoon-like, too caricatured. When you notice the line is bent, there's a tendency to want to bend it too much. That happens very often with things that don't have any high symbolic content. Like any kind of squiggly line sort of looks like hair, so if it's not the right squiggle you can get away with it, whereas if it's a nose or something you tend to be tougher. It's hard to maintain the same seriousness and care as much about it.

11:00 Elaine says "Bye, we love you" in her most obnoxious way. Even I can't stand this show! I don't know why I watch it and I'm pissed at myself that I just wasted the last half-hour watching it. Not that I actually watch. There's a quality to daytime TV that's very non-visual. . . . I used to paint to music, especially rock music and, because I always painted that way, I didn't realize how nervous it was making me. . . . Then for some reason—I guess my radio was broken or something—I painted two or three days without a radio, and I felt much better. So for a long time I worked with nothing on, and then I started working with the TV. I find it really is a tolerable kind of musak, and really a tranquilizer. Leslie can't stand to have the TV on if we're not watching it. The background noise drives her crazy. . . .

The next three hours are taken up with *Let's Make a Deal*, $10,000 *Pyramid*, consultations with a plumber who has work to do in the building, a lunch break at McDonalds, and a phone call from Leslie who is unhappy with the way that the Prince Street renovations are going—she wants Chuck to return home to take care of a problem. The underdrawing progresses to row eight.

2:30 I'm sitting and looking at the photograph of your face. I'm trying to figure out why the highlights are all blue. I'm not sure if it was like skin oil or some kind of bluish eye shadow. There's a brushstroke over your eyelid of eyeliner and in the photograph it's really a stroke which you've painted and now I have to paint. . . . You made a stroke with one gesture— one long, skinny stroke—which I then have to manufacture three times. I have to make a red line very carefully building up a red stroke, then apply a blue stroke on top of that, and then apply a yellow stroke on top of that, so that your single gesture becomes very complex. There's almost never anything, with the exception of lipstick, in my pictures that was man-made. Everything is made either by God or machine, like shirts and things, so this is the first time I've had something that's kind of a human gesture in a painting, which is nice. . . .

At 3:45, Leslie calls with a shopping list—currant jam, lingonberry sauce, and nine cucumbers. At four o'clock Chuck heads home, stopping to mail letters and to pick up groceries.

4:30 to 5 I'm in the Grand Union. There's absolutely nothing [there]. I don't know if the trucks didn't make the deliveries because of the bad weather or something, but there's nothing. Everybody in the store is angry. There are no lingonberries or jelly. I buy some skim milk and dog food and the cucumbers and go home . . . Home to confront the carpenters who are trying to rip me off with extra charges to run some BX electrical wiring through the walls. . . . Georgia screams "Hi, Daddy!" which she's been doing now for a week or so. It's a fantastic feeling to have someone run up and say "Hi, Daddy!" . . .

5:00 sit down with Georgia and Les, with Mister Rogers, while Georgia has her bottle. . . . 5:30 I play with Georgia and talk to the carpenters about the electricity some more. Mostly I'm trying to keep her out of their way. She wants to go pick up all the boards they nailed down. . . .

5:30 to 6:15—what I have to do is go out and get the jelly and take-home food we've decided on, so I go get the car and it's really freezing. I go to the bodega and they don't have the currant jelly, so I drive the car one block from the bodega to the Eva deli and I close the door, lock the car, and go into Eva. They don't have it. When I come out the lock on the car door is frozen, so I go back into Eva and they very begrudgingly give me a book of matches because I had just been in there and not bought anything, although I spend thousands of dollars every year in the joint. So they give me a book of matches and I have to heat up the key and unlock the door—so I drive to the Pioneer on Sixth Avenue and I forget and lock the door as I get out the car. . . . When I get back to the car the lock is frozen again. . . . The wind is blowing sixty miles an hour and I'm crouching down with my back to the traffic roaring along Sixth Avenue, trying to heat up this key without the matches blowing out. . . .

After further mishaps, and a trip to Kentucky Fried Chicken, Chuck returns to Prince Street triumphantly bearing currant jelly (though he accidentally leaves it in the car and has to unfreeze the lock one more time).

6:30 to 7:10 I try and entertain Georgia while Les vacuums up the mess in the studio. . . . 7:10 I put Georgia in her jammies and change her Pamper. . . . 7:15 to 7:30 I carry Georgia around and talk to Les about the loft renovation. . . . 7:40 I put Georgia to sleep. . . . 7:40 to 7:50, Les and I lay on the bed and talk about working on the loft, whether we're going to do the wiring or whether we're going to hire it done.

7:50 The dog and cat are both reminding me I haven't fed them. I go into what used to be the studio to sift through the rubble to find their bowls.... 8:30 Leslie accused me of not doing the dishes because I was taking notes [for this tape] and it really pissed me off. It was totally untrue. I do the dishes virtually every night and I would have done them anyway....

Chuck and Leslie watch *M.A.S.H.* on television and while doing so become depressed. Leslie says that it really bothers her to see perfectly good walls being torn down. Chuck agrees. He says that it has always bothered him to watch a building being knocked down or to see a car smashed up for a television commercial, and now it bothers him to see cabinets that he built with his own hands being ripped out, even though he was not particularly proud of the craftsmanship. Leslie sits on his lap "nervous and depressed" as they watch the rest of the show.

From 9:20 to 10:00 I work in the studio getting rid of the trash, putting it in barrels. I taped up some big boxes and filled them up with sheetrock and when I moved them they fell apart and all the sheetrock fell on the floor.... 10:15 to 10:30 Georgia is up crying. I spend fifteen minutes trying to feed her an aspirin in every possible way.... She's teething.... 10:35 Georgia's up again. We decide to let her stay up for a while with us. Leslie and I are having drinks. I'm having a scotch and soda and she's having a martini. We decide to read *Artforum* together. One of the things we've been doing recently, which is sort of fun, is to take the art magazines, especially the stuffier ones, and read them aloud to each other.... They're hilarious. But I must say *Artforum* isn't good for that—it's so humorless there's no way to make humor out of it....

11:05 Georgia wakes up again.... I'm dreading walking Ruby and taking the car to the lot because it's so cold.... I'm feeling very sorry for myself and I want to go to bed.

11:30 to 11:45 we watch Johnny Carson's monologue and at 11:45 I go out. The lock was of course frozen on the car and I have one match left. I manage to get the door open and I drive the car to the lot and park it and I run home with the dog. I run in the house and I leave her to work out her own problems between two parked cars. I'm damned if I'm going to stand there and watch her dump.

I come up and turn off Liberace and take a leak, and at 12:00 I go to bed.

The fact that Chuck had vacated the studio at 101 Prince Street meant that the stage was set for Leslie to expand an interest in horticulture into a vocation that would eventually evolve into a career. In this, she was inspired by Sandra Beal, who had long raised begonias on an ambitious scale on a lower floor of the building. Remodeled, the former seventh-floor studio space would be perfect for an urban "greenhouse," with its row of windows facing south, though it would require banks of grow lamps to provide an entirely hospitable environment for the plants Leslie intended to grow there.

By this point, Leslie had given up any serious ambition to be an artist, discouraged at least partially by the fact that she was inevitably in her husband's shadow. Leslie knew a number of women like Elizabeth Murray, Lynda Benglis, and Jennifer Bartlett who early on broke through the art world's glass ceiling, but they were all older and further along in their careers when feminism began to transform the landscape. Leslie had just earned her undergraduate degree, was not close to achieving a signature style, and probably was not entirely convinced—smart and talented though she was—that she even wanted to be a visual artist. The question arose, what should she do with her life? She and friends, including Susan Posen—mother of the future fashion designer Zac Posen—toyed with making money through craft activities such as selling hand-decorated belts to stores like Henri Bendel. When Susan Posen decided to attend law school, Leslie began to think more intently about raising plants, signing up for a course in city gardening sponsored by the New School and immersing herself in books on the subject. Taking care of Georgia kept her busy, but the fact that Chuck was now gone several hours a day provided a sense of freedom that she took advantage of by planning tiers of indoor seedbeds, ordering cuttings, or simply enjoying the poetry of plant names as she browsed through catalogues—Sweet William, Honesty, Job's Tears, Moonflower.

Very quickly, the urban nursery became a reality. Even as it took shape, however, Leslie worried about the inevitable issues that would arise when they went to the country for the summer, as they had planned to do that year. Chuck, she was sure, would insist she should pay someone to come to Prince Street and water the plants, but Leslie was certain that would be totally inadequate—the environment she was creating would be too delicate. She wanted to be taken seriously, feeling that some friends—and perhaps Chuck too—were not entirely convinced of her commitment and resolve. Chuck would bring his work with him that summer, and she was determined that she would too; so, in June of 1974, when the Closes traveled to a rented farmhouse in Garrison, New York, across the Hudson River from West Point, Leslie's plants, grow lights, and portable seedbeds—the entire contents of the nursery—were shipped there in a large truck.

Her commitment was no longer in question. Soon she would go on to earn a certificate in horticulture by way of a Penn State University correspondence course, before studying for a postgraduate degree at New York University. Nominally she earned her MA in women's studies, but the subject of her research was specifically women in the history of American landscape architecture.

While Georgia was still an infant, the Closes' routine was interrupted by an alarming episode that frightened both of them badly. Early one morning, in the darkness of the Prince Street loft, Chuck was woken by excruciating chest pain—as if his rib cage was being crushed—that also shot down his left arm. There was no dodging the obvious conclusion. Surely a heart attack? Leslie was asleep beside him but Chuck made no attempt to wake her. Despite the overwhelming pain, an ingrained fatalism kicked in, perhaps the product of growing up with an invalid father who had defied his disabilities.

"Denial runs in my family," Chuck would say when recalling this first angina episode, a phrase that would become a leitmotif.

As he lay there in the glow of the alarm clock, he saw everything reduced to a single binary consideration. Either he would die or the pain would go away, so he waited it out. The situation unfolded like a slow-motion horror film with the early morning dissonances of downtown Manhattan providing the soundtrack—garbage trucks rumbling over cobbled streets, the Doppler effect of sirens on Broadway and Sixth Avenue, none belonging to an emergency vehicle coming to his aid. Finally the pain subsided, and he woke Leslie. Anxious and angry at his reckless procrastination, she quickly arranged for a neighbor to stay with Georgia and rushed Chuck to New York University Medical Center where an EKG and other medical tests were administered. No definitive evidence of a heart attack was discovered. The triage nurse scolded that he should have called 911 as soon as the attack began. His delayed visit to the hospital meant that too much time had elapsed since the inception of the episode for a conclusive diagnosis.

Nonetheless, the attending doctor warned that a significant cardiac condition was strongly indicated, and Chuck was prescribed nitroglycerine to relieve the symptoms should they reoccur.

At dinner with friends a day or two later, chicken was served in deference to health considerations, and Chuck complained bitterly about having to give up so much that he loved. No more scotch, he lamented, no more butter and cheese, no more eggs and bacon, and worst of all no more cigarettes. But denial remained close to the surface, and despite all evidence to the contrary, he refused to accept fully that he was suffering from heart disease. At that time, the media had been devoting a good deal of space to the so-called "Type-A" personality described by Meyer Friedman and R. H. Rosenman in a 1974 book, *Type A Behavior and Your Heart*. "Type-A" personalities, according to the theory expounded in this volume, are driven, impatient, ambitious, yet insecure people—often hostile when frustrated—and highly prone to cardiac arrest. "Anyone can see," said Chuck that night, "I'm not a Type-A personality. I'm the most laid-back person I know." That got a laugh since—despite Chuck's frequent protestations that his success was due solely to never compromising his artistic goals—it would have been hard to miss the fact that his integrity was amply supplemented by a sizable helping of drive and ambition. When it came to the hostility component, however, Chuck did not come close to fitting the profile. Certainly he enjoyed a good argument with, for example, anyone foolish enough to assert in his presence that painting was dead, but overt hostility was alien to his character. In the fractious New York art scene, it was not unheard of for differences to be settled with someone being thrown through a window. This was not Chuck's style. On the contrary, he tended to be unfailingly generous towards his fellow artists, and during the political turmoil that had followed the Kent State shootings, his involvement had been characterized by a strong instinct for diplomacy.

In the days and weeks that followed that first angina episode, there were more tests, all inconclusive, and Chuck continued to protest that he could not believe he was a candidate for a heart attack. As it happened, he was not alone in this. The episode came to the attention of a prominent Chicago heart surgeon who was also an art collector, a patron of Chuck's downstairs neighbor, the painter Jack Beal. This surgeon—who knew Chuck socially and admired his work—contacted him to say that he found it hard to buy into the heart attack theory. His intuition told him that Chuck did not fit the profile, and he went on to explain that the most problematic branch of medicine is diagnostics, telling Chuck that a great diagnostician is as rare as a great artist.

This surgeon invited Chuck to Chicago to undergo three days of intensive testing. No sign of heart damage was found but the testing did raise another possibility, namely that the angina-like symptoms could have been caused by myasthenia gravis (MG), a disorder caused by the malfunctioning of biochemical transmissions between the neurological system and the muscular system. MG can be relatively mild or extremely serious, and in its early phases it is characterized by muscle fatigue and weakness. As described earlier, although six-foot-three and broad-shouldered, Chuck had suffered since childhood from neuromuscular disorders that fit in with the MG thesis. Tests for the disease were inconclusive, however, though the Chicago doctor was of the opinion that the results supported a tentative MG diagnosis. Later, in New York, Chuck repeated these tests, but neurologists who saw the results were by no means unanimous in their opinion, one dismissing the myasthenia gravis theory out of hand. What seemed highly probable, however, was that Chuck did *not* have a heart condition, and so the scotch, the butter, the cheese, the eggs, and the bacon crept back into his diet, and the Mount Rainier ashtray filled up with stubs once more, despite a serious attempt by both Chuck and Leslie to quit with the help of SmokEnders.

This first episode of angina-type pain proved not to be an isolated instance. Robert and Jane Cottingham recall another frightening occasion a few years later. The Cottinghams had become friends of the Closes around 1977, not long after returning from four years in London where Bob had enjoyed success with his Photorealist paintings of urban signage. Jane recalls how the two couples ran into each other at a brunch in New York.

"I remember that Chuck and Leslie both had on black leather jackets and jeans. Bob and Chuck had been in a few shows together so we knew them to say hello. That day, we gravitated to them and something clicked. I recall being very taken with Leslie's sense of humor—she's so smart and sharp—and no one's funnier than Chuck. The brunch must have been dull so we decided to leave together. I invited them up to our new house in Connecticut and soon after they came up with [the artist] John Clem Clarke. That was how it began."

"It wasn't a friendship based on art," says Bob. "Chuck and I would talk about art, but it was much more about family and having the same sense of humor. Our youngest was just a little younger than Georgia. We had a lot in common."

"We became firm friends," Jane continues. "Later they would come to us for Christmas, we would go there for Thanksgiving, and we would take trips together. Once—around nineteen seventy-nine or eighty—we drove up to Maine together, to visit Richard Estes who had a mansion up there he'd exchanged for one of his paintings. On the way back, Chuck had some sort of an attack—chest pains and stomach pains. He was doubled over on the backseat of the car—throwing up out of the car window."

In a small, run-down Maine village they found a medical facility of sorts—a shabby clinic—that was open. It was not the most reassuring of environments, but there was nothing else for miles.

"The waiting room," Jane recalls, "was unbelievable. There were women who looked like they were battered wives—black eyes and missing teeth. When the people on duty saw Chuck they were sure it was something really serious. I think there was talk of having him medivaced to Boston or somewhere."

Chuck remembers the occasion.

"The waiting room was probably the only place in town that had a television set and somewhere to sit down and drink coffee, so the homeless and the out of work would meet up there to pass the time—vacant-looking guys in bib overalls. The doctors there were convinced that I had appendicitis. They put me in this dark hole that passed for an emergency room and tried to get hold of a surgeon somewhere who could fly in to take my appendix out. By the time they found somebody, my appendix would have burst anyway, so luckily I still have it."

Before long, Chuck was feeling well enough to be released, and the Closes and Cottinghams continued on their way, taking a leisurely detour by way of the Massachusetts coast.

From then on, however, similar episodes, of varying degrees of severity, would be a recurrent part of Chuck's life.

Chapter 14

The Grid Emerges

In 1973, shortly after Georgia's birth, Chuck had had his third Bykert Gallery exhibition—a group of color portraits—having shown the last of the black-and-white heads there in 1971. Since 1971, his work had also been seen at museum shows in Los Angeles, Chicago, Akron, and New York, where the Museum of Modern Art featured him in one of their Projects exhibitions. He was by now widely recognized as an artist to be reckoned with.

If the big continuous-tone color portraits were the most ambitious products of this period, Chuck had by no means lost his interest in black and white. Back in the spring of 1972 he had traveled to California to create a work that he considers a landmark in the evolution of his commitment to process. Earlier that year, Robert Feldman of Parasol Press had asked Chuck to think about making a print, giving him virtual carte blanche to do whatever he liked. Having a sound basic knowledge of printmaking, Chuck eagerly accepted the challenge and threw down one of his own. What he wanted to do, he announced, was to make a mezzotint—a very large one.

"I wanted to do a mezzotint," he says, "because no one had done one for a hundred years."

Invented in Holland in the seventeenth century, the mezzotint was occasionally used by major artists—notably Goya—but was chiefly employed to make limited edition reproductions in the days before photogravure. Traditional mezzotints were printed from copper etching plates prepared by being pricked with tens of thousand of tiny holes. The printmaker would scrape and burnish his image into the plate, producing areas that would hold progressively less ink, or none at all, working from black to white—the exact opposite of the method used by Chuck in his black-and-white paintings.

The image Chuck selected to work with was the 1970 black-and-white portrait of Keith Hollingworth. Arrangements were made for him to collaborate with Kathan Brown of Crown Point Press, a highly regarded workshop that had recently relocated from San Francisco to Oakland. The plate size Chuck had in mind—the final image was 51 x 41 1/2 inches—was far larger than anything that could be handled by a standard press of that period, so one would have to be custom-built. Chuck's collaboration with Brown would entail three months of intense activity, much of it spent solving problems. One of these derived from the fact that Chuck began by working from the middle of the image—the central rectangle in which eyes, nose, and mouth are clustered. This part of the print was proofed so many times that the plate began to break down so that in the final image that rectangle printed significantly lighter than the rest.

In the end, the entire plate began to wear down and only ten satisfactory proofs could be pulled. Those, however, are remarkable examples of ambitious experimental printmaking, displaying all of the beauty of velvety blacks set off against pearly whites that only the mezzotint process can yield. For Chuck, this print has a special significance because it was the first work in which the underlying grid is explicitly revealed. This occurred by accident, a consequence of the building blocks of the image—the information contained within each discrete element of the grid—not quite matching with one another so that the image seems to be overlaid with a faint checkerboard pattern. Realizing that this was happening, Chuck accepted it as evidence of process and began to think about how he might explore and expand the possibilities implicit in this important transitional work.

While in California, Chuck and Leslie made a brief trip to Los Angeles to see friends, during the course of which Chuck visited two places that had long interested him. One was Walt Disney Studios, where Linda and I were working at the time. We took the Closes on a tour of the back lot and the animation department where Chuck was able to get a sense of the kind of work he might have found himself doing had he followed through on his job application fifteen years earlier.

More significant for his current art was the visit he made with Mark Greenwold to the studio of Foster & Kleiser, then the West Coast's leading billboard company. Here was a chance to study the methods of other artists working on

Keith/Mezzotint, 1972 (detail, left). Mezzotint on paper;
sheet: 51 1/2 x 42 in. (130.8 x 106.7 cm)

an enormous scale, producing paintings up to sixty feet long designed to be seen from a car traveling along a highway at sixty miles an hour. (Greenwold, who several times took his UCLA class to the Foster & Kleiser studio, was struck by the fact that the artists creating these iconic American images were almost all Europeans, some barely able to speak English.) Chuck was astonished to discover that the only time the Foster & Kleiser artists saw the image they were working on as a whole—at least until it was finished—was in the projection room, a huge space that permitted a small maquette of a piece of advertising art to be projected and traced in enlarged form onto the surface to be painted. Elsewhere, space was at a premium, and when the time came to actually apply the paint, it was done in very tight circumstances with the artists able to step back only a few feet from their giant paintings, so that they had to imagine how they would appear from a distance. Chuck was fascinated to see that some paintings were very loosely rendered when viewed up close while others were quite detailed and precise. He did not come away from Foster & Kleiser with any new insights as to how to fabricate his own paintings, but the visit provided a unique practical opportunity to confirm some of his theories about scale and distance as applied to two-dimensional imagery.

In *Keith/Mezzotint*, Chuck not only allowed the grid to emerge from behind its photographic veil, he also inaugurated another practice that has become a constant in his career, the habit of recycling images in different mediums, using imaginative variations on his basic methodology. The original 1970 photograph of Keith Hollingworth formed the basis, at various removes, for the mezzotint, for a 1975 lithograph in which the head appears four times in different sizes, and for two 1981 handmade pulp paper editions. Interspersed with these multiples were a number of drawings, beginning with a 1973 version on graph paper in which the likeness has been built from dots of spray-brushed black ink of various densities placed on a grid made up of penciled squares. Though little more than a sketch, this is an early expression of Chuck's grid process presented in its naked form, and it led to a long series of black-and-white sprayed dot drawings culminating in the nine-foot tall example *Robert* completed in 1974, the result of almost a year and a quarter of demanding work. This enormous "drawing" (it is actually rendered on canvas) is a tour de force built from what seems like a near infinity of dots (in fact there are 104,072).

(When making these variations, Chuck sometimes goes back to the original photographic maquette, but often takes a painting or some other work derived from that maquette as his source. For example, a drawing derived from the painting *Phil* might lead to an aquatint that could in turn serve as the source image for a paper pulp edition.)

In the summer of 1974, in the old farmhouse the Closes had rented in Garrison, visitors were asked to pose for a Graflex camera fitted with a Polaroid back which Chuck had set up for the purpose of making mug shot–type portraits. These became the basis for snapshot-sized drawings that featured in a rogues' gallery that was at the core of a dot drawings exhibition that traveled to seven museums and public galleries in Texas, Oregon, California, Ohio, and Maryland. Dominating the show were the large *Robert* and a self-portrait in ink and graphite on paper almost six feet tall based on a grid containing 58,424 squares.

The prominence of the grid in the *Keith* mezzotint was largely accidental. In the dot drawings, however, the grid was exploited deliberately and with consistency and, in retrospect, it's easy to see how these sober black-and-white images, both large and small, anticipate the prismatic brilliance of the paintings Chuck Close has made since the late 1980s.

Although throughout the 1970s Close's exploration of the grid's potential was carried out in black and white, he also experimented with color. The large, continuous-tone color portraits led to a number of investigations employing pastel, watercolor, and colored pencil. There were, for example, pastel versions—on watercolor-washed paper—made after *Linda*, *Leslie*, *Susan*, *Nat*, and *Mark*. These were dot drawings, but employing a full chromatic range. Chuck has said, "I would probably have done something like this earlier, but I couldn't afford a really good set of pastels. I would go to the art stores and look hungrily through big boxes of French pastels. Finally I could do it, and I had pastels handmade for me. Working with them was the opposite of working with the color separations. Instead of just three colors, I used a huge range of colors with just minute variations between different blues, or pinks, or greens."

These pastels proved to be an important development in Chuck's career, the beginning of an evolution that had far-reaching consequences.

Chapter 15

Widening Horizons

Towards the end of 1976, Chuck began work on a black-and-white self-portrait—watercolor on paper mounted on canvas—which now hangs in the Ludwig Museum in Vienna. At 80 1/2 inches by 59 inches, it's smaller than the 1968 *Big Self-Portrait* but is still rendered on an imposing scale. Except for the fact that watercolor was substituted for acrylic, the technique employed is identical to the technique used for the earlier, breakthrough painting, the photo-imitative image being built from transparent layers of pigment applied with an airbrush.

That said, though, the images could hardly be more different. The confrontational attitude that characterizes *Big Self-Portrait* has vanished. Nine years older, the artist now looks out from the canvas with a neutral stare. If the earlier painting was a mug shot, this is more of a photo for a passport or a driver's license, conveying the information needed for identification without betraying much in the way of psychological insight. The sense of neutrality is pervasive, emphasized by the rather flat lighting. The hair is much shorter and tidier than in the first portrait, and the beard—even though full and free of excessive grooming—is well-mannered compared to the punkish stubble of 1968. The subject's astigmatism is apparent as seen through the corrective lenses of spectacles that sport frames lighter and

Chuck Close at work on
Self-Portrait/Watercolor, 1976–77

somewhat less aggressive than those in *Big Self-Portrait*. This time, the subject is fully clothed. He wears a frayed work shirt of the sort favored by artists at the time, but he might just as easily be a folk singer or an automobile mechanic.

The painting is a tour de force but tells us surprisingly little about the Chuck Close who might have been encountered on the street in SoHo in the mid-1970s. In fact his life continued to evolve, though not as radically as SoHo itself.

A key event in the evolution of Chuck's life and career was his affiliation with a new gallery.

In 1975, Klaus Kertess left the Bykert and, although it stayed in business for a while under a new director, an era was over. Kertess was among the most astute and intelligent dealers in New York. His record for supporting and introducing artists speaks for itself, but beyond that he had encouraged the gallery to be used as an informal salon for his artists and others who shared their interests.[11] The back room at East Eighty-first Street contained a long, comfortable couch, and it was rare to go there without finding a couple of painters on it, just hanging out or thumbing through the latest *Artforum* together. On one occasion I recall coming across Joe Zucker spread out there sound asleep, and Chuck remembers the couch fondly because of the small change he could extract from between the cushions, sometimes needed to pay for the subway ride back to Prince Street.

Before SoHo completely took over as the primary location for cutting-edge galleries, it was a Saturday afternoon ritual to head uptown to see the new shows on Fifty-seventh Street and on or near Madison Avenue, shuttling between galleries like Pace, André Emmerich, Leo Castelli, Jill Kornblee, and Cordier & Ekstrom, maybe with a break at the Madison Pub. The New York art world was so compact you could see everything of note in an afternoon, and for one group at least, the place to wind up the proceedings was the back room at Bykert, which on such occasions often became crowded and noisy, and filled with cigarette smoke, with Kertess the benevolent host.

Bykert was more, then, than an influential gallery. It was also a meeting place—a haven on the Upper East Side. In addition, Kertess had been a dealer who did his best to look after his artists, sometimes lending them money when they were short, at least when he could afford to, for this was an era when spare cash was seldom plentiful, even at successful galleries.

Kertess was far less successful as a manager of assets than he was as a judge of talent, and this was one reason for his leaving Bykert as was the suicide of Jeff Byers, the gallery's backer. Once this phase of his career was over, Kertess went on to a distinguished career as a writer and curator, and his former artists began to look for new dealers.

There was no question of Chuck having any problem finding representation, his reputation having advanced to the point where there were a number of well-established galleries keen to take him on. Initially his first choice was Leo Castelli. By then, in addition to his East Seventy-seventh Street gallery, Castelli had opened a space at 420 West Broadway in SoHo where his stable of artists—which included Jasper Johns, Robert Rauschenberg, Andy Warhol, Roy Lichtenstein, Frank Stella, Donald Judd, and Bruce Nauman, among others—could show larger works. Castelli did not reject Chuck out of hand but rather, over lunch at the dealer's favorite Italian restaurant, told him that first he would have to prove himself by showing with Castelli's ex-wife, Ileana Sonnabend, who also had a gallery at 420 Broadway. Other prominent dealers, however, were actively courting Chuck, and he was taken to lunch at a number of fine restaurants. Rather low on his list was the Pace Gallery which—although it had made a considerable name for itself and showed some artists he admired—Chuck thought of as perhaps too "uptown" for his work. Nonetheless, Chuck arranged to meet with Arne Glimcher, the gallery's founder and director.

"I went there," says Chuck, "to ask him what he could do for me."

Everything about the meeting caught him by surprise. To start with, instead of taking Chuck out to yet another expensive lunch, Glimcher said, "I hope you don't mind eating in my office—we'll send out for sandwiches." This was the beginning of a very effective sales pitch. Glimcher's office in those days had a one-way mirror looking out into the gallery. The dealer explained that he had had this installed so that if a collector came into the gallery he would be certain to know he was there, and since there were collectors who came in on their lunch breaks, he always ate lunch in. "This," said Glimcher, "is the kind of thing I do for my artists and that I'll do for you if you join the gallery."

"Arne laid out a whole game plan," Chuck explains. "Nobody else had done anything like that. I went in there with zero expectations and came out completely sold. I knew this guy was really going to look after me."

One thing that Chuck quickly discovered is that Arne Glimcher is a dealer with enormous respect for artists, having himself painted before becoming a dealer, abandoning his ambitions because his work, in his opinion, lacked the quality to which he aspired.

"I made things that looked like art," he says, "but they weren't. They lacked that something extra." And so instead he turned to selling art, for which he turned out to have a natural gift.

Pace Gallery—named for Glimcher's father—first set up shop in Boston, then opened a second gallery in New York, while also for a time having a presence in Los Angeles. In Boston, Pace had a major success with a show of sculptures by European masters including Matisse and Giacometti, and also showed Pop artists including Warhol and Claes Oldenberg at an early stage in their careers. Since Warhol and Oldenberg and their best-known contemporaries already had representation in Manhattan, there was no question of showing them in New York, so Glimcher and his then partner Fred Mueller had to build a stable from scratch for their gallery, originally located at 9 East Fifty-seventh Street. Some came by way of a partnership with Los Angeles's pioneering Ferus Gallery; by the time Chuck Close joined Pace, the gallery's list of artists included major international figures such as Jean Dubuffet and Louise Nevelson (whose reputation Glimcher had revived), along with rising stars like Lucas Samaras, Larry Bell, and Robert Irwin. Pace also represented the estate of one of Chuck's biggest heroes, Ad Reinhardt.

"I'd been following Chuck's work for several years," says Glimcher, "since Lucas [Samaras] took me to see his first show at Bykert. When Chuck said he was looking for a new gallery, I was only too happy to offer him a home."

From a point of view of exposure to the wider art world, and of financial security, the change of gallery would have an enormous impact on both Chuck's career and his life.

By the mid-seventies, the center of gravity of the New York gallery world had shifted to SoHo. Spaces like the Paula Cooper Gallery and Ivan Karp's OK Harris had been there since the sixties, but the key date in the evolution of the SoHo gallery scene was a sunny Saturday in September 1971 when four major established galleries—Leo Castelli, Ileana Sonnabend, John Weber, and André Emmerich—opened to the public at 420 West Broadway. The big hit of the day was Gilbert and George performing infinite repetitions of the old English music hall song "Underneath the Arches" at Sonnabend, but all four galleries were packed to the rafters. (John Weber reported that his gallery clocked 12,000 visitors that day.) The stairways were clogged and a rumor spread that the Fire Department was ready to clear the building and close it down. Crowds lined the sidewalks outside and spilled over into the street so that taxis and limos bringing uptown curiosity-seekers could barely move. The former wilderness SoHo was gone forever, at least on weekends,[12] and the once-homegrown nightlife was gradually supplanted by bars, restaurants, and discos with well-heeled backers of various stripes.

What made the new SoHo galleries so refreshing was that they were essentially industrial spaces, much like the lofts in which the art they showed was created, and in this regard they were in complete contrast to the more genteel uptown galleries. Ironically, from Chuck's point of view, Pace Gallery was still located uptown—having moved from West Fifty-seventh to 32 East Fifty-seventh Street—which at the time was of some concern to Chuck, who would have preferred to have shown in SoHo, which he saw as integral to his identity. Before long, Glimcher would establish the first of several downtown spaces, at 142 Greene Street, but Chuck's initial Pace show opened on Fifty-seventh Street on April 30, 1977. The exhibition included the black-and-white self-portrait described at the beginning of this chapter and a similarly-scaled watercolor portrait of Klaus Kertess. The centerpiece of the show was the 108 x 84 inch acrylic *Linda*—the penultimate example of his airbrushed, continuous-tone, dye transfer–derived, super-sized portraits, which had cost him over a year of studio time. Also included was the pastel version of *Linda*, which inaugurated his series in that medium, a set of watercolors, *Linda's Eyes I–V*, and other works on paper.

This exhibition received more attention from national reviewers than any of Chuck's previous shows. John Russell remarked in *The New York Times* that these paintings stretched "the experience of looking at another human being."[13] Thomas B. Hess, in a four-column review in *New York Magazine*, reckoned that "[Close] has arrived at a classical kind of statement..." but detected "a howl underneath, a sense of outrage and of losses...."[14] And in a full-page feature in *Time* magazine, Robert Hughes observed that "[Close] is perhaps the only artist of his generation who has really extended the meaning of portraiture."[15]

Describing how *Linda* looked from close up, Hughes noted, "each wrinkle a canyon, the nose a mountain, lakes for eyes." Other reviewers made similar observations, David Bourdon writing in *The Village Voice*, "The network of lines under her eyes is so intricate as to suggest an aerial view of a dry lake bed in Nevada...." This is typical of how these early continuous-tone portraits—both the color paintings and the earlier black and whites—were perceived at the time. Now the brutal detail seems less shocking and Chuck believes, correctly I think, that these images had an influence on how portrait photography evolved at many different levels, especially in the magazine world. In those days, almost all magazine close-ups of people were airbrushed to eliminate blemishes. Today, despite the availability of Photoshop to clean up images even more efficiently, many publications prefer to go with the raw image, warts and all. (Often art editors actually choose to exaggerate the flaws.) Certainly photographers and magazine professionals were among the first to become aware of Chuck's work, and at least one major figure, Richard Avedon, acknowledged that he had been influenced by the giant heads as early as 1969 when he first encountered one at Bykert.

In 1977, along with the one-man show at Pace, Chuck's work was included in exhibitions at the Wadsworth Atheneum in Hartford (also a solo show), at Documenta 6 in Kassel, at the Whitney Biennial, at the Pompidou Center in Paris, at the Museum of Contemporary Art in Chicago, at the University of Michigan Museum of Art in Ann Arbor, and in a show titled *Representations of America* that was organized by the Metropolitan Museum of Art to travel to the Pushkin Museum in Moscow, the Hermitage in Leningrad, and the Palace of Art in Minsk.

His eminence in the art world had taken a quantum leap, but for the time being this did little to alter Chuck's lifestyle or work habits. He remained very much the family man, taking Georgia to the playground, walking the dog, helping Leslie around the loft, and always trying to work regular hours. One practical studio innovation was that he began using a Big Joe forklift when painting the upper portions of his canvases. This forklift was fitted with a platform on which was mounted a bench, an easel to hold the photographs from which he was working, and shelves for essentials such as an ashtray, a portable radio, and the small black-and-white television tuned, as always, to quiz shows or soap operas.

I recall visiting his studio one afternoon and asking what he saw in these programs. He invited me to stick around and watch for a while. In those days, at least some of the soaps were still shot live, without time delay, on rows of crude sets that resembled those built for school plays. The show he was watching was one of these, and soon enough that became evident. A doorbell rang and was answered by a woman who discovered a man shivering on her doorstep. Heavy snow fell in the darkness beyond him. The woman invited him in, took his coat, and opened a closet door to hang it up. It was snowing in the closet.

"Does that answer your question?" Chuck asked.

In fact, Chuck hardly *watched* these shows. (And in any case, Manhattan television reception was far from perfect in those days before cable, with signals bouncing off skyscrapers and causing multiple ghost images.) *As the World Turns* and *Guiding Light*, with their casts of adulterous and masochistic muses, functioned as distractions from the repetitive tasks he was performing (though he always denied that these were monotonous). He *listened* to the soaps, and to the game shows, rather than watched them, just as he'd listened to the radio soaps as he lay in his sickbed in Tacoma, and even so he was less interested in the plotlines than in the familiar mood that they enabled.

Bob Cottingham recalls that Chuck's existence in the studio was not always so solitary.

"Chuck's loft got to be like a salon. As he became more successful and he got to know more and more people—sometimes it felt like he knew everyone—there would be more and more visitors. People wanted to see his work—museum people, other artists. Chuck was in demand, and he reveled in it, but he still managed to get the work done."

This was the beginning of a period during which the most dramatic happenings in Chuck's life occurred in his work, which became increasingly experimental, not so much in terms of subject matter as in terms of process which as always was the engine that drove his creativity. Between 1977 and the mid-1980s, he would explore traditional printmaking techniques such as etching and classical Japanese woodblock printing. He would experiment with unlikely processes such as fingerprint painting and paper pulp collage, investigate the potential of Polaroid photography, and tentatively begin the return to his first love, oil paint. The evolution of Chuck's work during this period is fascinating to trace because of the cross-pollination that occurs between different groups of paintings, drawings, and prints.

In 1976, a number of artists had contributed to a portfolio of small rubber stamp prints, published by Parasol Press and distributed by the Museum of Modern Art. Chuck's offering was a hatched portrait of Phil Glass, just 7 5/8 by 6 1/2 inches. Because of this print, he had a stamp pad in his studio and a couple of years later hit on the idea of using his finger to transfer ink from such a pad to a support of gridded paper so as to create a portrait image. He began with small versions of *Keith* and *Robert*. In some of these early examples he applied the ink through an acetate stencil to obtain uniformly shaped marks—"square fingerprints"—but in one of the *Robert* drawings he took a much looser approach, at times straying over grid lines and coming up with a result that was therefore less systemic and more expressive. This in turn led Chuck to the thought that perhaps it might be beneficial to take a break from the grid—perhaps it was becoming too confining—and he embarked on a series of thumbprint drawings of Phil Glass, based on the original 1969 black-and-white image, that culminated in a huge example on a sheet of paper almost eight feet tall.

Departing from his established practice, Chuck made these images with the aid of a projector, a method he continued to use in subsequent stamp pad drawings and finger paintings. He did not trace the outlines of the projected image,

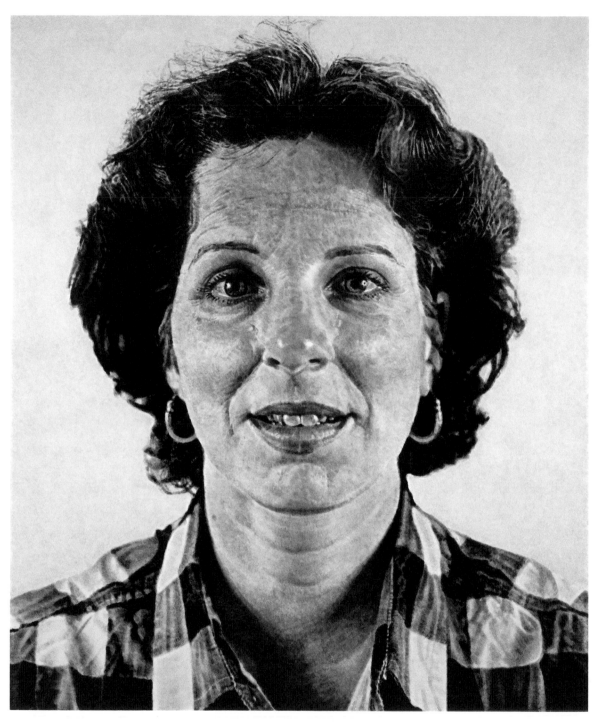

Leslie/Fingerpainting, 1985.
Oil-based ink on canvas, 102 x 84 in. (259.1 x 213.4 cm)

as is commonly done by artists wanting to make an accurate copy of something, but rather used the projection to establish key points on the paper support—points that would mark, for instance, the corner of an eye or the extremity of an ear—then proceeded to join the dots. This method would produce a number of ambitious images, at least two of which, both completed in 1985, are quite astonishing.

One is a portrait of Leslie Close; the other is a portrait of her grandmother, Fanny. Both are on canvases that measure 102 by 84 inches, just slightly smaller than the canvases used for the continuous-tone airbrush heads. The medium used in both cases is oil-based ink. (Chuck had abandoned stamp pad ink when his finger became numb and he discovered that it contained a chemical that could cause nerve damage after prolonged use. It also had the disadvantage of fading when exposed to light.)

The portrait of Leslie is in full color and employs essentially the same process as the airbrushed continuous-tone color paintings—transparent primary color placed over transparent primary color—except that the pigment has been applied with the fingertip rather than an airbrush. When a comparison is made with those continuous-tone paintings—and especially with the large watercolor of Leslie made a dozen years earlier—what is immediately apparent is that the anonymity of the airbrush has been supplanted by a sense of intimacy and immediacy that gives the painting a warmth and glow. Fingerprints become freckles, evoking Robert Storr's comment about these paintings that they are the product of flesh being used to evoke flesh.

Even more striking than *Leslie/Fingerpainting* is the black-and-white portrait, now in the National Gallery in Washington, of her grandmother. Fanny's face, as shown in this image, is ravaged yet immensely dignified. The finger-painting method proved especially well suited to evoking the weathered and wrinkled texture of her skin; with this technique Chuck could no longer distance himself from a subject as he had in his airbrushed portraits. Any vestige of his original commitment to the impersonal application of process had dissolved. This did not mean that he had abandoned process but rather that he had now become comfortable enough with his basic method to be able to apply its principles more flexibly. In that sense, *Fanny* and the other works that employed the fingertip application of pigment represent a watershed in his career. Until then he had been hiding behind a screen of studied detachment that he now felt free to abandon—at least up to a point.

Fanny/Fingerpainting, 1985.
Oil-based ink on canvas, 102 x 84 in. (259.1 x 213.4 cm)

A few years ago, the art historian James Elkins wrote a book titled *Pictures and Tears: A History of People Who Have Cried in Front of Paintings.* His research revealed that most art professionals—historians, critics, teachers, and so on—confessed to remaining dry-eyed in front of even the most staggeringly beautiful works of art. They admitted to thinking of paintings and sculptures as objects to be studied, deconstructed, and commented on, rather than as things to be moved by. It could be argued that the professed detachment of Chuck Close's early paintings invited such an objective response, though paradoxically it is that deliberate distancing that gives those works their emotional strength since the viewer is forced to challenge their apparent aloofness to find human content. (In fact some of them have become objects of great affection among patrons of the museums where they are housed.) It was inevitable, however, that sooner or later Chuck would begin to emerge from behind the screen of detachment. Family life has a way of playing into such things, and it was perhaps no coincidence that Leslie had given birth to the Closes' second daughter, Maggie, in 1984, shortly before *Leslie/Fingerpainting* and *Fanny/Fingerpainting* were made.

I recall visiting the National Gallery one afternoon, having a couple of hours to spare during a book tour, and coming upon *Fanny* unexpectedly. Luckily I always carry a handkerchief when visiting museums. The tear I wiped away was only partly inspired by the emotional content of the portrait, however. I was also moved because, not to put too fine a Lacanian interpretation on it, the painting is so bloody good. A tour de force of that order deserves either a laugh of delight or a tear of gratitude.

The series of stamp pad drawings and fingerprint paintings overlapped with another group of works that many art world observers found unexpected, a series employing pulp paper as the medium. The reader may recall that Chuck had unpleasant associations with pulp paper, having grown up in cities where paper mills filled the air with the stench that is a by-product of the process of commercial pulping. The reason that Chuck even considered making pulp paper pieces was due entirely to the dogged persistence of one man, Joe Wilfer.

Wilfer—who died in 1995 of a brain tumor that may have been induced by the chemicals he worked with on a daily basis—was a gifted printer and papermaker who had taught at the University of Wisconsin in Madison. In the late 1970s, he was brought east to Maine to become director of the Skowhegan School of Art. There he managed to step on a number of sensitive toes and was soon released.

Desperately wanting to stay on the East Coast, preferably in New York, he began to lobby artists to make editions using pulp paper. These proposed editions were to be made in Manhattan at the Dieu Donné Papermill, a nonprofit shop founded in 1975. One of the artists Wilfer targeted was Chuck, who was not enthusiastic, telling him he did not like the pulp paper pieces he had seen—too artsy crafty. Wilfer asked what it would take to change Chuck's mind. Chuck told him he would need to work with a whole range of different grays—as many as twenty or thirty calibrated from black to white. Wilfer brought samples. Chuck told him what was wrong with them. Wilfer made more samples until Chuck became caught up in the momentum of the printer's enthusiasm, and gradually they arrived at a point where there seemed to be possibilities. Finally, in 1981, Chuck agreed to give it a shot.

Arrangements were made to begin work at Dieu Donné, and the image he chose for his first pulp multiple was *Keith*. The idea was to build the image in much the same way as a black-and-white dot drawing, with wads of tinted pulp taking the place of the dots. Chuck and Wilfer came up with the concept of structuring the piece by means of a grill normally employed as a light filter placed over fluorescent lamp fixtures. Such grills are in fact readymade grids, meshes of small squares, half an inch deep, into which watery pulp can be injected one square at a time. As it dried, it would bond to a sheet of pulp, also wet, that dried at the same time, serving as the support for the whole.

To determine the pigmentation and placement of each wad of pulp, Chuck took a gridded watercolor of Keith as his maquette. Liquid paper, tonally matched to the squares of the watercolor drawing, was squeezed into the openings of the grill from plastic bottles. The system worked well, though not perfectly, so that when the pulp was in place Chuck would sometimes change the pigmentation of a given wad of paper that did not quite pull its weight in the overall constellation. He also manipulated the still soggy wads to give them texture and a sense of hands-on intervention, so that each example of a given edition was slightly different from every other one.

Keith (which as an edition took almost a year of experimentation and work to complete) was the first of these pulp paper multiples. Later, pulp editions were made under the auspices of Pace Editions in a variety of locations, employing a level of improvised technology that Chuck has compared with making bathtub gin. Wilfer remained the principal printer, with Ruth Lingen—a former student of Wilfer, who had become his chief assistant—playing a key hands-on role.

Georgia, 1982.
Pulp paper collage on canvas, 48 x 38 in. (121.9 x 76.2 cm)

It is characteristic of Chuck's devotion to process, and to the inquiring nature of his imagination, that he soon began to invent new ways of using paper pulp. As work progressed on the grid editions, blobs of liquid paper sometimes fell to the floor where they flattened and hardened into what Chuck has described as "miniature meadow muffins the size of Pringles potato chips,"[16] in the two dozen shades of gray employed in the prints. The artist began to pick up these chips and save them in a cigar box. In spare moments, he would make little heaps of overlapping paper discs, noting, "The edges of these little chips were beautiful—natural, irregular outside edges formed by gravity, not by artistic decision."[17] Assistants began to produce more of these gravity-generated pulp paper patties, which when dry were collected by tonality into trays, providing Chuck with an unlikely "palette" that he employed to create collage portraits by gluing the irregularly shaped chips to canvas.

One image in the series was a 1982 *Georgia*, which prompted Chuck to create an edition using irregularly shaped wads of pulp paper. In a multiple, these could not be left to gravity, so he made a tracing of the collage, which indicated the edges of all the patties, simplifying where necessary. This was passed on to Wilfer, who translated the resulting diagram—which resembled a paint-by-numbers image—into a stencil-like mold soldered together from bent strips of brass, a process that took four hundred hours. From this, a handmade paper multiple was produced in an edition of thirty-five.

During the period in which he was creating the fingerprint images and the pulp paper pieces—not to mention large black-and-white watercolors, as well as important color dot paintings and drawings that are discussed in a future chapter—Chuck also found time to embark on a new career. His work since 1968 had been rooted in photography, but as mentioned earlier he had never thought of the photographs of his subjects—his maquettes—as anything but source material, and although he had taken comprehensive photography courses at school, he did not consider himself a photographer.

In 1977, Chuck was given the opportunity to work at the Polaroid Corporation's Cambridge, Massachusetts, research center, using a large format—24 x 20 inch—custom-built Polaroid camera. Nothing came of that, but two years later Kathy Halbreich, then director of the Massachusetts Institute of Technology's Hayden Gallery, in Cambridge, invited Chuck up to work with the same camera, which Polaroid had now made available to MIT. This time the experiment proved more fruitful.

The big Polaroid was an oversize view camera that had been fitted with a special back designed to carry the instant developing film invented by Dr. Edwin Land in the 1940s. Chuck accepted Halbreich's invitation, thinking this camera might be ideal for taking photos that could serve as source material for his paintings. In fact, he found that it offered far more than that. The images it produced were characterized by intense natural color and a degree of resolution, which, at that size, provided a level of scrutiny that recalled the unforgiving detail found in Chuck's large continuous-tone portraits. In addition, Chuck was stimulated by the immediacy of the process—the fact that he could see the image barely a minute after the shutter had been released.

When shooting with standard film, his practice had been to shoot multiple versions of a sitter, bracketing for minor variations of exposure or focus, because there was no way of checking the image till it came back from the lab. Working with the big Polaroid, he could immediately see what he had got—instant feedback—so for the next shot it was possible to set things up differently, change the lighting, ask for a different expression, or whatever. Chuck also liked that the subject received the immediate feedback too and had a chance to react—to participate in a dialogue and become a collaborator.

The first straightforward Polaroid heads he shot were striking enough, but they were soon surpassed by an extraordinary work, a self-portrait that stands, I believe, as a milestone in the history of photography. The title of this 1979 work is *Self-Portrait/Composite/Nine Parts*, which describes the piece succinctly without conveying any of its visual drama.

This huge photo assemblage demonstrated how Chuck's incremental process could be applied to photography. It is made up of nine 24 by 20 inch Polaroids, each an extreme close-up of part of the artist's face, each separate and distinct but marginally overlapping its neighbors when mounted on the wall in the form of a tick-tack-toe grid, making for a cumulative image with overall dimensions of 83 by 69 inches. Seen today, the piece remains extremely powerful. In 1979 it was positively shocking. At that time, large-scale photographs—so commonplace in galleries now—were seldom encountered except in the form of advertisements such as the backlit Kodak billboards then a feature of Grand Central Station's main concourse, installed so as to be seen from a distance. The nine-piece portrait was intended to be seen from close up, and the shock value of the scale, combined with the fragmentation of the image and the merciless detail provided by the Polaroid system, was enormous. Fragmentation is particularly shocking when applied to the human face, especially since in this instance the edges of some sheets actually slice through the eyes, metaphorically assaulting the very notion of vision.

While working with the MIT Polaroid camera, Chuck learned of an even larger instrument that the Polaroid Corporation had installed just a couple of miles

Self-Portrait/Composite/Nine Parts, 1979.
Polaroid photographs, 83 x 69 in. (210.8 x 175.3 cm)

away in an empty gallery at the Museum of Fine Arts, Boston, one that could take 80 by 40 inch instant prints. This had been built on Dr. Land's orders to show off the product in a spectacular way at a shareholder's meeting. After that event, the monster camera had no obvious practical use until it found a home in the museum, where it was utilized for making high-quality life-size images of works of art. Chuck approached Polaroid, and the company, somewhat reluctantly, gave permission for him to experiment with the camera which was in fact a room-sized, light-fast box, sixteen feet deep and twelve feet tall and wide, at one end of which was a lens board into which a rather basic optical system—lens and bellows—was fitted. The person or object to be photographed would be placed in front of the lens in a space equipped with strobe lights that could produce 30,000 watt-seconds of flash power. The room-sized camera was furnished with a focusing screen on which an inverted image of the subject projected by the camera lens could be adjusted. (Sometimes this was done simply by having the model move an inch or two towards the lens or away from it.) When focus was achieved, an oversize strip of Polaroid negative would be lowered in front of the focusing plane, where it was held flat by suction provided by a simple vacuum device. After final adjustments, the exposure could now be made. Often the lens used was from an enlarger rather than from a camera, so that no mechanical shutter was involved. Instead, a piece of cardboard was held over the lens and removed by hand for a fraction of a second as the strobes flashed.

Along with a couple of technicians, Chuck would actually be inside the camera for the crucial moments leading up to and during the exposure:

"For a while, you'd be in total darkness. Sometimes I'd wear a night-vision headset like the FBI and the army use, so I could see what was going on—people moving round like ghosts. Then, when the strobes were triggered, it was amazing. You saw the whole image in an instant—every detail. You could tell if the model had shut her eyes. I mean, you may have known before how a camera worked, but here you were actually inside the damn thing. It was like that Raquel Welch movie where they shrink people to go inside the human body."

Once the exposure had been made, the next task was to manhandle the negative and a sheet of printing paper, between which developing chemicals were spread, through a set of rollers that squeezed the layers of the "sandwich" together, allowing the chemicals to stimulate the Polaroid dye-printing process as paper and negative spilled out onto the floor. When the two sheets were pulled apart, ninety seconds later, the image materialized.

When first given the opportunity to work with what was then known as the Museum Camera, in 1980, Chuck made a number of head and shoulder portraits of friends and a gigantic six-panel self-portrait that was an extension of the ideas explored in the nine-sheet self-portrait of the previous year. When he used the big Boston camera again in 1984, he departed from his seventeen-year, single-minded devotion to the portrait and produced a series of nudes which also differed from his paintings, drawings, prints, and earlier photographs in that he employed models, both male and female, from outside his immediate social orbit, some of them professional dancers. The images produced included diptychs and triptychs that recorded partial torsos, as well as seventeen-foot-long, five-panel reclining nudes that inevitably recall the big black-and-white nude of 1967 (though these Polaroids were in color).

One reason for Chuck's disappointment with the 1967 *Big Nude* derived from the fact that the figure's erotic hot spots tended to distract from the uniformity of visual information for which he was aiming. If anything, the obtrusion of erotic hot spots is even more characteristic of the 1984 nudes in which breasts, male genitals, and pubic hair jump out at the viewer thanks to the way in which they have been both magnified and intensified by the camera. Instead of trying to find a way around this, Chuck—perhaps because he had developed more confidence in his vision—now insisted on forcing the viewer to confront these areas. Chuck's photography dealer Peter MacGill recalls that when these nudes were first exhibited at his Fifty-seventh Street gallery, in January 1985, Chuck insisted that he build false walls that would oblige the viewer to encounter the images at close range.

The most successful of these giant Polaroids are the truncated torso diptychs and triptychs precisely because they exploit this immediacy most effectively, confronting the viewer with anatomical hot spots that cannot be ignored. Not many years earlier, Chuck had shocked school authorities at the University of Massachusetts by including frontal male nudes in his Amherst exhibition. One wonders what they would have made of a photograph like *Mark Diptych II*.

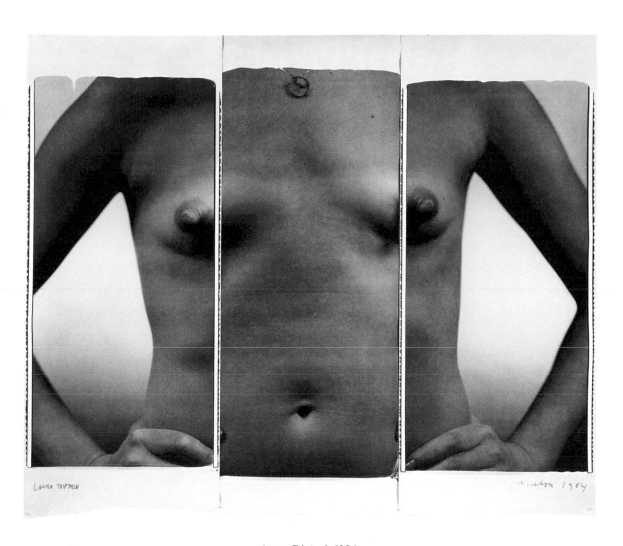

Laura Triptych, 1984.
Polaroid Polacolor II photographs, 102 x 128 in.
(215.9 x 325.1 cm)

Chapter 16

Family Matters

On Saturday, September 27, 1980, Chuck and Leslie Close were in Minneapolis for the opening of his first major museum retrospective, organized by Martin Friedman and Lisa Lyons, at the Walker Art Center. The occasion drew a diverse crowd, with local grandees—families like the Daytons and the Pillsburys—rubbing shoulders with prominent members of the New York art world and curators from around the United States. One person conspicuous by her absence was Chuck's mother. She languished at her home in Lake Stevens along with her second husband, Art Sipprell.

Chuck had helped Millie build the Lake Stevens house—a handsome and spacious structure in a loosely post-Bauhaus idiom that, though starker, bore comparison with Rus Day's modernist home. Sited on a hillside overlooking the lake, it had been completed in the late sixties. While it was under construction, Millie had lived for two years in a dilapidated frame house in a working-class neighborhood, paying for her future home by putting in long hours as a real estate agent for the Green Gables company, the job that had made her blue Austin Healy coupe a familiar sight as she drove clients around Everett and the surrounding communities. On weekends, when conditions were right, she would strap her skis to the little car and head up Highway 2 to the Stevens Pass ski area. She still gave piano lessons, and she continued as organist and deaconess at the Memorial Baptist Church until a sharp disagreement with the church fathers caused her to resign the membership she had held there for many years.

This incident illustrates clearly that Millie's steely sense of right and wrong, which had served as such a strong example for her son, was still very much intact. It had come to her attention, through her real estate work, that a family was in need of temporary accommodations. A property belonging to the church

Mildred Close at her home overlooking Lake Stevens, 1972

was empty at the time, and she asked if it could be made available to these unfortunates. Her request was granted until it was discovered that the family was Hispanic, at which point the offer was hurriedly withdrawn. During services the following Sunday, Millie denounced the church leaders as hypocrites before marching out, never to return.

After her 1970 marriage to Sipprell, Millie, with her usual passion, had joined in her new husband's enthusiasm for offshore sailing. Messing around in boats is almost a prerequisite for anyone who lives near the shores of Puget Sound, but Sipprell was an ambitious amateur sailor who harbored dreams of undertaking long-distance voyages, and who chose to bypass reliance upon modern navigational aids, preferring to employ time-honored tools such as the sextant to practice celestial navigation. This approach to sailing undoubtedly appealed to the sense of adventure which Millie had been forced to suppress during the years when she was caring for her ailing first husband and performing the duties of a highly proactive single parent. She was probably never happier than when aboard the Sipprells' boat *Arabesque*.

An extended cruise to California, Hawaii, Alaska, and British Columbia was intended as a warm-up for a round-the-world voyage to be made without benefit of radio communications. More modestly, in 1975, they arranged a boat swap with East Coast sailors that permitted them to cruise out of New Rochelle, New York, and to spend time with Chuck, Leslie, and Georgia. Again, the following year during the U.S. bicentennial celebrations, they visited New York and Long Island, where Chuck and Leslie were renting a house in Springs, not far from the home of Chuck's hero, Willem de Kooning.

Chuck and Leslie had made occasional visits to Washington throughout the seventies, though these became less frequent as the decade progressed, partly because Georgia's arrival made travel more of a chore—cross-country driving was no longer a comfortable option—but partly because Leslie in particular did not look forward to these family get-togethers.

The relationship between Leslie and Millie, never entirely relaxed, had become increasingly strained. It was Leslie's sense that Millie had become obsessed with aging, an obsession that had been heightened by the fact that recurring breast tumors—although deemed nonmalignant—had resulted in a double mastectomy. Leslie, who was still in her twenties at the time, reports that she was disturbed to find that Millie was complaining in private to Chuck that she, Leslie, was flaunting her youth in order to make Millie feel old. More disturbing was the fact that Millie began to make it clear that she disapproved of the way that Georgia was being brought up, hinting that Leslie did not employ a firm enough hand and was too protective, failing to imbue Georgia with the fearlessness that Millie considered the child's birthright. Leslie found this intolerable.

Chuck tried to mediate but ultimately was caught in the middle between two strong-willed and opinionated women, intensely suspicious of each other, neither prepared to give an inch. Inevitably he sided with Leslie, believing that the problem was rooted in Millie's chronic blindness to anything that called for empathy or psychological insight.

Things came to a head in 1977 when Chuck, Leslie, and Georgia traveled to Lake Stevens for what proved to be a traumatizing visit. Childrearing was the explosive issue, but, almost comically, it was Millie's cooking that provided the incendiary spark. Every evening Chuck's mother served the same meal, her famous—or infamous—beef Stroganoff. It was bad enough for Chuck and Leslie, but it was hardest on Georgia, who was four at the time. Confronted with the Stroganoff yet again, she would refuse to eat. Millie's attitude was, 'Why should she be spoiled? She eats what we eat.'"

Finally, on what was scheduled to be the last evening, Leslie could take it no longer. After dinner she went to the kitchen and opened a can of Spaghetti Os, or some such delicacy, for Georgia. Millie was outraged. Having gone upstairs, she and her husband could be heard ranting against Leslie. Chuck had had enough and told Leslie to pack. Now Millie and Art came downstairs and a violent quarrel ensued, which culminated with Art grabbing a log from the fireplace and lunging threateningly at Chuck. Before any physical harm was done, Millie rushed from the house, screaming, and ran off into the woods. Chuck went out to find her and eventually brought her back. The argument then started up again, but finally the bags were thrown in the trunk of Aunt Bina's car, which Chuck had borrowed for the visit, and he, Leslie, and Georgia were aboard, ready to drive off. Hysterical, Millie now prostrated herself on the driveway, in front of the car, to prevent them from leaving. Chuck was finally able to get his family to a motel by backing the car around the circular drive, but the next day there was another equally melodramatic scene at the Seattle airport where Millie and her husband confronted Chuck at the departure gate.

Chuck is still not sure why they were there.

"Maybe they came to apologize, or maybe to continue the fight, or maybe they were just there to get the keys to Bina's car."

In any case, Millie became hysterical once more, and when the Closes got back to New York, the phone calls began.

"My mother's hostility towards Leslie made for an intolerable situation," says Chuck. "It reached the point where I would feel sick to my stomach every time the phone rang, in case it was her. I told her we couldn't talk or see each other for a while."

For a considerable length of time—Chuck thinks as much as a couple of years—there was no communication between them, and after that only very limited contact. With the Walker retrospective coming up, Chuck faced a quandary. He really did not want his mother there at the opening ceremonies, and the same went for Leslie, though even more so. Chuck also suspected that his mother probably would not want to be there, but at the same time, given all she had done for him as a child, he could not imagine barring her from this moment of major recognition. As best he can recall, Leslie lobbied for no invitation to be sent, but in the end one was, possibly at the last minute.

But Millie remained in Lake Stevens, responding to the invitation with a letter dated September 23, 1980, the day of the opening reception. Written in her emphatic, cursive longhand, it combines sorrow and bitterness with love and anger barely moderated by restraint.

Dear Chuck,

We want to thank you for the invitation to meet you in Minneapolis. As the day draws near I am overwhelmed with longing to see you. However, I cannot quite take that step. Perhaps in time I can face it.

I want you to know how much I love you and Georgia. I am so proud of you and your family. I am very proud of your success in your career, moreso [sic] over the fact you are a fine husband, father and family man. No matter what recognition you receive in the eyes of the world—it is not as important as the *kind* of person you are in your private life. As a father, you now know how it feels to be proud of your child. Imagine how you will feel 30 years from now when Georgia is a fine woman. Isn't she the one? I do so pray her life will go forward in the direction she chooses and all will go smoothly and well. Certainly with her family environment and love, life should be [what] anyone would desire for her. I do hope my life will be long enough to see her as an adult. Not that I'm worried. Short of an accident, I look forward to many years of active life. I am amazed at how well I feel. I still am strong and quite able to do most anything I want to. . . .

The letter continues after a paragraph of family news:

Thank you for the snaps. You all look so happy. Georgia is so tall and grown-up looking. Looks more like 10 or 11 years instead of 7.

I am very happy for Leslie and her success in her new career. It must be a joy for her to be able to create the beautiful gardens and then receive recognition for them and advance in her profession. It will be hard when she is back in school, however. I know you and Georgia will do everything to help her.

I have rambled on too much, I know. It is hard to express myself for what is in my heart.

Anyway, I just wanted you to know how much I love you and appreciate you.

Love to you

Mom.

The standoff continued for a while, but Chuck maintained conciliatory contact with his mother. Finally an understanding was reached that she would attend the New York opening of the retrospective scheduled for the Whitney Museum in April 1981.

Once again, though, Millie would be absent.

On Christmas Eve, 1980–Chuck and Leslie's thirteenth wedding anniversary–Millie began to suffer chest pains at the Lake Stevens House. Sixty-seven years old, she had seemed in excellent health (as she had boasted in the September letter), but the pains became severe and her husband tried to persuade her to go to an emergency room. She refused, insisting that she knew what a heart attack would feel like and this certainly was not one. To prove her point, she stubbornly went out to chop wood, then walked briskly up a steep hill. On her return to the house, she collapsed and was rushed to the hospital. Chuck immediately flew out to be at her bedside, but by the time he arrived she was in a coma. On December 30, she died.

"I still feel terrible that I didn't have a chance to reconcile with her," Chuck says. "I never felt totally estranged from her–she was my mother. I'm still very conscious of what she did for me when I was a kid, but she was a difficult, stubborn woman and I was very angry at her hostility towards Leslie. It made things impossible. It's very sad, really. I've always been sorry that I never photographed her for a painting."

Why, in fact, did he never photograph her for a painting? When that question is posed, his immediate answer is, "I never expected her to die. She was so tough, so formidable–I just didn't expect it."

After a moment's hesitation, he adds, "I didn't photograph her because I was angry at her."

Given Chuck's time-consuming work methods, and the daily intimate confrontation with a particular face that is involved, it's difficult to imagine him painting someone with whom he had such a long, intense, and complex relationship as his mother. He may have started his portrait career with the presumption that he was painting "heads" or "mug shots," but inevitably personality was an underlying factor. His paintings of Leslie, for instance, have a very different flavor from those of almost anyone else, including other family members. The images he presents of his daughters are bathed in benevolence. The images of Leslie can be seen as responses to the complexities that inform any marriage. She is not treated as a muse. None of his portraits of her can be said to be flattering, though at the same time none conceal the fact that she is an attractive woman.

Mildred Close Sipprell aboard the Arabesque in the late 1970s.
"Art [Sipprell] said I looked so happy he had to take [a photograph]. A great life!"

It's true, of course, that none of his other portraits seek to flatter either, yet there is something about those of Leslie that suggest that in her case this principle is carried to an extreme, as if the artist is trying to strip the image down to basics. In the continuous-tone watercolor of 1972–73 and the marvelous finger painting of 1985, Leslie is permitted lipstick, but otherwise it's as if her skin has been scrubbed. These are naked faces in which every freckle is exposed.

Perhaps it's easy to read too much into this. Leslie's explanation of her appearance in the watercolor portrait is that, since she is extremely sensitive to light, the photographer's lights were almost painful so that her eyes were watering and she had to struggle to keep from squinting.

Nothing, however, can detract from the fact that this is a very intense painting. Could Chuck have painted his mother with that same intensity? The decades of wear and tear on their relationship would have made it difficult, yet it's even harder to imagine that he could have painted her any other way.

Chuck had observed that his mother had two faces, one resembling the mask of comedy and one the mask of tragedy. Looking at her life as a whole, Chuck had two mothers—the one who gave unstintingly, determined to ensure his success, and then the one who could not or would not let go: not an unusual conjunction, but one that in this case was unusually dramatic in its dynamics. If we consider how Mildred Close struggled with her own frustrated ambitions, how she fulfilled her family duties while attempting to transcend the limitations of her background, how she fought for just causes without being inhibited by public opinion, then it must be agreed she was a remarkable woman, and that is without even considering everything she laid on the line for her son. Yet at the same time she had a highly developed knack of driving wedges between herself and her only child. She might take satisfaction in his success, but at the same time she could never forgive that success for taking him away from her.

In the end, the only mask that fits is the mask of tragedy.

Mildred Close died with a secret she had kept from her son for forty years.

Not long after his mother's funeral, Chuck received a phone call from a man named Martin Close. He told Chuck that he was his brother.

The story that emerged was that Leslie Durward Close had been married in Illinois before he moved to the Pacific Northwest. A single child, a boy, was the product of this union that had fallen apart in the early years of the Depression. When Chuck checked this out with his Great Aunt Bina, she confirmed that the facts had been known to Millie and other family members but that Millie had chosen to keep them from Chuck. In retrospect, Chuck recalled that his mother would sometimes receive upsetting letters from someone she described as "an old girlfriend of your father's." She would add, without giving any specifics, that the woman was crazy and was harassing her.

Martin Close was a retired aerospace engineer, successful enough to have owned a California beachfront home. Chuck and Leslie invited Martin and his wife to visit them in East Hampton. They drove up in a large Winnebago that they parked outside the Closes' house on Newtown Lane. Chuck was quite excited to meet this half-brother, but Leslie's last words before they went out to greet the arrivals amounted to a warning. "Don't expect him to agree with all your political opinions," she cautioned, adding, "he might be a Republican or something."

This proved to be sound advice. Over the next couple of days—which seemed an eternity—Martin expressed right-wing views that Chuck found appalling and bigoted. The visit did provide some fascinating revelations, however. Martin had brought black-and-white snapshots taken in Illinois decades earlier—Chuck's father with his arm affectionately draped around a woman Chuck had never seen before, and cradling a child who decidedly was not Chuck. It was disturbing for him to be confronted with these photographs. Later, he would learn from his Aunt Bina that the version of the story which had circulated among the Albros and Wagners was that Les Close had married his first wife reluctantly, and then only to give the child a name. It was even hinted that the baby was not his to begin with, and it was understood that the marriage had been dissolved almost immediately. These snapshots did not bear that out. To Chuck, they looked like pictures of a real family, and in some of them young Martin was significantly beyond infancy.

After the breakup of the marriage, Martin's mother had moved to Los Angeles, where Chuck was told she had had a very hard time. Presumably it was from there that she had written to Millie, possibly, Chuck speculates, asking for money. Perhaps the most shocking piece of information Chuck was given was that his mother had contacted Martin—who would have been a young adult at the time—and told him not to come to his father's funeral. Chuck found this upsetting, but it did little to soften his feelings towards his newly found half-brother whose political and social postures he found so abhorrent. When the Winnebago drove off, it would be the last time the siblings set eyes on each other.

Chapter 17

Leaving SoHo

When Georgia was born, SoHo had been a place almost devoid of young children, and of facilities to care for them. There was a small urban playground on Thompson Street where toddlers sometimes had to be discouraged from picking up used hypodermic needles—Georgia was briefly in a playgroup there—or you could walk the kids up to Washington Square Park in search of a little shade. Slowly, as couples settled down, things began to change. In the late seventies, my own daughter attended a preschool program in the basement beneath Food, which later, after an infestation of rats, relocated to a city-owned structure in the Thompson Street playground (where needles remained a hazard), while some parents sent their children to the nursery school in the NYU Silver Towers highrise complex just north of Houston Street. Beyond that—and despite the relentless gentrification of SoHo—local schooling remained an issue. Greenwich Village offered nearby options such as Little Red Schoolhouse, Village Community School, and St. Luke's, as well as a couple of well-regarded public schools. Initially the Closes enrolled Georgia at Grace Church School, a conservative establishment on Fourth Avenue, a dozen blocks from the loft. Chuck would walk her there before heading for the studio, but later they switched Georgia to the Dalton School, an Upper East Side preparatory school with a reputation for channeling its pupils into prestigious Ivy League colleges.

One outcome of this, which manifested itself quite quickly, was the discovery that, for children accustomed to Park Avenue, SoHo in the early 1980s might just as well have been a shantytown slum in Calcutta or Rio de Janeiro.

"Georgia's friends would come down to Prince Street for a sleepover," Chuck recalls, "and they'd never seen a wino passed out on a loading dock before, or a police lock on a loft door. They'd never been in a loft. They thought they'd been kidnapped and taken to a Third World country."

Leslie Close, pregnant with Maggie,
posing with Georgia and Ruby, the family dog, 1984

In 1984, partly because of this, and partly because Leslie was expecting a second child, meaning that more space would be needed, the Closes decided that it
was time to move. Since joining Pace, Chuck's income had increased to the point
where they were able to afford a spacious apartment on Central Park West, at
Eighty-seventh Street. On moving day, March 24, Leslie went into labor, and
Maggie Close was delivered a few hours later.

Chuck admits to having had a good deal of reluctance about moving uptown,
but he quickly discovered that living so close to the park had its compensations.
Unless it was raining–his Washington upbringing has left him with an abid-

ing hatred of rain—he would walk through the park each morning, emerging at Columbus Circle where he boarded a downtown subway train to take him to his studio. For a few months this meant the West Third Street studio, but soon he acquired a new work space on Spring Street, thus maintaining a daily connection with SoHo.

In the late seventies, the Closes had purchased a modest summer home near the railroad station in East Hampton, on the South Fork of Long Island—the one visited by his half-brother and his wife—and in 1986 they bought a larger property a dozen miles away in Bridgehampton, with a pond and space for a freestanding studio for Chuck, and a substantial garden for Leslie that would become a local showpiece, as was already the case with the smaller garden of the East Hampton house.

In the early eighties, Leslie devoted much of her time to working at Wave Hill—the Riverdale estate famous for its public gardens—where she became the founding director of a program in the history of American landscape architecture, and cofounded its Catalog of Landscape Records which has since been moved to the New York Botanical Garden in the Bronx. Her association with Wave Hill, which began as an internship, was an outcome of her postgraduate work at New York University. Among her achievements at Wave Hill was a 1983 exhibition *Portrait of an Era in Landscape Photography: the Photographs of Mattie Edwards Hewitt*, for which she prepared a handsome illustrated catalog. She was also responsible for organizing a number of seminars involving experts from fields related to landscape architecture. Her association with Wave Hill continued until 1987.

The year the Closes acquired the Bridgehampton property, Chuck turned 46. He was on the art world fast track, and it is hard to imagine how things could have looked rosier, at least from the outside. That same year, however, there was an episode that recalled an earlier scare and hinted at troubles to come. In October, Chuck traveled to Kyoto to work with the master printer Tadashi Toda—officially a National Treasure—on a traditional Japanese ukiyo-e-style woodblock print, a portrait of Leslie. Leslie stayed behind, since Maggie was just two years old, and Chuck traveled with Kathan Brown of Crown Point Press, with whom he had produced *Keith/Mezzotint*, and Hidekatsu Takada, a printer with wide experience in both Japan and America. Takada's presence proved essential to bridge cultural differences and misunderstandings. The print was to be based on a watercolor

Chuck had made earlier in the year, which had been sent on ahead. He understood that Toda would have cut some blocks, and proofed them, before he arrived, but when he got to Kyoto, he was shocked to find that Toda had gone much further than he expected. In Japan, a printmaker of Toda's stature is considered the equal of the artist whose original he is interpreting, so he had simply started without Chuck. This was not what the artist had had in mind.

Mark Greenwold and Chuck Close at Close's home in East Hampton, c. 1984

"I pointed to a specific shape and said to Takada, 'Tell him it is too green.' Takada started talking and talking, and there was an intense reaction from Mr. Toda. Finally I asked, 'Why is it taking so long?' Takada said, 'You don't understand, what I have to say is "Chuck is thrilled with what you have done, he thinks you are a genius. He thinks it is perfection. Beyond his wildest dreams. Nothing could be done to improve it. However, in the interest of intellectual curiosity, not that it would be better than what you have done, just to see what would happen, could you possibly make it a little less green."' We had to go through this process every time. . . . I found it strange yet interesting to let someone interpret the work, to make decisions about color and separations. I realized we had to work together to make a good print."[18]

The Close family, c. 1986: Leslie, Maggie, Chuck, and Georgia

The print turned out well—and Chuck has said that it taught him many things about the importance of collaboration—but while in Kyoto, Chuck once again suffered severe chest pains. Again he was rushed to an emergency room. Again there was no definitive diagnosis, and again he was given nitroglycerine in case of a recurrence. He returned safely to New York, complaining that he had been forbidden to eat the delicious Japan Airlines food.

Chapter 18

Prismatic Grids

The woodblock print of Leslie that Chuck produced in Japan belonged to an evolving sequence of images that can be said to have been launched with the series of pastel drawings, beginning with *Linda/Pastel* in 1977 and including *Leslie/Pastel* (1977), *Susan/Pastel* (1977), *Nat/Pastel* (1978), and small and large versions of *Mark/Pastel* (1978 and 1978–79, respectively). These all relate to large continuous-tone paintings, but it should be emphasized that they were not studies for those paintings but rather explorations carried out using the completed paintings as starting points. The idea was to build an image from hundreds of tiny chromatic units juxtaposed within a grid in such a way that when seen from an appropriate distance the viewer's eye would perform the task of assembling the dots into a clearly photo-derived likeness of the sitter. When studied closely, there is a surprising variety to the pastel series, which evolves from images that rely on relatively straightforward juxtapositions within the grid, to the large version of *Mark/Pastel* which displays more complex handling of the individual components of the grid so that any given colored dot may be modified by the superimposition of a touch or touches of another color, thus allowing for more chromatic subtlety.

It was almost inevitable that Chuck would explore the possibilities inherent in these pastels by developing the same idea in paint on canvas. Pastel is a very sensual medium, which came as a release after years of working with an airbrush. Chuck's first love had always been oil paint and now these richly chromatic pastel drawings led him back to using oils for the first time since he had terminated his romance with Abstract Expressionism. Back in the sixties, giving up oil paint and using an airbrush had been symbolic of abandoning the possibly un-American pleasures of traditional fine art fabrication—an indulgence associated with ateliers rather than lofts—in favor of a quasi-industrial process that provided a very different kind of satisfaction, evident primarily in a finished product as beautiful and untainted by artsy self-indulgence as a Ford truck fresh off a Detroit assembly line. To hold a brush once again, and to squeeze sweet-scented, oozing color onto a palette, was a voluptuous pleasure waiting to be rediscovered.

Chuck made the transition back to oil paint in two versions, small and large, of *Stanley* produced in 1980 and 1980–81. The subject was Stanley Rosen, a business-man Chuck and Leslie had met—along with his wife Phyllis (the subject of a pulp portrait)—when their children became friendly on the beach at East Hampton. Rosen was photographed looking somewhat formal in a suit and tie, but both the large and the small portrait are clearly rendered with an enjoyment of tactile values that owes nothing to the anti-painterly detachment of the continuous-tone portraits, though it does share a good deal with the hands-on intimacy of the pulp paper pieces and especially the finger paintings (some of which utilized oil-based inks). Conceptually, these first mature forays in traditional oil paint emerge directly from the pastel drawings, and from a watercolor of Leslie made as a maquette for the Japanese woodblock print, but they provide the added di-mension of brushwork. With the continuous-tone portraits, Chuck's virtuosity, though always implicit in the finished product, is veiled by the anonymity of the execution. In both versions of *Stanley*, we find a record of the artist rediscovering gratification in his own mastery of brushwork.

The paintings were built by laying an evenly spaced grid of plump, lusciously pigmented dots over a warm, flesh-tinted ground, then modulating the impact of almost every primary dot with smaller dabs of color in order to build patterns that from a distance would read as highlights and shadow. Especially in the larger painting, an enormous amount of visual information was introduced in order to achieve these effects. Here and there, colors were permitted to spill over the grid lines, and in some areas dots were stretched into wiener-shaped directional markers to suggest, for example, hair follicles or the weave of a fabric. Because the squares of the grid were small in relation to the size of the canvas, allowing for a dense texture, the image attained a distinctly photographic sense of "real-ism" when seen from a distance, almost as if constituted from the halftone dots used in photoengraving. From close up, however, it dissolved into thousands of tiny nonfigurative elements organized according to an apparently self-sufficient pictorial logic.

In 1986, Close further refined this technique in a medium-sized (54 1/2 x 42 1/4 inch) oil on canvas self-portrait. From a distance, this painting reads in much

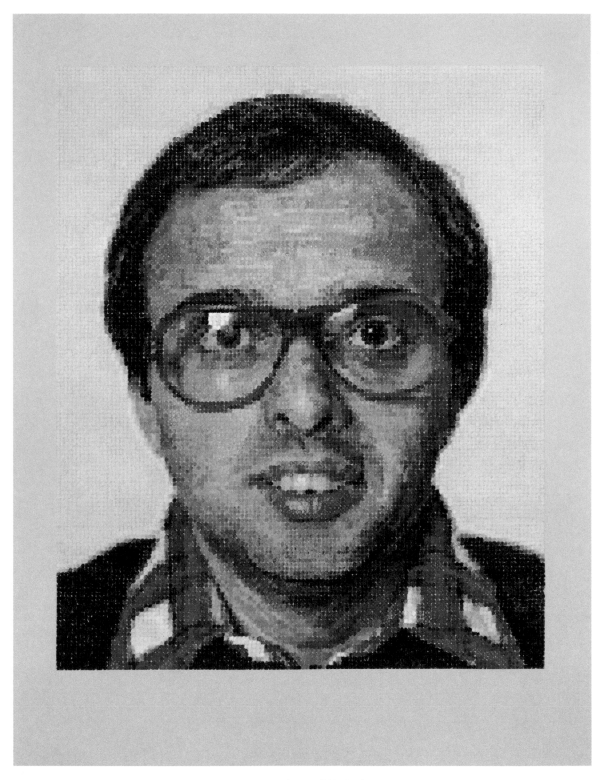

Large Mark Pastel, 1978–79.
Pastel on watercolor, 56 x 44 in. (142.2 x 111.8 cm)

Leslie, 1986.
Woodcut, 32 x 25 1/4 in. (81.3 x 64.1 cm)

Self-Portrait, 1987.
Oil on canvas, 72 x 60 in. (182.9 x 152.4 cm)

the same way as the large pastel version of Mark and the two oils of Stanley, but the constellation of dots possesses a somewhat more expressive character. Colored marks were superimposed upon one another in ways that suggest sections through olives stuffed with pimento, and some brushstrokes—though tiny—became almost gestural. The artist who had formerly suppressed overt expressiveness to create an image that was fully satisfying only when completed had found a way to put explicit pleasure back into the *act* of painting.

The following year, Chuck painted a larger, 72 x 60 inch self-portrait that is a fully realized example of the idiom that has occupied him ever since. The 1986 self-portrait had been very much a figure on ground image, the head silhouetted against a light-colored background. The 1987 self-portrait has much more of an allover character, with a dark background woven from skeins of red and blue paint, further animated in some areas by superimposed dots and dabs of pigment. Despite the fragmentation, the image still reads photographically when seen from a distance—helped by lighting that is much bolder than in the 1986 self-portrait, creating strong contrasts. As the viewer approaches the canvas, however, the shift to reading the imagery as a collection of abstract notations becomes extremely pronounced, far more so than was the case in the preceding paintings. In this work, the artist confidently calls on the viewer to fully employ his or her powers of perception as an active—even interactive—player in experiencing the painting, as blobs and flecks and speckles of paint first take on then divest themselves of descriptive roles.

Chuck recalls that at around this time he made a visit to the National Gallery in Washington and afterward began to think about the portraits he had seen that day.

"I was going over them one by one in my head—Holbein, Ingres, Vermeer, and so on—and my thoughts were about the importance of pose, the different angles used in various paintings, the lighting, and especially the eyes. I was struck by the fact that so few of the sitters had eyes that looked directly at the viewer."

Given his original emphasis on the mug shot, it is hardly surprising that almost all of Chuck's portraits had featured eyes that *did* look directly back at the viewer. Now he began thinking about alternatives and this line of thought would begin to have an impact on the new series he was about to start. His subjects had always been family and friends, and inevitably many of these friends were artists. For this major new group of works, he decided to concentrate entirely on artists—not necessarily artists he knew particularly well, but all artists who had made something of a specialty of self-portraiture, the chosen subjects being Cindy Sherman, Lucas Samaras, Francesco Clemente, and Alex Katz, artists he thought of as "professional posers." The resulting paintings would employ Chuck's new overtly incremental approach to create works as implacable and monumental as any of the continuous-tone portraits. At the same time, the increased flexibility in paint handling that the new approach encouraged would permit the artist to bring an emotional intensity that was evident in every brushstroke. This visceral feeling had been present in works like *Fanny/Fingerpainting* but was now achieved with brushes, a development that opened up new possibilities. In reality, of course, Chuck's art had always been impassioned, but the openness with which the passion was now expressed—the clear pleasure he was taking in the manipulation of pigment—made this group of works striking in a fresh way.

The nearer the viewer comes to the surface of these paintings, the more the play of pigments ravishes the mind. These are intensely retinal paintings, built from thousands of bits of chromatic information, pointillist at least to the extent that a comparison with the work of the Post-Impressionist Georges Seurat is begged. (Chuck in fact dislikes the term "pointillism" as applied to his own work.) But whereas Seurat's system depended, nominally at least, upon the scientific theory of the prismatic division of light into the colors of the spectrum, Chuck's approach is entirely more pragmatic, though its effect is decidedly prismatic. His own description of his method is strikingly down to earth: filling each square of the grid, he has said, is like playing a hole of golf.

By this analogy, Chuck means that a series of strokes brings him incrementally nearer to his goal. Let's say that an individual square of the grid is set to represent part of the sitter's face, just where the edge of a plane creates a shadow so that flesh begins to shift from light to dark. The underpainting of the square is perhaps cadmium orange (the underlying color is deliberately arbitrary). To come closer to the desired effect, the artist might cover most of the square with a patch of pale blue. That first brushstroke might be compared to the golfer's tee shot, striking the ball as far as possible in the direction of the flag. On the canvas, the patch of blue falls short of achieving the required end result, so a little loop of orange is applied (the approach shot) which begins to establish the basic tonal and chromatic value demanded. It does not yet indicate quite the shift of luminosity needed, however, and so a touch of turquoise is added to one side of the evolving cluster (the chip shot to the green) and offsetting touches of pink and yellow to the square's opposite edge to complete this tiny component of the illusion (the putt finally sunk). Richly inhabited by blobs and squiggles of color, the square is now ready to fulfill its role in the evolving mosaic, modifying adjacent squares and in turn being modified by them. (To add to the golfing analogy, the larger paintings in this first artists' group were equivalent to playing as many as 8,000 holes, or more than 400 rounds.)

The method that Chuck refined between 1986 and 1988 generated enormously rich broken textures—greens sitting alongside pinks, pinks by purples, purples next to sapphire or cerulean, in tightly packed constellations that constituted a shimmering record of the artist's career-long obsession with process, and at the same time served to herald the rebirth of his long-suppressed love of the painterly. As the viewer stepped back from these canvases, those constellations of lenticular dots and Froot Loops circles began to read as faces with a degree of definition and articulation that gives them an intensely photographic presence that never allows the viewer to lose sight of the fact that a lens has intervened in the process.

This group of works broke new ground in other ways, too. While some were built on the conventional vertical/horizontal grids Chuck had favored until then, others employed variants. The two versions of *Francesco* painted at this time, and one version of *Cindy*, were based on diagonal grids. This has a subtle yet significant influence on the way the paintings are perceived. There is a gain in dynamism but a loss of some of the bricks-and-mortar solidity provided by the vertical/horizontal grid. They sit differently on the support, just as a garment cut on the bias hangs differently on the torso.

Versions of *Cindy* and *Lucas* were painted on grids defined by concentric circles and spokes extending from a central hub. Such a grid inevitably has a marked effect on the image represented within it, since the work's compositional energy collects at the center and diminishes rapidly towards the edges of the canvas. *Lucas II*, a frontal image, concentrates energy right between the sitter's eyes with startling psychological impact. The progressive lessening of pictorial density as the viewer's eye is drawn centrifugally towards the perimeters makes it seem as if the image is about to fly apart. This portrait evokes thoughts of entropy and the progress of the universe towards chaos, a condition countered only by the fragile ability of the human imagination to give meaningful shape to random events.

The sense of disintegration in *Cindy II*, also painted on a circular grid, is less pronounced. One reason for this is that the painting is far larger than *Lucas II*, making the components of the grid much smaller in proportion to the size of the canvas as a whole. This tends to create a greater sense of unity throughout the picture plane. Also, this painting is one of Chuck's rare profiles. The fact that the grid is centered on the sitter's right earlobe, rather than between the eyes, gives it an entirely different psychological impact. A person gazing sideways into space registers very differently from one staring directly at the viewer, especially when the artist's incremental method demands that the viewer work at putting the elements of the likeness together.

(Chuck recalls that Cindy Sherman was difficult to photograph in that she was accustomed to being photographed, for her own works, while playing a role, as in the case of her Untitled Film Stills series. "She didn't seem to know how to be just Cindy—was quite uncomfortable with the idea. Finally, for the profile, I said, 'Imagine you're the Queen of England on a postage stamp.'")

In all the paintings in this group, the background itself is as alive as any other part of the image. Its share of the grid is vitalized by thousands of dabs of variegated color that seem to vibrate as in an exercise in optical art by Bridget Riley. By activating the entire picture plane in this way, Chuck reemphasizes his ideal of Pollock-like allover composition, creating a painting that is a kind of prismatic grid, at the same time reinventing chiaroscuro for the age of quantum physics and DNA.

The last of this group of portraits to be painted was *Cindy II*. Chuck has declared that the final painting he makes in any particular sequence is in a sense also the first of a new set, since it generally leads him in a new direction. In this instance, the connection to his future work is not immediately obvious, largely because the concentric circle format of the grid is so dominant a feature. Although Chuck has occasionally employed that format again, it certainly has not been central in his later work.

What makes the work significant for paintings to come can be understood only on close inspection. If one compares its incremental units to those of other paintings in this group, it will be seen that *Cindy II* is notably looser in its handling—its loops and dabs more gestural and expressive than those found in its immediate predecessors.

This would prove to have a significance far greater than the artist or anyone else could have predicted at the time.

Lucas II, 1987.
Oil on canvas, 36 x 30 in. (91.4 x 76.2 cm)

In the fall of 1988, these new paintings were exhibited at the Pace Gallery's Fifty-seventh Street headquarters. Simultaneously, Chuck had exhibitions of photographs at Pace/McGill and multiples at Pace Editions. (The photographs included some stunning floral images that were in part a response to Leslie's career in horticulture.) The reception to all three shows was enthusiastic. The paintings in particular were welcomed as a sign that the artist was in top form. Chuck Close, it was widely acknowledged, had successfully reinvented himself.

Part III

Cindy II, 1988.
Oil on canvas, 72 x 60 in. (182.9 x 152.4 cm)

Chapter 19

The Event

The reception that followed the opening of Chuck's 1988 Pace Gallery triple exhibition was held at a Midtown Chinese restaurant. He was in excellent spirits that night and had every reason to be. Three months past his forty-eighth birthday, he was at the pinnacle of the New York art world. His work was featured in prominent public collections, he had had a mid-career retrospective that traveled to major museums around the country, a dozen one-man shows in New York alone, important exhibitions in other American cities, as well as in Europe and Japan. His work was even becoming known in Russia and China, where it was awakening the imaginations of artists trained in the traditions of social realism. He had been featured in *Time* and *Newsweek*, and his work had appeared on the cover of every major art magazine. He had earned the respect of his peers and the admiration of the gallery-going public. He had, in short, achieved just about everything that an artist could have hoped to by this point in his career and, as a family, the Closes appeared to have it all, living in a spacious Central Park West apartment with celebrities like Meryl Streep and Jane Pauley for neighbors. They had two smart and attractive daughters, Georgia, fifteen, who would soon be looking at colleges, expecting a top placement, and Maggie her junior by eleven years.

Then, on December 7, 1988—just six weeks after the three one-man shows had closed—it was all thrown into jeopardy by a catastrophic episode that Chuck refers to in retrospect as "The Event."

The artist had been suffering from what appeared to be a severe cold, accompanied by a hacking cough that showed no signs of letting up. Mark Greenwold, who had seen him in New Haven a few days before, remembers that he looked and sounded awful, haggard and pale, and was so wracked by coughing that at times he was doubled over. Chuck had not visited his regular doctor, but had stopped by a SoHo clinic, near his studio, where an antibiotic had been prescribed.

"Chuck was neglectful of his health," says Leslie Close. "He had a doctor but used the walk-in clinic because it was less of a hassle."

The antibiotic prescribed there had very little effect.

"The fact is," says Chuck, "I was always sick and wheezing and feeling run down. This was worse than usual, but I just took it for granted."

Leslie is convinced that stress was a big factor in this illness.

"It started before the shows opened. With Chuck, there's always a lot of stress before an opening. He's never satisfied with the last painting he's been working on–every day he'll say it's not going well. Then maybe finally he's happy with it, but when it leaves the studio and he sees it in the gallery, he's unhappy all over again. Hanging a show is always stressful because there are so many control issues involved, and when it comes to his work, Chuck is a control freak. The lighting has to be just right. He has a heightened perception about these things, but sometimes that means he gets lost in the details–can't see the big picture.

"That [1988] show was especially stressful. He wasn't sure how people would react to the new paintings [because they were radically different]. Then after a show opens there's always the wait for the reviews, and for the feedback from other artists. And then inevitably there's an emotional letdown when something is over–plus it was that crappy time of year when the days are getting shorter."

Leslie believes there was an additional reason for Chuck's stress this time. He had reached the exact age–48–at which his father had died, and the trauma of that event still haunted him. Chuck had wrestled with the inevitable feelings of guilt attached to the fact that he had been there alone with his father at the time of the fatal stroke–could he have done anything more?–and with the tangle of emotions brought on by his mother's blindly inappropriate behavior in the aftermath. He had struggled with his confusion in therapy, and had resolved some important aspects of it, but the fact of his father's death, and at that particular age, loomed large. There must have been times when Chuck thought about what he had lost when his father died, and perhaps about what his children would lose if anything were to happen to him.

Alone in the Central Park West apartment that morning, Chuck was preoccupied by a recurrence of the sharp chest pains he had experienced years earlier on Prince Street, and then again in Kyoto, this time aggravated by the insistent cough. He did not call 911 or even phone Leslie, who had left earlier for her office. The girls were in school.

His fatalism kicked in, and inevitably one is reminded of his mother's refusal to be taken to the hospital on another December day eight years earlier. Chuck's case was different, he believed. He had been through this before and had had tests that indicated he was not suffering from heart disease. There must be another explanation—stress, probably. This was just some kind of anxiety attack.

The pain grew worse, accompanied by nausea and shortness of breath, but still he took no action other than to press up against the kitchen table in an effort to relieve the symptoms. Normally Chuck would commute downtown to his studio on a workday, but in this instance he was scheduled to be interviewed for the public radio show *All Things Considered* and to present an award on behalf of the Alliance for the Arts at a ceremony to be held at Gracie Mansion. It was a bright, breezy morning, and as the pain finally began to subside, Chuck left his apartment building, crossed the street, and entered Central Park near the reservoir, traversing the park diagonally—past a playground where he often brought Maggie, past the Delacourt Theater and the Turtle Pond, coughing and sniffling through a familiar world of squirrels, joggers, dog walkers, hot dog vendors, and tourists taking in the skyline from horse-drawn carriages—emerging eventually onto the cobblestone-trimmed sidewalk that edges Fifth Avenue, where banners flying from the spars of the streetlights promoted the Metropolitan Museum's retrospective exhibition of the Italian Futurist painter and sculptor Umberto Boccioni.

Chuck made his way to East Fifty-seventh Street, where he noticed, in the window of a jewelry store, an antique brooch which he thought would be a perfect gift for Leslie on their upcoming wedding anniversary. After making that purchase, he continued to the Fuller Building, an art deco skyscraper that is one of the architectural gems of Midtown Manhattan and home to some of the city's most prestigious galleries. He took the elevator to the second floor where the Robert Miller Gallery was then located. With Howard Read, the gallery's director of photography, he looked at some examples of flower photographs by Robert Mapplethorpe, thinking that one of these would be perfect as his principal anniversary gift to Leslie. Read provided him with Polaroids of a couple of the images he was most interested in, then Chuck continued downtown to National

Public Radio's Forty-third Street studio to be interviewed by Susan Stamberg, the topic being changes in the character of the art world.

Although still feeling under the weather, he soon warmed to the subject, responding energetically to Stamberg's questions, offering spirited opinions on how the art world was changing, for the worse in his opinion. He placed blame on the power that had accrued to a new breed of collector equating ownership with the acquisition of prestige. He complained that whereas art once belonged to the part of the brain that thinks, it seemed to have shifted to the part of the brain "that chooses what covering you'll put on the seat of your car."

Emerging from the interview, Chuck found that he still had a couple of hours to kill before he was due at Gracie Mansion. On foot once again, in the gathering wintry gloom—the sky cloudy now, the wind gusting—he headed for Eighty-eighth Street and East End Avenue, past the Chrysler Building and Citicorp Center, past the brightly lit storefronts and cafés of the Gold Coast and Yorkville, past the glowing Chanukah candles and blinking Christmas lights.

Arriving in the vicinity of Gracie Mansion, he found he was still a little early. The cough had erupted again and, thinking a scotch might help, he stopped into a neighborhood tavern where he killed a few minutes at the bar, sipping his drink and idly watching a local newscast.

The most poignant story that day was the continuing coverage of the role of former children's book editor Hedda Nussbaum in the prosecution of her common-law husband Joel Steinberg, accused of beating to death their illegally adopted daughter, Lisa. The district attorney had dropped second-degree murder charges against Nussbaum in return for her testimony against Steinberg. Inevitably she was cast as the star witness. The presence of television cameras in court-rooms was a novelty in 1988, and the case had provoked a media frenzy, to a large degree because Nussbaum's battered face had become etched into viewers' minds, her flattened nose and haunted eyes suggesting that she herself was a victim. The alleged crime occurred a short walk from Chuck's studio, and prior to their arrest, Nussbaum and Steinberg had appeared to be a typical bourgeois-bohemian downtown couple—the kind of people Chuck might have rubbed shoulders with at a party or a museum opening—and as it happens, he knew one of Nussbaum's attorneys, who lived in the Closes' building. It was an ugly story made uglier for Chuck by a sense of proximity.

The scotch proved to be a bad idea. It made him feel worse. The nausea had returned, but he gathered himself together and walked the short distance to Gracie Mansion where he was directed to a reception room in which hors d'oeuvres were being served. He saw people he knew—the poet John Ashbery; Kitty Carlisle Hart, chairman of the New York Council on the Arts; and Agnes Gund, a trustee of the Museum of Modern Art—but he was preoccupied with his extreme discomfort. The program for the awards ceremony listed him as the third presenter. The pain was increasing, and he became concerned enough to approach the woman in charge and request that the order of the program be changed. She told him it would be impossible because Hart, scheduled to make the first presentation, had another engagement to attend.

Chuck was feeling worse by the minute. During the course of the pre-awards gathering, he was approached by Gund, who took the opportunity to ask if he would consider painting her portrait. He snapped her head off, feeling she should know he never accepted commissions.

The ceremony proper began, and the pain got worse. A discursive speech and prolonged glad-handing by Mayor Ed Koch meant that considerable time passed before Chuck, who had finally insisted on being moved to first presenter, was introduced. He got through reading the citation and handing out the award, but instead of returning to his seat on the dais, he staggered off the stage. Minutes later, still on his own two feet but accompanied by a police officer, he arrived at the emergency room of Doctors Hospital, just across East End Avenue from Gracie Mansion, where he received immediate attention. By now the chest pains were excruciating. A cardiac problem was indicated, and the staff administered shots of intravenous Valium for the pain.

Still fully aware of his surroundings and able to communicate, Chuck asked a nurse to call Leslie, who was on the point of leaving their apartment en route to the Pace Gallery Christmas party, where he had been scheduled to join her.

She jumped into a taxi and headed for East End Avenue, not greatly concerned because similar previous episodes had amounted to nothing. As soon as she arrived at the emergency room, she realized that things were far more serious this time. What made everything especially terrifying was that no one could give her any clear idea of what had happened, let alone exactly what was wrong, though a heart attack still seemed the likeliest explanation. Immediately following another dose of IV Valium, Chuck experienced a violent spasm, his arms and legs thrashing.

"Not an unusual response to pain, or to Valium," one nurse told Leslie.

Within minutes Chuck was paralyzed from the neck down but still conscious. Breathing took great effort and his lungs began to flood, a condition that was aggravated by his head cold. Nurses rushed to suction the fluid from his respiratory system. Had he been anywhere else but in a medical facility, he would have suffocated.[19]

Leslie claimed Chuck's possessions, and in his jacket she found the antique brooch he had bought for her earlier that day. Also in the pockets were the Polaroids of the two Mapplethorpe photographs between which he had been planning to have her choose. The atmosphere, Leslie recalls, was surreal, compounded by the fact that the ER doctor kept looking at her in a way she found disturbing. Finally he introduced himself—or, rather, reintroduced himself. By a strange coincidence, they had been at junior high school together and he had taken her out on her first real date, but given the circumstances, she had failed to make that connection.

Friends began to appear, the first to arrive being Herb and Emily Kramer, though Leslie has no memory of having called them, nor of calling Helene Steel, who was soon there too. Emily Kramer phoned Bob and Jane Cottingham, saying, "Chuck's in the hospital," but without being able to offer any explanation as to why he was there. The Cottinghams jumped into their car and drove down from their home in Fairfield County, Connecticut. Jane remembers walking into the emergency room and finding herself in a dark area—"No one seemed to be around"—and then spotting Leslie in the shadows. She took them to a curtained-off room where Chuck lay, paralyzed from the shoulders down but still fully aware of everything that was going on.

Jane's first knee-jerk reaction was to say, "Chuck—you'll do anything for attention." When she later expressed her embarrassment to him for saying this, he told her, "You weren't the only one to have that reaction. When Arne [Glimcher] saw me the first time, he said exactly the same thing." (Glimcher acknowledges as much. "I thought it was a panic attack or something.")

No one could offer a definitive explanation for what had happened. There were checks for possibilities such as Lyme disease, by then rampant in the Hamptons, but Leslie's old classmate told her that he believed the problem was likely to be neurological and advised her to get Chuck to a hospital that could provide a complete neurological workup as quickly as possible.

"We could see it was bad," says Jane Cottingham, "but somehow we thought that he'd be okay. We didn't realize just how bad it might be."

Still conscious, Chuck would remain at Doctors Hospital for two days, with Leslie at his side, joined on the ninth by Barbara Harshman, Mark Greenwold's ex-wife, who had traveled from upstate to lend support. It was Barbara's voice, over the phone, which alerted many of Chuck's friends and colleagues to what had happened.

One of the first people Leslie herself had contacted was Arne Glimcher, who helped her to arrange for Chuck's transfer to the intensive care unit at Tisch Hospital, part of the New York University Medical Center complex that stretches south from Thirty-fourth Street along the FDR Drive, the expressway that skirts the East River. This occurred on the morning of December 10, a Saturday, and in the midst of the holiday season to boot, so two more days passed before any specialists would see him. Meanwhile, Chuck continued to have no voluntary movement from the shoulders down, could breathe only with great difficulty, and had to have his lungs drained every two hours because only 25 percent of each was functioning.

Finally, an investigation was initiated to test the neurological damage hypothesis.

Two doctors who specialized in imaging the spine with tiny fiber-optic cameras carried out a procedure and afterward stood with Leslie and her mother in a hallway as they gave the results.

"Their expressions are among the most lasting memories for me of this whole unfolding event," says Leslie. "They looked right in my face and said, '. . . blah, blah, blah—occluded spinal artery—blah, blah—C6, C7—blah, blah—paralysis below C6 . . .' and so on. They waited very quietly, while both my mother and I absorbed this, asked what it meant, etcetera. The grim, professionally sympathetic expressions on their faces told me that this was very, very bad. That was the moment when I realized how really awful this might be."

The essential diagnosis was "spontaneous occlusion of the anterior spinal artery, of unknown genesis"—sometimes referred to as a spinal stroke. The anterior spinal artery is a key blood vessel in the central nervous system. The type of paralysis Chuck had experienced is most often the result of physical trauma caused by an accident, but spontaneous occlusion, although very uncommon, was not unheard of, according to the doctors. The earlier episodes of angina had probably been instances of occlusion that had passed without permanent damage being sustained. Another doctor later told Leslie that there was some possibility that weeks of continuous and violent coughing might have helped precipitate the final catastrophic event, though other physicians suggest that such a theory is, to say the least, highly speculative.

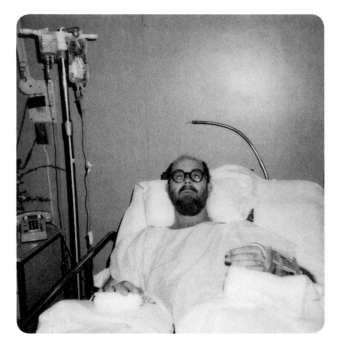

In the intensive care unit, New York Hospital, 1988

To counter the secondary swelling of the spinal cord that follows any spinal injury, spontaneous or otherwise, Chuck was given massive injections of steroids. Had they been applied earlier they might have helped, but now all that they did was to keep him awake for twelve days straight, during which time he suffered hallucinations that were liable to erupt at any time of the day or night.

"The effect of the steroids," he recalls, "mimics schizophrenia. I would be lying there, flat on my back, unable to move, and I would look at Leslie and say, 'Did you feel that?' 'What?' 'That earthquake …' 'There was no earthquake.' 'But I felt the bed shake—I know there was an earthquake.' And then the bed would take off and I'd be hurtling along at tremendous speed—it was like being on some kind of rocket sled out of *Star Wars*, and I'd be zooming through these Germanic, proto-

Nazi baronial halls that were right out of paintings by Anselm Kiefer—those long rooms he paints, with pillars and beams and lots of wood grain detail, all rendered in black and white, rooms that have a single vanishing point, and I'd be rushing towards that vanishing point, and there'd be a door there—a closed door—and it would seem I was about to smash into it, but at that last minute it would open and I'd be in another of those rooms, and it would happen all over again, one room after another after another. I would be flying a few inches above floor level, always just above those wooden planks disappearing in one-point perspective, and the velocity was tremendous. But it wasn't that scary, somehow. Or, rather, it was scary but in an almost fun sort of way, like being on a roller coaster."

Leslie remembers being told that he was in a state described as "Intensive Care Psychosis," having to do with the constant light, the hospital noises, and things of that sort. During this phase, Chuck told her about an incredible, ironclad system he had devised to beat the stock market. For a couple of days he repeated this totally incoherent and grandiose scheme to anyone who would listen.

I was in Europe on December 7 and heard about Chuck's plight by telephone. I returned a couple of days later and visited him in the hospital as soon as I was allowed in. In the meantime, I had received a phone call from Mark Greenwold warning me that Chuck was upset about something. Shortly before his September openings at Pace, I had written an essay about the new grid paintings for *Art in America*. Mark had been one of the first people to visit Chuck in the hospital and—despite everything that had happened to him—Chuck had asked Mark to check the latest issue of the magazine to see if the article was there. It wasn't, and Chuck had insisted that Mark contact me to find out why.

Sure enough, practically Chuck's first words to me when I got to the hospital were, "What's happening with the article?"

I had been warned, but I remember being astonished by the intensity of this demand, which verged on vehemence. Chuck might not be able to move, but this was really important to him. I told him why it wasn't surprising that the article had not appeared yet, explaining that, in order to avoid the appearance of publishing promotional puff pieces, the magazine's policy was not to print feature stories until some time after exhibitions in commercial galleries had closed. Chuck accepted the explanation, reluctantly, but felt that surely enough time had lapsed by now. Having been out of the country, I did not know what the magazine's plans for the piece were. I promised to get in touch with the editor, Betsy Baker, to find out, and in fact the article was published as a cover story a couple of months later.

Next I remember Chuck telling me that he envied me for being a writer. When I asked why, he said that if he were a writer he would have no problem being able to continue his career. He would be able to dictate if necessary, or learn to use a typewriter with something attached to his nose. He went on to talk about his fears that he would never be able to paint again.

(Later, Leslie would tell me that during this period—although Chuck was hopeful of making a full or fairly complete recovery—he often brought up the names of artists he respected, such as Sol LeWitt and Donald Judd, who had other people manufacture their pieces. Mark Greenwold recalls Chuck saying, "I'll spit paint onto the canvas if I have to.")

Only after he had raised these career-related issues did he give me an account of what had happened since I had last seen him. He talked about the period of total neck-down paralysis with a combination of horror and humor—"It feels like you're in the ultimate Samuel Beckett play and it's never going to end . . ."

He told me too about the hallucinations. The one that had been tormenting him that day was less benign than the Anselm Kiefer theme park ride.

"It's horrible," he said. "I'm up near the ceiling of a room, and it's in the Hedda Nussbaum–Joel Steinberg house, and I'm watching terrible things that are happening to that little girl—and I can't turn it off, it just goes on and on."

(Chuck has no memory of this particular hallucination, but as mentioned he does recall that he had watched the local news in the bar while on his way to Gracie Mansion. It was only later when I researched what was being covered by local news shows that evening that I saw a possible connection.)

He told me how strong Leslie had been in handling the emergency, how worried he was about how Georgia and Maggie would respond to what was happening. He also talked about the tremendous support he was receiving from Arne Glimcher. It was thanks to him that Chuck had health insurance sufficient to cover the enormous expenses involved in responding to the catastrophic event that had overtaken him.

"The gallery's insurance plan," Leslie explains, "provides all the artists with the same coverage that Arne has for himself and his own family. This was and is far from usual in the art world, and without it we would have lost everything—

I can't even begin to contemplate how devastating the financial impact would have been."

Foresight and sound planning were far from being the only things Glimcher brought to the situation, however.

"Arne was very much involved from the first," Leslie says. "He visited daily, or if he couldn't be there, he phoned. He and Milly [Glimcher] would bring cookies and flowers for the nurses. It seemed they were always looking for excuses to be there, and Arne was an extremely reassuring presence. From the earliest days of the paralysis, he told Chuck that whatever happened we were not to worry about money, that we were family to him, and that with or without paintings to sell we would be okay. He repeated this as often as Chuck needed to hear it—and as often as I needed to hear it.

"Arne gave us that assurance even when we were contemplating the possibility that Chuck would never be able to paint again. He and I told Chuck constantly that art is made more in the head than in the hands. Sometimes Chuck laughed about that, saying that he might have to make art *with* his head since it was the only part of his body that moved."

As word of Chuck's plight got around the New York art world, a stream of visitors began to appear at his bedside, and despite his situation he clearly enjoyed the company and drew strength from it. In one-on-one situations, however—especially when he was alone with Leslie, and the realization began to sink in of how limited his recovery might be, his mood was sometimes bleak as he talked about his future prospects in general, and specifically about his anxieties regarding what began to seem like almost insurmountable odds against him being able to resume his painting career. As limited movement slowly returned to parts of his body other than his neck and facial muscles, finding a way to make art was something that was constantly on his mind, but before that could be addressed on anything but a purely speculative level, more general therapeutic goals had to be achieved. How could Chuck's condition best be treated? What kind of therapy would be most effective, and what degree of rehabilitation was it reasonable to expect?

At this point, Chuck was still flat on his back, unable to elevate himself to even the smallest degree. Whatever therapy was employed, it would have to start from the most basic level. Determined to stay on top of the situation, Leslie set out to learn as much as she could that would help her make informed decisions, the most pressing of which was which rehab facility to use. Chuck's doctors were urging her to choose the Howard A. Rusk Institute, NYU Medical Center's own facility located on the same campus as the hospital.

Probably nothing can prepare a first-time visitor for the spectacle of human tragedy found at an institution like Rusk. Leslie has a vivid recollection of her initial visit.

"A very nice woman—a social worker—offered to take me to see the rehab facility. Mark [Greenwold] was at the hospital that day and I asked him to come with me on the tour. The woman walked us through wards filled with patients with various levels of horrendous brain and spinal cord injury, people strapped into wheelchairs, terrible smells of incontinence, the stunned faces of devastated spouses and children, a surreal aura of catastrophe and horror, all presented to us with cheerful social worker optimism. I remember the lump in my throat growing to the size of a golf ball. When the social worker left and we were finally alone in a corridor, Mark and I looked at each other and we both broke down and sobbed. Then we pulled ourselves together and talked about how to sell the place to Chuck."

Among the shocks of the tour had been a visit to the physical therapy room, where the facilities seemed incredibly primitive, with patients waiting in line to use archaic-appearing weight and pulley devices that looked as if they belonged in a museum, relics of a medieval torture chamber perhaps. Leslie scouted out other rehab facilities, in and around the city, and discovered that similar contraptions, with leather straps and webbing belts, were standard equipment. These rudimentary but proven machines were all that was available to provide the kind of workout that could reawaken vitality in frozen limbs and wasted sinews. If he wanted to be able to feed himself—let alone apply paint to canvas in any meaningful way—Chuck would have to work as hard as a bodybuilder preparing himself for the Mr. Universe contest.

It became apparent that Rusk was the most feasible choice. One of its virtues was that it could offer a well-equipped physical conditioning pool—aquatic exercise being a key element of the kind of rehab Chuck would need. Also, it was conveniently located so that it would be easy for family and friends to visit. This was especially important where Georgia and Maggie were concerned since the support offered by their presence was of inestimable value. Georgia's first response to the catastrophe had been one of adolescent shock and denial. She and Chuck had always been close, but as a teenager Georgia now had her own exciting life and a wide circle of friends, and initially she experienced Chuck's hospitalization as an interruption to that life. She soon realized the seriousness of the situation, however, and became the model daughter, trying to help out Leslie when she could and buckling down to do her schoolwork–improving her grades so that these would not become an additional worry. Just four years old, Maggie probably could not fully grasp the gravity of what had happened to her father, but the affection she displayed towards him was always very direct and physical. She would cuddle up to him in his hospital bed, and later, when he was in a wheelchair, she would climb all over him as if he had become a living jungle gym.

At Rusk, they could continue to see him often after school, as they had been doing. Leslie's grueling routine would remain the same: take the kids to school, head for NYU Medical Center (often to do battle with the staff), spend the day there, pick the kids up from school, take them to see their father, take them home, feed them, and help them with their homework. Sometimes this would be rounded off with a late-night trip to the hospital.

"I had to rely tremendously on friends and neighbors, and my parents," she remembers, "especially my mother. To all intents and purposes, she moved in with me for the first several weeks of the disaster."

Jane Cottingham, a frequent visitor, offers a telling vignette from this period, describing how she came across Leslie in a corridor one day–Georgia on one side, Maggie on the other–clutching a huge bag of sheets and pajamas that she was dragging home because she was not satisfied with the way things were being laundered in the hospital. Jane remembers how exhausted Leslie looked.

After a six-week stay at Tisch, Chuck was moved across the campus to Rusk, where he tried to prepare himself mentally for the battle ahead. He knew that the place was, in his words, "a snake pit," a nightmare environment full of reminders about how thin the line is between having it all and having nothing. He recalls one man he saw every day, beautifully dressed in a Harris Tweed jacket and tie, out in a corridor sitting quietly in his wheelchair. Chuck discovered that this unfortunate person had been a top conservator at the Metropolitan Museum–a man who had done exquisite restoration work on paintings by the great masters– who now didn't know where he was or even who he was.

But at the time Chuck could not afford to think about that kind of thing. He had to concentrate on finding the inner resources he would need to get through this hell, and one thing that helped him was the fact that he had had to learn to deal with his dyslexia and his other disabilities when he was a kid. In Rusk, he drew on the same resources that had carried him through those long hours in a bathtub filled with lukewarm water, memorizing information on index cards; or that had enabled him to ignore the looks of other students in the gymnasium when he was unable to climb a rope. It was remembering how he'd been able to cope with things like this that gave him strength. He understood how tough this was going to be and knew that he had to stay completely focused.

Above all, though, Chuck drew on the memory of how he had survived the painful period after his father's fatal stroke. At the age of twelve he had been robbed of the presence of a loved parent, whose death could not have come at a more crucial moment in his son's development, as he recovered from a debilitating illness and reached the threshold of puberty. Chuck experienced the loss of his father from his own point of view, and in a sense from his mother's too as she desperately turned to him for solace, clinging to him and diverting all her love and her aspirations towards him. Chuck's inability to help his father when he suffered the fatal stroke meant guilt had been piled on top of loss, and for a while this guilt transformed the possibility of having fun—simple preadolescent fun—into something forbidden, almost a sin.

Yet, in retrospect, Chuck came to view his father's death as something that ultimately had enhanced his life.

"It wasn't until I was an adult and in therapy that I understood that my father had given me an extraordinary gift. I loved my father and I grieved for him—I grieved for him terribly—but I found out you don't grieve forever. Eventually you will be happy again. I learned that lesson at an early age, and it's intertwined with who I am—who I became. When I found myself flat on my back in the hospital, as horrendous as it was, I was able to believe that one day it would be over."

Believing is one thing; implementing that belief quite another.

"Finding the strength to survive—to get through this thing any way I could—defined my whole experience of Rusk, and still colors my memory of the place. I've shut most of the bad things out. That's why you'll find that my memories of those months are very different from Leslie's. Of course I would get panicked about my career, and what was going to happen to my family. Of course I got depressed. But I had to try to find positive things to hang on to, otherwise I was sunk."

Staying strong and focused was not easy. Challenges to concentrated thought are endemic to a facility like Rusk, where humiliation is a constant companion.

One thing Chuck quickly learned was that everything was always done for the staff's convenience, not the patients. Say some kind of lab test was scheduled for Monday morning. At 9 a.m., all the patients taking that test, two dozen maybe, would be wheeled downstairs on gurneys and lined up in a corridor. They might then be left there for hours, lying helpless under their sheets, missing physical therapy, missing lunch, incontinent. It never seemed to have occurred to anybody that people could be taken down for testing one at a time. It was easier to do it the other way.

Leslie would complain about such indignities on Chuck's behalf but soon discovered that in this environment it did not pay to be a squeaky wheel. On the contrary, protests to the administration were apt to be met with reprisals on the part of orderlies. A patient could be left to lie for hours in his own excrement. When a bath was finally administered, it was like being sent through a car wash, with jets of water turned on the naked patient as he passed through the shower room in a wheelchair.

It was not only the orderlies. Sensitivity, Chuck discovered, was not a strong point of some members of the medical staff. If Leslie was pushing Chuck in his wheelchair, a rehab doctor was likely to talk to Leslie as if Chuck couldn't speak for himself or even understand what was being said.

"What did he do before this happened?"

Certainly many of the Rusk patients were unable to communicate, but the assumption seemed to be that all patients without exception were completely gaga.

"You'd think," says Chuck, "that they'd give these people some sort of training to clue them in."

But if some of the Rusk doctors were less than empathic, this was compensated for by the compassion and concern demonstrated by its highly trained and experienced therapists. Meg Sowarby was assigned to be Chuck's physical therapist, Phyllis Palsgrove became his occupational therapist, and it's fair to say that the art world owes a debt of gratitude to these two women. For the next seven months, they would work with Chuck five days a week.

What he was facing up to now—and his family, too—was the knowledge that he would be an "incomplete" quadriplegic; meaning that the best he could hope for was limited movement in all four limbs. The doctors had told him he could expect some improvement in his condition over a period of two years, but beyond the first six or seven months, the rate and degree of improvement would begin to diminish rapidly. The hard work of the long weeks at the institute would be the key to determining whatever extent of recovery was possible.

(Retroactively, Chuck is skeptical about the effectiveness of physical therapy, saying, "Your body gets better if it wants to get better." That said, he makes an exception for some of the more specialized therapies he encountered, such as the "feedback" therapy mentioned later in this chapter.)

At Rusk, one of the first challenges was reintroducing Chuck to something most of us take for granted: the experience of being in an upright position, which was absolutely essential to the stabilization of his blood pressure—low blood pressure being a by-product of spinal cord injury—and by extension to any further physical progress. This was tackled with the help of a tilt table—basically a board with a central pivot, like a seesaw, to which the patient is strapped and eased, in tiny increments over a period of weeks, towards a vertical position. Any attempt to increase the angle too rapidly would cause the patient to pass out.

As Chuck became accustomed once more to being upright, work with weights and pulleys and pool therapy became possible. But nothing came easily. For a while he was forbidden to use the pool because a doctor, who should have been seeing him daily but did not meet with him for weeks on end, discovered a burn from a heating pad that he claimed could become infected and thus endanger other users of the pool. (Burns of this kind were frequent because damaged nerve endings do not respond rapidly enough to temperature extremes. To this day Chuck has to be careful with hot coffee and the like.)

To an occasional visitor, the bitter realities of the Rusk experience—the hours of boredom and despair, the routine self-torture—were not readily apparent since more often than not Chuck was able to put on a good show at the end of the day when friends stopped by, especially since he was hungry for art world news and gossip to offset the awfulness of the rest of his routine. His room at Rusk overlooked the East River and the traffic streaming along the FDR Drive. Noisy choppers descended to a nearby helicopter pad, so that the atmosphere was rather like something out of *M.A.S.H.*

Late in the afternoon, Chuck would sometimes transform himself into a gracious host, inviting friends to pour themselves drinks from the bar he managed to maintain despite the institute's strong disapproval (another *M.A.S.H.*-like aspect of the situation). Presumably, most participants in these festivities suspected that life must be difficult on either side of the "happy hour." Looking back on those days, Leslie regrets that these "happy hours" have come to be, in her view, cloaked in art world mythologizing, a tendency promoted by the fact that Chuck *did* succeed in overcoming his disabilities and thus provided the world with an upbeat Hollywood ending. For participants in the immediate drama, and Leslie in particular, the denouement was not so clear-cut.

"A lot has been said and written," she says, "about those times at Rusk when there were visitors in the room and scotch in the refrigerator. In fact those moments were the exception, and the reality of that period was mostly made up of the grinding sameness of very long, sad days. When friends were there, they put on a good show of being cheerful for Chuck's benefit, but there were times when I escorted someone out to the elevator and they would break down in tears at the shock of seeing him in that condition."

Chuck acknowledges that Leslie has a point, and that some people were shocked when they saw him, but he insists that these "happy hours" served an important therapeutic purpose. He needed to convince himself that life went on—that gossip and laughter and all the good things did not have to stop because of what had happened. He had to believe that he would be happy again.

"Leslie," Chuck says, "is intuitively a glass half-empty type and I'm a glass three-quarters full type. On top of that, we were in very different positions. I had to stay focused on getting through this mess as a functioning artist and human being, otherwise I was finished. She was more focused on coping one day at a time. Unfortunately, she couldn't let herself share the enjoyment I had from partying with friends, or from the comradeship I felt socializing with other patients. I think it seemed to her like a betrayal of her misfortune."

It's commonplace to say that the wife of a victim is herself a victim and that certainly applies to Leslie Close's case. Her lasting memories of Rusk center on the terror that came with being in that situation—gruesome procedures, depression and anxiety attacks, constant concern about the pain the children were feeling, and, on top of those big issues, having to deal with the everyday annoyances inherent in such places. She emphasizes how it would have been impossible for her to cope without the support of friends.

"I would never have made it without Barbara [Harshman], who came down from Albany every weekend, holding my hand for the entire miserable year. My mother literally moved in with me for the first shocking weeks—both my parents were and [still] are great supports. Helene Steel sat [with me] at my table most nights, into the wee hours, crying in our beer. Actually vodka.

"Arne and Milly Glimcher offered comfort and unflinching support. Dick and Ann Solomon were always there, and I could always rely on a tight circle of old friends—Bob and Jane Cottingham, Herb and Emily Kramer, Diane Rothschild, Amy Newman and Bud Shulman, Carol and Sol LeWitt, Kirk Varnedoe and Elyn Zimmerman, Katherine and Ken Snelson, Barbara and Gene Schwartz, Bob Elson, David Pease, Joe Wilfer, Joyce Robinson, Bob Shapiro, Joe Zucker, the Augers—all of them were constant presences at the hospital. Robert Friedman and Louise Yelin [came to my rescue] taking Maggie under their wing many days and nights when I couldn't be in two places at once. They were all wonderful."

A memorable event took place when Chuck had made enough progress for the Glimchers to take the Closes to dinner at the Water Club—an upscale restaurant

Chuck Close undergoing rehabilitation at Rusk Institute, with physical therapist Meg Sowarby

not far from Rusk, with spectacular city and river views—one of Chuck's first social outings since his hospitalization. Pushing the wheelchair, Arne Glimcher was nervous—afraid that he might accidentally tip Chuck into the street. Sensing this, Chuck told him to relax.

"If I fall out of this thing, what else could happen to me?"

Another early expedition was a visit to the Museum of Modern Art—organized by Kirk Varnedoe, then MoMA's chief curator of Painting and Sculpture—to see the Andy Warhol retrospective. Chuck was taken to the museum by ambulance and pushed around the exhibition in a wheelchair, even though he could barely sit up at the time. During a break for lunch, there was a chance encounter with MoMA's director, Richard Oldenburg, who had not seen Chuck since his hospitalization and was clearly shocked by his appearance.

"Is there anything we can do for you?" Oldenburg asked.

Chuck thanked him and said, "You can give me a retrospective."

Despite the days of routine misery, hard work in the physical therapy room along with Leslie's persistence in badgering the staff started to pay off. Chuck was beginning to regain some useful movement in his biceps, but very little in the hands or forearms. If he was to manipulate a brush, or any other tool, the power would have to come from the shoulder and upper arm, and he would have to control movement from his elbow.

Dr. John Gianutsos
instructing Chuck Close in
biofeedback technique at
Rusk Institute

When Chuck was at Yale Summer School, Philip Guston had encouraged his students to make drawings using a long stick dipped into ink, the idea being to challenge acquired reliance on eye-hand coordination. If Chuck were to paint again, his hand and forearm would be reduced to serving much the same function. At least he knew that such a way of working was not out of the question.

Before he could contemplate that possibility, however, he had to overcome yet another problem. Although his biceps were functioning, he had almost no use of his triceps: there was feeling in those muscles, but they did not respond normally to neurological signals. In order to be able to paint, biceps and triceps would have to work together. Luckily, a research physician—Dr. John Gianutsos—introduced Chuck to a biofeedback technique that enabled him to regain strength in the triceps while at the same time teaching them to coordinate with the biceps once again. (Biofeedback therapy involves teaching a patient to control body functions by means of relaxation, visualization, and other techniques, the results of which can be seen on a monitor.)

As Chuck's physical condition improved, the occupational therapy dimension of the program became more and more important, and his case required some special fine-tuning. Rehab therapists are trained to teach skills that will be useful when the patient returns to the outside world. They start with really basic exercises like stacking spools and boxes, which is tedious but important in rebuilding muscle strength and coordination. Then they move on to more practical tasks. One day Phyllis Palsgrove told Chuck they were going to practice doing laundry. It took him an eternity just to get a couple of pairs of underpants into the washing machine, using a stick and a hook. He told her, "This is ridiculous. I've never done laundry in my life." This was not true, but his point was that he didn't see doing laundry as a priority, given his limited strength. "What was the point? I could hire someone to do that for me." Smart and practical, Palsgrove grasped that a different approach was needed, then Leslie went to work on getting a program put in place that would focus on the assumption that he could revive his career. She lobbied the doctors, worked with the therapists, and got on the case of anyone who might be able to help or who she thought wasn't doing enough.

"I was at the hospital at least six hours a day," Leslie remembers, "so I didn't miss much that was going on. After watching Chuck's first sessions in occupational therapy, I cornered Phyllis in the cafeteria and told her it was absolutely essential that Chuck's therapy used the tools of his trade, not spools and pipe cleaners, and that his mental health depended on his being able to reassure himself that all was not lost—that he would be able to paint again."

After that, everything was geared towards making art. Leslie paid a visit to the Rusk workshop where adaptive equipment is made and designed. She talked with the man who ran the place, and he set about designing and constructing a wheelchair attachment to hold a palette and cobbling together an easel so that it could be used by somebody in a wheelchair.

Meanwhile, Palsgrove worked with Chuck to develop techniques that would be useful to him as he attempted to paint again, beginning by introducing him to a kind of "splint" that allowed him to hold a pencil. (In this context, a splint is a prosthetic device that immobilizes, and hence supports, parts of the hand/wrist system while allowing enough freedom to grasp and control various implements.) He discovered that he had more control than he had feared might be the case and that he could use the pencil to form letters and words. As she worked with him, Palsgrove thought about how the splint could be adapted to holding a paintbrush.

The first tentative steps towards a return to painting were taken in the occupational therapy room. Leslie fit a brush loaded with cheap poster paint into the modified splint, and Chuck attempted to make meaningful marks on a sheet of cardboard clamped to the easel cobbled together in Rusk's shop. The physical effort involved was enormous, and inevitably the first results were unsatisfying. Gradually the marks on the cardboard did begin to coalesce into something that resembled a painting, though Chuck occasionally lapsed into tears as he looked at the results of his efforts.

"I told everyone that it was no good, I couldn't do it—but the truth is I was looking for reassurance. I was actually thrilled to see that I was able to put paint onto cardboard, and I wanted people to tell me it was okay."

The evidence of these first sessions was that the project was worth persevering with. It was arranged for the experiment to continue in the art therapy room—a grim, cavernous space overlooking a bleak, windswept courtyard—which was normally used for basket weaving, raffia work, and other simple therapeutic activities. The setting itself was depressing enough, but what made it worse was the evidence of human misery all around—people's sad efforts to make something with fingers that did not work properly.

Michael Volanakis, Chuck's longtime studio assistant, brought in art supplies from Spring Street, and now Chuck began an effort to paint in earnest on a small canvas installed on the customized easel. This was the start of a lonely struggle witnessed by only a tiny handful of people.

There were no overnight miracles, only long hours of pain and frustration, punctuated by frequent moments of despair and occasional glimpses of a possible successful outcome. Everything depended on the encouragement of the small support group, and ironically upon Chuck's Type-A personality, which made the thought of failure impossible to contemplate.

Slowly a degree of motor control and firmness of touch returned, and the marks on the canvas began to display a hint of authority. Soon it became apparent that Chuck's belief that he could renew his career was not as crazy at it had seemed a few short months earlier. By the time I was invited to visit that dungeon-like art therapy room—on a gray, windy day not long after the process of rebirth had begun—a grid made up of dabs and swirls of pigment was beginning to take shape.

The paint was applied in a loose, almost expressionistic way, yet the method and image clearly derived directly from the paintings that had made up Chuck's most recent Pace Gallery show. For me the impact was as miraculous as if he had gotten up from his wheelchair and not only walked but performed a soft-shoe shuffle.

Dancing did in fact feature in this final period of hospitalization.

There was a good deal of socialization among a small group of rehab patients and their therapists, among whom bonds had formed. Along with Chuck, the patients included a former college basketball star injured in a car accident, an ex-military intelligence officer, and a charming young paraplegic woman who always seemed to be helping someone worse off than herself—painting the nails of a fellow patient who could barely move, brushing the hair of a woman unable to reach above her head. On weekends, these patients would be pushed in their wheelchairs to an Italian restaurant on Second Avenue for lunches that were notable for their quotient of good humor and laughter—the unrestrained laughter of people who were happy to find themselves alive and functioning in the world once again, understanding from daily contact with the hopelessly maimed and brain damaged that they were by comparison the lucky ones. Occasionally too there were nighttime expeditions—wholly against regulations—to cafés and bars. Once Chuck was equipped with a self-propelled wheelchair, he would sometimes break curfew and sneak out alone. It was like playing hooky from school.

The Cottinghams remember taking him out for a drink one evening around this time.

"Chuck didn't want to leave the bar," Jane Cottingham remembers. "He didn't want to go back to that awful place. Finally, we got him out of there, and it was pouring with rain—coming down in buckets. I was worried that the rain would do something to the electrical system of the wheelchair—that it would blow a fuse, burst into flames, or something. Chuck didn't care. He hates the rain, so he just took off as fast as he could go, leaving us there in the street to get drenched."

On another memorable occasion—to celebrate a therapist's retirement (burn-out being commonplace in that Bosch-like world of horrors)—half a dozen patients and as many staff members invaded an Upper East Side disco and took over the floor, broken bodies shaking themselves to boisterous life in wheelchairs, while caregivers, released from their monstrous chores, boogalooed with the wheelchair-bound and with one another.

Chuck recalls this as one of the most memorable nights of his life.

Chapter 20

Alex II

Chuck's first fully-realized post-catastrophe painting was *Alex II*–completed in the summer of 1989 in that most dismal of ateliers, the Rusk art therapy room. Painted on a 36 x 30 inch canvas, this work was made from an alternate Polaroid maquette of Alex Katz that had been shot at the same time as the one used for the larger portrait included in the 1988 Pace exhibition. If Katz, known for his prickly temperament, was shown as looking dyspeptic in that earlier work, he appears somewhat melancholy in this version. A more important difference, however, is that whereas the first version was executed with highly refined brush marks applied to a fine grid, giving the feel of a tightly woven Persian silk rug, the newer one was loosely painted on a more open grid and has more the texture of a Norwegian sweater. Clearly the looseness of the paint handling derived in part from the fact that Chuck was at an early stage of regaining control of the brush. This is nonetheless a wonderful painting, in no way aesthetically compromised by the artist's physical condition or by the circumstances under which it was made. It maintains the essential balance between photo-derived imagery–an iconic head evoked in terms of highlights and shadows–and almost mathematical rigor of execution (however free the paint marks may be) that typifies all of his work.

Prior to his hospitalization, Chuck had employed many different ways of constructing images, and each–from the continuous-tone airbrushed paintings, to the fingerprint drawings, to the paper pulp pieces–had involved adapting his philosophy of process to changing mediums, some of them newly minted to give fresh expression to that philosophy. It was the continued adherence to the principles of process that would enable Chuck to revive his career so rapidly. Had he been a painter dependent upon bravura gesture or the careful modeling of surfaces (both areas in which he had once excelled) he might never have been able to pick up where he had been forced to leave off. On the other hand, the fact

Alex II, 1989.
Oil on canvas, 36 x 30 in. (91.4 x 76.2 cm)

that he had been constructing images from small increments applied to a grid meant that he could continue to work in much the way he had when producing the paintings for his 1988 exhibition at Pace. The appearance of the individual increments might change—though in detail of touch and timbre rather than in essential character—but *Alex II* and the paintings that followed demonstrated that continuity with the earlier work was entirely feasible. It's almost as if the artist, while healthy, had anticipated a need for devising a way of working that would stand him in good stead for the future.

Leslie Close makes the point that, prior to the Event, the course of Chuck's career had been determined by sets of self-imposed restrictions that defined each specific process. One consequence of the Event was that now a set of restrictions was imposed on him by traumatic circumstances. Since that time he has worked with that set of external restrictions just as he previously worked with those that were self-imposed.

The mental aspect of painting had not changed, but the physical aspect involved unimaginably daunting challenges. Chuck's arm below the elbow remained deadweight: the sheer brawn required to move it came almost entirely from the muscles of his shoulder and upper arm, and at the same time those muscles were required to do much of the work of precisely controlling the handling of the brush in contact with the canvas. To maximize this control, he used two hands—as he still does—one steadying the other, the left hand, as best he can judge, doing more of the work. In those early days, the effort and pain involved were considerable, but were trumped by his determination.

"Pushing myself to achieve something I really wanted was nothing new—I had been through all that before. The physical side of it was different, but the resolve and the obstinacy I needed were the same."

"Some people," says Chuck, "imagine that they see something different in the work I did when I started to paint again, but I don't buy that."

If one considers the conceptual similarities that link *Alex I* and *Alex II*, it's easy enough to acknowledge that he has a strong point, and it's not difficult to see why it is vital to the artist to perceive that continuity since it helped him validate the work executed after he became a quadriplegic.

Is it possible, though, that there *is* some essential difference between the work on either side of the catastrophic event? Looking at *Alex II*, we find the beginnings of what might be thought of as an almost expressionistic trend that would inflect much of the later oeuvre. Chuck prefers to emphasize the fact that, as noted already, he sees this trend as having been anticipated in *Cindy II*, the last painting made before the Event. (He was delighted when Robert Storr, installing Chuck's 1998 retrospective at the Museum of Modern Art, made a point of hanging pre-Event and post-Event canvases in close proximity.)

In the post-Event *Alex II*, the loops and lozenges of pigment, the bold dabs and dynamic doodles, display an unfettered freedom that belies the physical pain and psychological uncertainty that must have been a constant accompaniment to the making of the painting. What one finds expressed in this treatment, I suggest, is pure pleasure in having overcome extreme adversity—the simple joy of being able to paint again. As one studies the face from up close, it dissolves into a vibrant array of free-form touches of color—coral and crimson and saffron and turquoise and orange and emerald—like a spectacular sunrise reflected on a lake, or the scales of a tropical fish. The touches themselves are no longer slaves to discipline as they were in the majority of paintings for the 1988 exhibition. They do not forget their places in the matrix—their responsibility towards pictorial definition—but they shimmer and burst over grid lines, like dancers who have abandoned the strictures of ballet to join in some barefoot improvisation without forgetting where they came from. In *Alex II*, Chuck challenges conventions regarding the kind and quality of information that is required for portraiture, conjuring features out of a carnival of color and gesture that at times threatens to swamp the imagery (look closely at the treatment of the eyes) without ever quite doing so.

Painted in that gloomiest of ateliers, this canvas offers passages that are Fauvist in their effervescence, yet its impact is by no means entirely sunny. Katz's brooding features would be enough to ensure this, but beyond that there is something about the way the face, with its bubbles and buttons of bright color, dissolves into the far more somber background that has the effect of giving the painting a moody gravity despite the exuberance of the handling. This is a work of rich and profound contrasts, both aesthetic and psychological.

Chuck had started out his portrait-making career twenty-two years earlier, citing the models of the mug shot and the passport photograph with their implied nonaesthetic objectivity. This first painting to be completed after his catastrophic injury was something very different. The artist may not have set out to produce a painting that has a powerful emotional impact—to produce a painting *period* was his goal—but he had done so nonetheless. *Alex II* is a modestly-sized work, but one with a great deal of heft, an image that is at the same time optimistic yet informed by Chuck's face-to-face encounter with despair and possible extinction.

The completed painting became a gift for Leslie.

Chapter 21

Regeneration

Chuck was released from Rusk Institute towards the end of July 1989, after almost eight months of hospitalization and therapy.

For all the stress and tribulation of the hospital and the rehab, Leslie had been warned that the biggest challenge she would face would come when Chuck returned home. Helping him adapt to the everyday world—and helping the family adjust to having him back at home in a wheelchair—would present enormous demands, many of them impossible to anticipate.

"I knew it wasn't going to be easy," she says. "At the same time it was a relief to have him out of there, because I hated the hospital so much—going there every day, spending so much time there fighting with the doctors and the nurses, then picking the kids up and trying to be a family. The whole situation was so traumatic for them. Georgia was a teenager. It hit her very hard at the beginning, seeing her father in that state, but then she really threw herself into her schoolwork and started getting straight As. Maggie was very young, and for her I think it got harder as the months went by. I was determined that when Chuck finally got out I would try to make things as normal as possible."

She figured that this would be easier to do at the Bridgehampton house than in the city. Leslie had battled the authorities so that a swimming pool could hurriedly be put in, enabling Chuck to continue aquatic therapy, and the house was partially retrofitted, ramps being installed and doors removed to accommodate the passage of a wheelchair. Finally the big day arrived. Chuck was wheeled into a specially fitted van, which from now on would be his lifeline to the world, and was driven out to the South Fork where a large "welcome home" sign had been hung and Leslie's friend Diane Rothschild was waiting to greet them, with Brenda her housekeeper.

"We were there for three months," Leslie recalls. "The first couple of weeks the girls may have been in camp, but then we were all there, the four of us—with no one else except for the nurses who came four times a day."

The nurses were required to catheterize Chuck, to monitor his cardiac and respiratory systems, and to perform other necessary medical tasks.

"The problem was," Leslie continues, "that the nurses were trained to function in an institutional world, and after all those months Chuck had become institutionalized too. So you'd be in the kitchen, putting food on the table, and there'd be a bottle of urine sitting there. I wasn't going to have that, but it took a lot of effort to get the point across because the nurses took that for granted, and so did Chuck. He'd become inured to that kind of thing. I didn't want the kids to have to deal with that. There was an occasion when Maggie walked in on Chuck when he was with one of the nurses—she just wanted to see her father—and the nurse chased her away. I went ballistic. That just wasn't acceptable. This was a home, not a hospital."

When they moved back to the city, there was a new routine to adapt to. In Bridgehampton, Chuck had his studio adjacent to the house so he was able to roll over there in his wheelchair. In the city, in order to paint he had to commute to Spring Street in the specially equipped van. Once he began working on large paintings again, he had to be strapped to the forklift to work on their upper sections. Often he would stay up there all day with an assistant bringing him meals and refreshments. Just getting in and out of the building was a challenge. Chuck's loft was on an upper floor, and to reach it, he had to use the elevator, but the door to the elevator was too narrow to accommodate a wheelchair unless it was folded. In rehab, Chuck had learned to take a few clumsy steps, like Frankenstein's monster lurching to life. Now he had to use this painfully reacquired skill to access the elevator, with someone supporting him to make sure he didn't fall. Having the right people around to help was crucial. Leslie emphasizes the importance of Michael Volanakis's continued presence—his longtime familiarity with Chuck and his work was vital—but Michael alone could not handle everything.

"We needed someone else to help out," says Leslie, "and we got very lucky finding Andy Tirado."

The young artist from Colorado had the necessary skills to assist Chuck in the studio and for the next eighteen months played a major role in the Closes' lives. Big, capable, and personable, Tirado moved into Chuck's studio, sleeping on a futon. In Bridgehampton, Leslie found him a room not far from the house.

"I don't know what we'd have done without him," she says. "He was indispensable. He did everything—getting Chuck to the studio, or to therapy—whatever was needed. Somebody had to be there all the time. When I couldn't be, Andy stepped in. He got along with people, he was discreet, he was competent, and he wasn't afraid to use his own initiative—plus he was sensitive with the kids. That was very important."

Chuck's life was busier than ever, rebuilding his career while still putting several hours a day into strenuous physical therapy. His condition had evolved to the point where he could function in the outside world, if not easily. He could take a few steps with the help of strap-on quad crutches. Using his teeth, he could fit a fork or a paintbrush into the prosthetic splint, and he could get around in a motorized wheelchair, but his reliance upon the daily attention of nurses was never going to change. Outpatient rehab continued, as it still does, but he knew that only some small amount of continued physical improvement could be hoped for. It was more a question of learning how to maximize the skills he had been able to salvage, and that came with practice—something that applied

Chuck Close painting *Janet*, 1989

to everything from painting to handling the wheelchair in city traffic. Soon he was zipping around downtown streets with an aplomb that occasionally verged on the reckless. The paintings that he produced speak for themselves.

Adjusting to home life, though, proved to be far from easy, and the acclimation was equally difficult for Leslie and the children. There was always some new crisis to deal with. Chuck was still having severe breathing problems; he had choking fits; he fell out of bed, and out of the wheelchair; he suffered from terrible bladder infections and urinary tract infections that came on without warning, calling for heavy-duty antibiotics that sapped him of his strength. Problems with his circulation meant that he had to sleep in a woolen hat and scarf, and that he constantly burned his fingers on things like coffee cups because there was no feeling there until it was too late.

"Dealing with all that was bad enough," Leslie continues, "but in many ways what was worse was adjusting to the different notion of privacy that applies when you're living with a quadriplegic. That was obvious from the first—those weeks in Bridgehampton—and it didn't get easier. There was no privacy anymore. Someone was always there—a nurse, a physical therapist, someone waiting to drive Chuck to the studio. There were times I felt I'd never be alone again, and there was no longer any such thing as spontaneity. You couldn't just say, 'Let's go to the movies,' and go. It had to be planned as a major expedition. I don't know how I would have managed without my mother, and without my friends. So many people pitched in."

She recalls too how she found it difficult to deal with social situations that to an outsider might seem trivial but that to her were important.

"I sometimes felt that Chuck couldn't quite imagine how other people saw him. When he was in the hospital, he didn't realize how upset people were to see him in that condition—now he didn't realize how it might bother someone when he offered them this dead hand to shake. That made me very uncomfortable. He didn't see why. I would talk to him about it, but he couldn't see it."

Chuck, for his part, says he never thought of the hand as being dead.

"I was able to paint using that hand. What was so terrible about expecting someone to shake it?"

He adds that for him the emotional connection to a person involved in touching and being touched—whether a hug from a friend or a handshake with a stranger—has always been essential to his well-being. After finding himself a quadriplegic, unembarrassed physical contact with other people became in effect a form of therapy. If that contact was withheld, it was painful.

As had been the case with the period of hospitalization and rehab, Chuck and Leslie experienced their radically changed home situation in very different ways, with such questions as whether or not to shake hands with strangers symptomatic of larger problems. Chuck makes the point that, although he now spent most of his waking life in a wheelchair, he did not feel like a different person. He still looked out at the same world in the same way and responded to it in the same way.

Maggie and Chuck Close, early 1990s

This is not to pretend that his condition did not have an impact on the way he experienced life. He recalls the frustration of returning to familiar surroundings without being able to enjoy "normal" activities, especially when it came to interacting spontaneously with his daughters, who, he felt, were missing out on many things he wished he could do—simple, everyday things like taking Maggie to the playground. He was appalled too to find that when he showed up at their schools in his wheelchair he wasn't treated like other parents, a fact that his daughters could not help but be aware of. Retrospectively, Chuck feels especially sad for Maggie, who can barely remember him as an able-bodied parent. Georgia, since she had a life of her own, with school and friends to occupy her outside the home, was able to cope relatively well with the changed situation, though she certainly missed many activities she had once taken for granted. On the other hand, Maggie—though by now she too was in school—was still at an age when the family unit is pivotal to healthy development. Support for her was there from both parents, but for Maggie it was hard to adjust to Chuck being in a wheelchair since it robbed her of so many outings and interactions that previously she had taken for granted, especially since Chuck had been very much a hands-on parent who instinctively had tried to pass on the fearlessness instilled in him by his mother.

"As a quadriplegic," says Chuck, "you face a steep learning curve. You quickly discover that many theaters and movie theaters are not wheelchair-friendly, that there are a lot of places where there are no curb-cuts—all that kind of thing. I learned that [back then] there was not a single handicapped parking space in the entire city. Then there's the whole business of dealing with strangers. You still run into people who seem to think that being in a wheelchair is some kind of punishment from God."

More important, though, was the question of his interactions with friends and, especially, family. He might see them as he always had, but how did they see him? Did they recoil from his frozen hand or from his wheelchair-bound body? He chose not to believe so. In fact, he was always very forthcoming about his disabilities, often making light of them, so that most people were quickly put at ease, which made Leslie's stance on the handshake issue, and other matters pertaining to his body, difficult for him to understand or accept. What did it say about her attitude towards him? Had the Event and its aftermath irrevocably altered their relationship? Chuck's initial response was to refuse to acknowledge that possibility, but there was mounting evidence that things had in fact changed. There were no more moments of casual intimacy, in part because of the physical strictures caused by his disability, but also in part because he sensed that he was being perceived as a different person. Since he did not feel like a different person, and since he still possessed the same emotional appetites, and in many ways the same physical appetites, this was a situation that could only become more painful as time went by. Chuck could understand why Leslie's perception of him might have changed, but that did not make things easier.

It seems reasonable to assume that both parties hungered to return to the way things were before the Event threw their lives into chaos, but their perceptions of that simple but charged phrase "the way things were" were completely different. Leslie felt deprived in terms of a loss of privacy, Chuck in terms of a loss of intimacy. For Chuck, things were most the way they had been when he was in his studio working or interacting with colleagues in the art world. For Leslie, things returned to a semblance of normality when she was in her garden.

For both of them, things were the least normal within the context of everyday domestic life, but binding the two of them together was the commitment they had made to being a family, and the traumatic experiences they had so recently shared—experiences that no one else could ever fully comprehend since that comprehension was measured out in pain, frustration, anger, and endless days and weeks of anxiety and despair. For the time being, separation was impossible to contemplate, especially since their daughters had years of school ahead of them, with Georgia not yet in college. There were difficult times to come, though it should be emphasized that there were also interludes of relaxation and family enjoyment—Christmas vacations on the island of Captiva, Thanksgiving celebrations with friends, weekends at the Bridgehampton house—when everyday conflicts did not get in the way.

Chuck believes that for a long time both he and Leslie were in denial about the deterioration of their relationship, perhaps because there were so many practical problems to be dealt with. Personal matters can dissolve into the background, at least temporarily, when the apartment has to be retrofitted with ramps and special bathroom furniture, and family privacy protected by creating a separate entrance for nurses.

"A lot of our energy went into remodeling," Chuck says, "both in the city and in the country. It's what we did best, and it helped take our minds off other things."

One of the biggest problems with suddenly finding yourself a quadriplegic is that nothing can prepare you for what to expect. Coming to terms with the unexpected—whether in the studio or the home—was a constant challenge. Chuck emphasizes, however, that he was extraordinarily lucky to be in a position financially to modify his environment to minimize his disability. Additionally, he had tremendous support from the art community, and—most important of all—he was able to continue the activity that gave meaning to his life.

Head-On

The first large painting Chuck made after leaving the hospital was a portrait of the painter Elizabeth Murray. *Elizabeth* (1989) is six feet tall and constructed on a diagonal grid. Chuck had been working on another version at the time of his hospitalization, but started from scratch when he was able to return to his studio. A six-foot canvas was as large as he could manage at that point.

The palette of *Elizabeth* is somewhat unusual, having a distinctly acidic cast to parts of the background, and being keyed to especially bright highlights in the facial area, with less reliance on evoking full flesh tones than is typical in the grid paintings. In this example, Chuck succeeds in achieving an allover quality as fully as in any canvas he has ever produced. As with *Alex II*, the background has a loosely woven or braided quality—almost a plaid effect—which extends into the sitter's hair, and even into shadowed planes on the face. This woven texture is broken up with blobs and swirls of pigment that perform a variety of functions, ranging from emphasizing highlights in the hair to giving focus to the eyes which, as with *Alex II*, are far more fragmented and less graphically literal than was the case with the paintings shown in 1988.

Although plainly photo-derived, this painting threatens to disintegrate into pattern even from some distance, the essential descriptive information materializing from ribbons of color. On closer inspection, the individual units that make up the grid are remarkably similar to those to be found in *Cindy II*. The way the components of the image do manage to hold together seems somewhat looser, but that is partly because of the different type of grid employed.

Chuck's reintroduction to the public art world came in the form of an Artist's Choice exhibition at the Museum of Modern Art, which he organized at the invitation of Kirk Varnedoe. Titled *Head-On/The Modern Portrait*, this was installed in a smallish room at the museum, from January to March of 1991, and was seen again at the Lannan Foundation Gallery in Los Angeles from June to September of the same year. It was like no other show that had ever originated at MoMA in that it featured scores of works by dozens of artists, chosen from the museum's various departments—painting and sculpture, drawings, prints, photography—installed salon style, which is to say crowded together in layers around the walls of the gallery, many on shelves with very little breathing space between one portrait and the next—mats and frames sometimes overlapping—the very opposite of the orthodox contemporary museum installation pioneered by MoMA.

Chuck's first thought had been to do something more conventional, namely to mount a show of the greatest de Koonings in the collection. He quickly dismissed this idea as something any competent curator could do and turned his attention to the portrait as subject matter. Briefly he considered the possibility of making a selection of the museum's best examples to demonstrate that there was a place for the portrait within the modernist tradition. He abandoned that approach on the grounds that the idea of the artist playing connoisseur was not particularly interesting, noting that he had always learned as much from work he did not like as from work he loved. Rather than being selective, he decided it would be far more interesting to have an exhibition that included *every* portrait in the museum's collection.

This inclusiveness meant spending days in each of MoMA's departments going through the inventory, sometimes finding works that had not been hung in the museum for years or decades, or not ever in some instances. The result was a radically eclectic selection of works that included not only obvious examples by the likes of Van Gogh, Picasso, Matisse, Duchamp, Man Ray, Diane Arbus, and Max Beckmann, but also dozens of lesser-known pieces by artists ranging from Max Pechstein and Jean Crotti to Hugo Erfuth, David Park, Arnulf Rainer, and Ray Johnson.

Chuck points out that these works had come to be acquired by the museum's collection in many different ways, which gave the ensemble a somewhat arbitrary character. Some were purchased, many were donated by friends of the museum, and others were bequests from artists or their families. In the case of the Johnson work—a small photocopied print labeled "Bill de Kooning"—it came into the collection by the back door, having been mailed to MoMA's head librarian, Clive Philpot, setting up a situation in which the print was routinely entered into the library's catalogue without any curatorial intervention. This was in fact a strategy devised by Chuck with the cooperation of Philpot because Chuck had been distressed to

Chuck Close in the exhibition *Head-On/The Modern Portrait*, 1991

find that Johnson, whose work he greatly admires (and who since his death in 1995 has belatedly been accorded some of the recognition he deserves) was not represented in the collection. It's the one instance in which Chuck bent the rules he had set for himself in making a selection for the show which otherwise reveled in the often capricious nature of the museum's inventory.

In his foreword to the booklet that accompanied the show, Varnedoe made the point that the exhibition, and the installation itself, emphasized the role of the museum as a repository of information—"a data bank"—as opposed to its role as an arbiter of taste. In addition, he pointed out that the installation to a large extent followed the principles that Chuck employed in his art, namely constructing an entity from related incremental elements.

In talking about the installation, Chuck picks up on the same general point—

that the way in which he had assembled the show related to the way in which he made his paintings, explaining that he was trying to share with the viewers some of the pleasure that he gets from making art. A key intention of the exhibition was to present works in a jarringly unfamiliar way, with unexpected juxtapositions, so that someone visiting the show might have a fresh experience even when confronting images seen many times before.

By the time of the Artist's Choice show, Chuck's painting career was fully revived. Three 1989 paintings were followed by four completed in 1990, and no fewer than five in 1991, a relatively large number for the artist at any point in his career. The new work had its first public exposure at a large Pace Gallery exhibition that opened on November 2, 1991, closing on December 7, the second anniversary of his hospitalization. If the Artist's Choice show had reminded people that Chuck Close was still very much alive and active, the Pace show provided ample evidence of his continued ability to make art at the highest level. By the time he painted *Bill* (1990), *Eric* (1990), and *April* (1991)—the artists William Wegman, Eric Fischl, and April Gornick—Chuck was in full control of his medium.

In 1992, Chuck moved his studio to new ground-floor space on Bond Street in the NoHo section of downtown Manhattan, which, like the Central Park apartment and the Bridgehampton house, had been retrofitted to meet the needs of someone forced to live largely in a wheelchair. Shortly before his hospitalization, he had installed in his Bridgehampton studio a device for dealing with the problem of working on the upper sections of very large paintings, a narrow, slotted pit built into the floor, flush with the wall, into which a painting could be lowered. (He had first seen such a system, which is extensively used by theater scenery painters, in Willem de Kooning's studio in nearby Springs.) When he moved to the new Bond Street space, he installed a basic version of this system, eventually adding motorized tracks that permitted canvases to be raised and lowered and otherwise manipulated mechanically. This allowed him to leave behind the inconvenience of working while strapped to a platform mounted on a forklift.

One of the first paintings to be made in the Bond Street studio was *John* (1992), a portrait of the sculptor John Chamberlain that holds up as an especially strong example of the artist's prismatic grid idiom. Chuck has often said that he only paints a small percentage of the people whom he asks to sit for photographs, and it's easy to see why this particular image caught his fancy. Chamberlain, whose face had been familiar to Chuck since the max's kansas city era—he claims that Chamberlain once threw him down a flight of stairs—shows ample evidence of worldly wear and tear and is caught from the marginally three-quarter angle that was becoming a Close favorite. Staring into the camera's lens, Chamberlain's features are lit as if for a climactic movie close-up, his moustache in itself a graphic statement, his silver hair a reverse silhouette against the dark background. The sitter even thought to wear a chromatically lively shirt and a patterned jacket that offered opportunities for visual grace notes.

In this painting, Chuck arrived at a particularly satisfying balance between description and abstraction. Circles and dots of bottle green, modified with touches of yellow, white, and blue, more than adequately evoke the irises of the subject's eyes (which seem all the more alive because of the fragmentation). It takes very little shift in focus, however, to experience these same circles and dots as elements in an abstract field.

In 1994, one of the most famous faces in the New York art world, Roy Lichtenstein's, was the subject of two striking portraits, one not quite full face, the other one of Chuck's rare profiles. *Roy I* is a trifle unusual in that it shows the subject with a half smile on his face—not common in Chuck's work—giving the artist an opportunity to work a little magic with the teeth. The roughly rectangular shapes that represent one tooth are stretched out over two squares to emphasize the three-quarter view of the face by introducing a comic book–like, shorthand illusion of foreshortening (certainly appropriate in a portrait of the master of the blown-up comic strip). For the most part this is a fairly straightforward painting except for some clever exploitation of the grid to square off the subject's jaw, and for a tendency for Lichtenstein's cheeks to "disintegrate" into the background, a kind of "edge erosion" that had appeared in a modest form in some earlier paintings. This edge erosion is more strikingly apparent in *Roy II*, in which bits of the prow of the subject's prominent nose have been allowed to drift off into the background. Chuck points out that he could get away with this only because he was working with a simple vertical-horizontal grid. Had he employed a diagonal grid, Lichtenstein's nose would have turned into an avalanche.

In the mid to late 1990s Chuck painted more artist friends, ranging from Dorothea Rockburne and Lorna Simpson to the veteran Paul Cadmus. A 1997 portrait of Robert Rauschenberg is one of several from that period to employ very tight cropping of the face as yet another way of achieving an allover effect. Simultaneously it places an emphasis on the subject's smile, one that is far more explicit than the tentative smile found in *Roy I.*

"I always tell sitters not to smile," Chuck says, "but when it came to Bob, there was no way I could get a picture of him when he was not smiling. He was the exact opposite of Jasper Johns, who makes a thing of *not* smiling for the camera."

The Rauschenberg painting is also amusing for the way in which the treatment of the eyes evokes a pair of hearts, an example of presumably unintended symbolism that fits well with Rauschenberg's genial personality.

During this period, Chuck created several new self-portraits, including a tightly cropped version in 1997, which followed an even more tightly cropped version he had painted the previous year. Earlier, in 1995, Chuck made a pair of black-and-white self-portraits that can be seen as a return to the mug shot ideal. Full-face and profile, the maquettes for these paintings present the artist in unflattering likenesses worthy of any FBI Most Wanted list. The paintings themselves are equally unflattering, but they are animated by the liveliness of the handling.

By the time Chuck was making these paintings, his reputation stood higher than it ever had, and more than one New York museum was vying to stage a new retrospective exhibition. Kirk Varnedoe wanted such a show for the Museum of Modern Art, but initially it appeared that the Metropolitan Museum would be the venue. Chuck withdrew from the Met, however, on the grounds that the museum was proposing to give him only half the gallery space he felt had been promised, and also planned to trim the size of the catalogue. At that point, MoMA took over, offering more space and a comprehensive catalogue. Varnedoe was originally scheduled to curate the show but was prevented from doing so by ill health. Robert Storr took his place, though Varnedoe remained involved, contributing a major essay to the catalogue. The exhibition ran at MoMA from February 26 to May 26, 1998, before traveling to the Museum of Contemporary Art in Chicago, the Hirshhorn Museum in Washington, DC, the Seattle Art Museum, and the Hayward Gallery in London.

In his essay for the catalogue, Storr addressed the primacy of process in Chuck's art, saying of Close and his peers, "The gamble they have taken is that the unique products of programmatic artistic choices will defy generalities and exceed any foreseeable result.... Chuck has spent the last thirty years pushing representation to its limits. In the process he has won his aesthetic wager many times over."[20]

Inevitably, Storr also touched on what Chuck Close had had to overcome in terms of catastrophic injury. Many of those present at the gala opening for the exhibition had visited him in the hospital or in rehab less than a decade earlier. The contrast between the grim corridors of Rusk and the hallowed precincts of MoMA was something that was palpably on people's minds, and must have had a special significance for members of his family. Given the severity of his trauma, a better outcome could hardly have been hoped for, and this sparkling occasion was the apotheosis of his recovery. There was a moving moment at the celebratory dinner when Varnedoe asked all those present who had been portrayed by Chuck to rise. At almost every table, one, two, or sometimes three and four people got to their feet. The extended family that Chuck had acquired through his pictorial skills was out in force, providing assurance that the only child—now an orphan—was no longer alone.

Roy II, 1994, in progress, and *Roy I*, 1994, in the studio on Bond Street

The following day there was a gathering for out of town friends at the Closes' apartment, and on that occasion, hosted by Leslie with her usual aplomb, one was inevitably more aware of the difficult realities that continued to impinge on the family's everyday routine. Ramps and other signs that this was a world created for a wheelchair were everywhere, and at one point Chuck quietly disappeared to rendezvous with his nurse, who came and went invisibly through the special entrance created for that purpose, like a conjuror's assistant performing some crucial task unseen by the audience. Later there was a moment of near panic because Chuck was running late for a television interview with Charlie Rose and his driver remembered that the van would have to be fetched from several blocks away, since that had been the best parking spot he had been able to find the previous night after the gala. Good conversation and delicious food masked these incursions, but they were apparent nonetheless, and one understood that for the Closes they were things that had to be dealt with day after day, to the point of tedium, the inescapable routine that was Chuck's lifeline and the bane of Leslie's existence.

The exhibition itself underscored the astonishing variety that exists within Chuck Close's oeuvre. The show contained all but one of the black-and-white continuous-tone portraits from the sixties, and five of the continuous-tone color portraits. There were key fingerprint paintings and pulp paper pieces. There were drawings and watercolors and pastels and prints and photographic maquettes, and Polaroids; and also on display was the comprehensive unfolding of the prismatic grid series, from the first version of *Stanley* made in 1980 to a 1997 self-portrait.

If you knew the New York art world, as most at that MoMA opening did, you could walk from gallery to gallery spotting familiar faces—"Here's Richard Serra . . . there's Phil Glass. . . . Here's Lucas Samaras . . . there's Roy Lichtenstein. . . ." The longer you spent with the show, however, the less that became the point of the exercise. This lavish temporary assemblage of works provided the perfect occasion for the visitor to consider the whole nature of Close's subject matter. Is it the human face? Or photography? Or the process of making art? At one extreme it became possible to see Chuck Close as a nonfigurative artist. Brice Marden (someone who has chosen not to be the subject of a Close portrait, although invited more than once), for one, has asserted with conviction that Chuck's work is abstract, but how can that be when it is so clearly representational? The retrospective reminded the thoughtful viewer that in Chuck's work the features of the

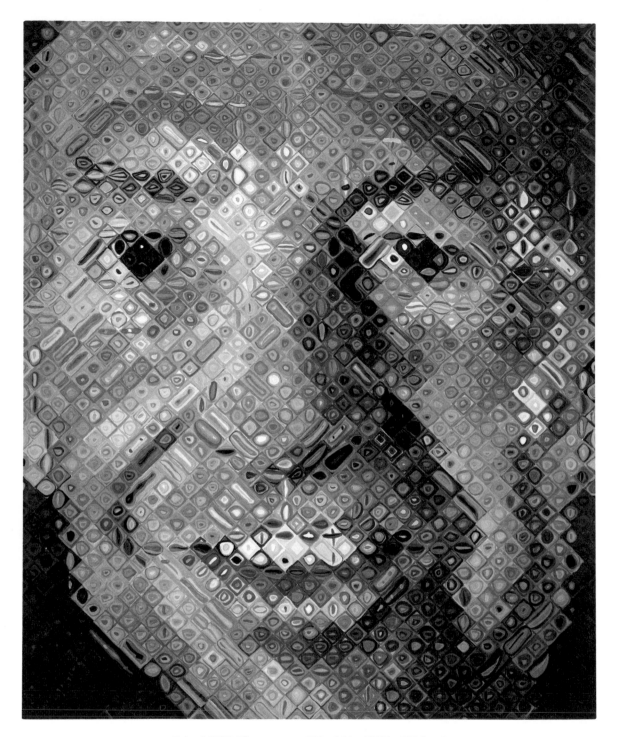

Robert, 1997. Oil on canvas, 102 x 84 in. (259.1 x 213.4 cm)

human face are, in a sense, perhaps no more important than rectangles were to Mondrian; but if you spent a little longer at the exhibition, the humanity of the subject matter began to reassert itself, inescapably so in some works such as the great 1985 finger painting *Fanny*.

In the end, what the retrospective illustrated was that for a quarter of a century Chuck Close had succeeded in making extraordinary work by walking an aesthetic tightrope stretched between two concepts of what constitutes authenticity in art—representation and abstraction—effortlessly balancing above an abyss like Philippe Petit poised on a wire between the twin towers of the World Trade Center.

Chuck Close and Robert Storr supervising the installation of
Chuck Close: A Retrospective, at The Museum of Modern Art,
New York, 1998. Photography by Tina Barney

Self-Portrait (1997) in progress

Chapter 23

Process and Pragmatism

Having earlier compared Chuck to a magician, and in the last chapter to the world's greatest high-wire artist, I am now going to add the thought that he is an accomplished juggler, keeping more balls in the air than almost any other artist I can think of. Only at the very beginning of his career was he exclusively a painter. Starting in 1972 with *Keith/Mezzotint*, he branched out into areas as varied as Polaroid photography and paper pulp multiples, while embracing a remarkable variety of printmaking techniques. Such activities have in fact increased as his career has progressed, stretching in recent years to include daguerreotypes and tapestries.

Many painters create prints that are essentially peripheral to their primary concern of working with paint on canvas, seeing them perhaps as a way of making their imagery available to a wider audience. Chuck Close, by contrast, embraces printmaking as an activity integral to his overall program of producing art by different methods while remaining faithful to both his subject matter and to his reliance upon process as a way of generating imagery. In recent decades, only a handful of major artists—Jasper Johns is the example that springs most readily to mind—have articulated their ambitions as effectively by means of editions of multiples, and Chuck is perhaps alone in the range of techniques he has embraced. Since his hospitalization, he has become more protean than ever, producing soft-ground scribble etchings, spitbite etchings, relief prints, linoleum cuts, silkscreens, and two kinds of woodblock prints. Even when he is working with traditional media, he has a habit of devising new approaches that derive from his obsessive need to understand and rethink the technology he is employing.

His ability, both intuitive and intellectual, to grasp print technologies was already apparent in his student days at Yale. On one occasion while there he was given the assignment of figuring out how the Dutch printmaker Hercules

Seghers (circa 1590–1645) was able to produce etchings that looked like aquatints, a process not invented until after his death. Chuck approached the problem by practical experimentation. The aquatint method produces a grainy, granulated texture, the result of the printmaker working through an acid-resistant ground, like a conventional etching ground but evenly loaded with a powdery substance, usually rosin dust. Rather than approaching his task as a purely art historical question, Chuck asked himself, "How would *I* get that effect without the aquatint ground?" He knew that Seghers's etchings came out in small editions, and that provided a clue. It suggested that the copper plates had been submitted to some pretty rough treatment that made them break down quickly. It occurred to Chuck that the Dutchman might have saturated his plate with acid till its corrosive action began to pit the copper, creating a grainy, aquatint-like texture. When he tried this out, he found that he was able to approximate Seghers's effects. It was not conclusive proof that the printer had used this method, but it certainly made for a very plausible theory, and it demonstrated that Chuck had a sophisticated grasp of the medium, as would prove to be the case with other methods of printmaking.

Chuck likes to say of printmaking in general that something always goes wrong, and there is always a solution. A spectacular example of this is the *Alex/Reduction Print*, an edition dated 1993. This started out as a reduction-block linoleum print—a method of printmaking invented by Picasso. The Spaniard had never envisioned using it to create prints of 79 3/8 x 60 3/8 inches, but that was what Chuck had in mind. In February 1991, he traveled with Joe Wilfer to Tandem Press, in Wisconsin, one of the few shops that could handle this kind of print on that scale. There were nine days in which to complete the job, and from the beginning everything seemed to go wrong. A roll of so-called battleship linoleum—a form of floor covering used aboard naval vessels—had been ordered. Made with linseed oil and sawdust, the material comes in a neutral gray on a canvas backing and, to quote Chuck, "it cuts like butter." Unfortunately, before it reached the studio floor, it was speared by a forklift and rendered unusable. Then standard vinyl flooring material was bought from local store and mounted on Plexiglas. Alex Katz's likeness was projected onto this, and Chuck prepared to go to work, cutting into the surface with electric tools he had previously used on smaller prints. Given his lack of strength, however, he found the improvised surface intractable and so a new approach had to be adopted. Now Chuck drew onto the surface with a Sharpie and assistants did the carving. When carving was completed for the day, printing commenced, and this system made it possible for one color—specifically one shade of gray—to be printed in each twenty-four-hour period.

Another problem had arisen, however. The custom-made paper ordered from Japan at great expense proved to be highly unsatisfactory. Chuck could see he would not be pleased with the end product so he ordered each block to be printed

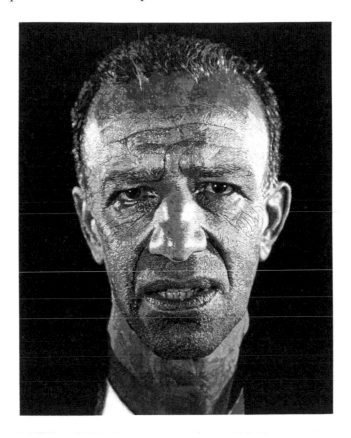

Alex/Reduction Print, 1993. Silkscreen, 79 3/8 x 60 3/8 in. (201.6 x 153.4 cm)

on Mylar as well as on paper, realizing that images recorded on Mylar could be transferred to fine mesh screens that could then be used to create silkscreen prints, meaning that the edition could be salvaged in an alternative medium. This was subsequently done at Brand X, a New York print shop, and the resulting edition was issued in screenprint form though its character had been determined entirely by the reduction-block method.

Chuck points to this as an example of how, while process is central to his working method, he is not rigid about its use.

9/15   Chuck Close   2000

Self-Portrait/Scribble/Etching Portfolio Final Print, 2000.
Final signed print from portfolio of 12 states and 12 progressives,
18 1/4 x 15 1/4 in. (46.4 x 38.7 cm)

"An uncompromising process artist would have gone with the woodblocks on the flawed paper, whatever the imperfections. That would have been true to the process—and it's actually what Joe Wilfer wanted to do. I will stay with the process all the way *only* if it gives me the results that I want. I'm not a purist. The quality of the end product is what I'm interested in."

Prior to this, Chuck had never had any interest in making screenprints, thinking of them as suitable for posters, commercial reproductions, and for the kind of art that draws directly upon mass-market imagery—he quotes the examples of Lichtenstein and Warhol—but certainly not for his own work. The experience with *Alex*, however, convinced him that he had underestimated the medium's potential.

Alex in fact helped launch a continuing relationship with the Brand X studio, where over the next several years he produced a number of editions. The first of these, issued in 1995, derived from his 1991 self-portrait in oil on canvas. Although not as large as the painting, this is still a very large print—64 1/2 x 54 inches—that presented the printmakers with a considerable technical challenge. At first glance, this is a black-and-white image, but on closer inspection it proves to be made up of many different colors—from pale flesh tones to rich blue-blacks—in a variety of different densities, shades, and tints. In fact, this is an 80-color silkscreen image, each color requiring a different drawing on Mylar and a fresh screen.

Subsequent screenprint editions have included highly chromatic images such as *John* (1998), which employed 126 colors; *Self-Portrait* (2000), utilizing a modest 111 colors; *Lyle* (2002), requiring 149 colors; and a 2007 self-portrait, which called for 187 colors (and hence 187 Mylars and 187 screens). Each of these derives directly from a preexisting painting, which in part accounts for the scale—all are more than five feet tall—because it is important to the artist that they have the same quality of "bigness" found in the original.

Chuck's entire career in printmaking is a story of high ambition and high achievement. One outcome has been perhaps the most successful print show ever, the exhibition *Chuck Close: Process and Collaboration*, organized by Terrie Sultan of the Blaffer Art Gallery at the University of Houston, Texas, where it made its debut in 2003. From there it traveled to the Metropolitan Museum in New York, the first stop on a tour of more than a score of museums and public galleries that at the time of this writing is scheduled to continue into 2011 and possibly beyond. Not just a selection of finished prints, this retrospective is a model of curatorial thoroughness brilliantly illustrating the relationship between process and achievement in a way that an exhibition of paintings and drawings never could. By seeing sequential proofs, and sets of progressives, the viewer is able to grasp exactly how Chuck Close goes about creating a work of art, and the insights provided apply not only to prints, since the presentation makes it possible to interpolate how the paintings are made as well.

Since 1990, Chuck Close's involvement with photography has become more varied in its scope, both from the point of view of technology—most notably in his successful attempts at producing modern daguerreotypes—and also in the range of projects he has undertaken. Since the nudes and flowers of the previous decade, Chuck had looked on photography as an opportunity to relax somewhat and play by a different set of rules. He remains firm about not accepting private portrait commissions but is willing to take on appropriate assignments from publications for which he feels comfortable working. Thus, for example, he has photographed Hillary Rodham Clinton for the *New York Times Sunday Magazine*, the editors of which have also commissioned him to tackle subjects such as Broadway actors and actresses, and popular female singers.

To be photographed by Chuck Close is a memorable experience.

The space housing the big Polaroid camera that he uses is located a few blocks from his studio, a large room with blackout shades over the windows. In many ways it's like any other photography studio, with a range of lights, umbrellas, power packs, flags, and scrims available for the photographer to select. The outstanding difference is the camera itself, a monster the size of a small refrigerator, mounted on a hefty dolly. Essentially it's an old-fashioned view camera with a flexible bellows, much like the cameras used in the Victorian era by men like Eadweard Muybridge, though even larger in order to accommodate the 28 x 24 inch Polaroid film pack.

The subject perches on an adjustable stool against a black background (for a black-and-white shoot). For a typical sitting, a "softbox" lighting setup is to one side, providing diffused light to minimize wrinkles and blemishes. A more focused lamp on the other side is filtered by a fiberglass screen, and a "snoot"—a light in a cone-shaped housing—is used to paint light onto one side of the face. In the shadows behind the camera, Chuck and the operator peer into the ground glass viewfinder. Adjustments to the focus are made. At the end of the bellows, the lens seems to lurch towards the subject as if alive—the cyclopean eye of a tourist from Mars out of some lost story by Jules Verne or H. G. Wells. The artist calls out directions: "Head up a bit.... Try not to squint." At last, the ground glass is replaced by the film pack, and suddenly there is a blinding flash, followed by a moment of silence. The pack is removed from the camera and, after a short wait, is stripped open. The developed photograph is pinned to a wall covered in corkboard. The subject approaches with trepidation as Chuck grins in anticipation of a horrified reaction.

Chuck has often expressed his dislike of being termed a realist painter, pointing out that he is just as interested in artifice as in realism. This applies equally to his photography, and is implicit in the daguerreotypes he began producing in 1999, this being a medium that combines a striking ability to convey pictorial information with great intensity and an elusive, shimmering surface quality that makes the image seem like something conjured up by an illusionist.

A century and a half after it went out of fashion, the daguerreotype is typically seen as being representative of a certain era—the 1840s and 1850s—it having been launched to astonishment and acclaim in 1839 by Louis Jacques Mandé Daguerre. The labor-intensive technology began with a sheet of copper coated with silver. That silvered plate had to be buffed until it was as reflective as a mirror, then placed in a container into which bromine and iodine fumes were introduced, rendering the plate sensitive to light. That plate was then exposed in the camera, using a very wide aperture, and developed using highly toxic mercury vapors. This rendered a unique and fragile image that sat on the mirrored surface of the plate. The mirror effect meant that the image had to be viewed from an angle at which it was not obscured by reflectivity, but it gave that image an almost hallucinatory character, and the definition was stunning.

The opportunity for Chuck to explore the daguerreotype came about in 1997 when Colin Westerbeck, then curator of photography at the Art Institute of Chicago, asked him if he would be interested in working with Grant Romer of Eastman House. The project was facilitated by a grant from the Lannan Foundation, and the resulting small self-portraits were interesting but flawed, lacking the kind of consistency that would be required if the project were to be pursued further.

A couple of years went by before Chuck decided to take another shot at mastering the medium, this time in collaboration with Jerry Spagnoli, a photographer

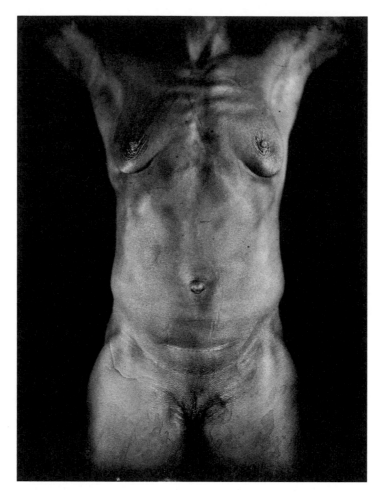

Untitled Torso Diptych, 2000. Two daguerreotypes, each 8 1/2 x 6 1/2 in. (21.6 x 16.5 cm)

who already had a good deal of experience with daguerreotypes. At first, they worked with natural light and long exposures, just as operators did back in the nineteenth century. The first efforts were self-portraits because Chuck did not want to subject anyone else to the discomfort until the system had been debugged. The key breakthrough came when he decided to do away with natural light and replace it with banks of strobe lights. In part at least this came about because he wanted to use the daguerreotype system to shoot nudes, and that presented a very specific problem. Long exposures in natural light were okay for portraits, because the head could be held in place with a hidden clamp. When it came to shooting a bare chest, however, there was no way for the subject to suppress breathing for long enough to allow a clean exposure. Strobes would do away with that problem, and it soon became apparent that they would also give the image

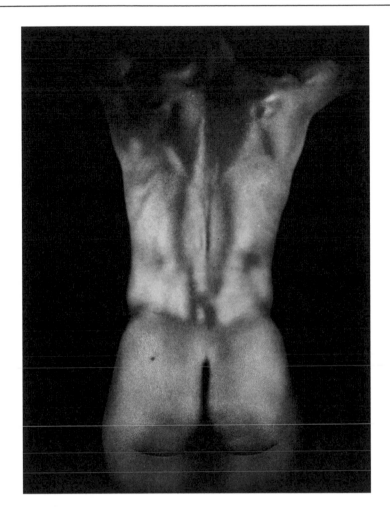

a look that was entirely modern, without losing any of the unique qualities that made the medium so appealing in the first place.

The largest of Chuck's daguerreotypes are just 8 1/2 x 6 1/2 inches, the biggest size used for classic nineteenth-century plates. Chuck points out that, although best known for his oversize paintings, he has always been equally interested in making small-scale images. When it comes to daguerreotypes, he particularly likes the intimacy of the viewing experience—the fact that you pick one up and look at it the way you would pick up a book, which was in fact the preferred way of viewing them in Victorian times. People would keep them in velvet sleeves, treating them as precious objects, almost like icons.

In the case of Chuck's contemporary icons, a sitter's expression sometimes betrays the fact that he is posed twelve inches from banks of strobes that produce a 30,000 watt-second burst of light. One version of *Robert* (2001) captures the subject—the stage director Robert Wilson—with his eyes closed and a grin on his face as he reacts to the blinding flash. Normally, Chuck selects only exposures that show the subject with eyes fully open (and reflecting the strobes). In these images, what gives away the power of the light source is the astonishingly high definition texture of skin in the areas of the image that are totally in focus. Moles, freckles, lines, wrinkles, and other blemishes are pitilessly recorded, and yet the effect of these portraits is not cruel. On the contrary, they have a unique beauty that comes from their ruthless veracity.

The daguerreotype nudes that Close began to produce in 2000 are characterized by the same pitiless beauty as the portraits. These differ from the Polaroid nudes he had made back in the 1980s in that, instead of using dancers and professional models, he persuaded friends and acquaintances to pose for him. When shooting those 1980s nudes, he had talked of sparing his friends the embarrassment of taking their clothes off. Now he reversed that policy, saying that times had changed and he had fun convincing people he knew that they should serve as nude models. More significantly, this was a way of guaranteeing himself subjects who did not match up to fashionable ideals of youth and beauty.

"I've watched people at the gallery looking at the nudes," he says, "and I find it interesting that they don't spend the most time in front of the beautiful bodies. I've photographed Kate Moss nude, but even [young gallery-goers] seem to be more involved with the bodies that show signs of wear and tear, the ones that show evidence of having been lived in."

Although he persuaded friends to stand naked in front of those banks of strobes, he did spare them to the extent of not identifying them, and not showing their faces. Like the best of his Polaroid nudes, these images make the most of the tension that can be set up between representation at its most literal and abstraction at its most ambitious. And like those Polaroids, they are far removed from the "abstract" nudes of photographers like Edward Weston and Bill Brandt in that they avoid all compositional artifice, depending instead on the basic symmetry of the body when seen from a full-frontal or rear view.

A remarkable offshoot of the daguerreotypes is the series of portrait tapestries, which Chuck has been producing since 2006. Developed in collaboration with Donald Farnsworth of Magnolia Editions, a company based in Oakland, California, and woven at a centuries-old family-owned factory in Belgium, these portrait tapestries exploit the possibilities inherent in the jacquard weaving technology developed in the Victorian era. In those days looms were programmed with the aid of then-revolutionary punch cards—the kind also used in player pianos and which found an updated use in the early days of computers. Today the process begins with the scanning of a photographic image that becomes the basis for the digital file that will control the loom. Although the images scanned are just 8 1/2 inches tall, the tapestries that result are almost nine feet high, a degree of enlargement that is made possible by the fact that a strobe-lit daguerreotype contains so much information.

This is not just a simple matter of scanning then weaving, which would produce something that was little more than an expensive reproduction. Rather, the artist modifies the digital information at every stage of production, first of all online and then by reference to samples of woven imagery that travel to and fro between Brussels and New York.

Remarkably, these large tapestries—woven from archival cotton—are able to capture something of the sheen and much of the elusive character of the tiny daguerreotypes from which they are derived. From a distance they appear to be black-and-white images—or more accurately, images made up of photographic grays—but close inspection reveals that they are in fact woven from a multitude of colored threads, ranging from primaries to tints, with more than a hundred used to achieve the desired effect in any one tapestry.

These tapestries effectively illustrate Chuck Close's approach to art, both intuitive and intellectual, which is to innovate by using a modern form of imaging—photography—as the starting point from which to re-explore traditional methods of image-making, some of which, like weaving, have been around since prehistoric times. The incremental and time-consuming processes he has adopted since the outset of his career contrast utterly with the ability of a camera to capture an image in a single gulp. His art is suffused with a kind of aesthetic and ethical tension between the instantaneous and the labor-intensive. The subjects of his portraits are captured by the camera for a fraction of a second. Reconstructing a facsimile of that moment—sometimes years later—whether as a painting or a multiple edition—demands the artist's attention for months at a time. In the case of the prints and multiples, it also involves the concentrated labor of collaborators who may be preparing batches of tinted pulp or transferring images on Mylar to screens ready to be proofed, while Chuck is in his studio confronting a

Self-Portrait, 2006. Jacquard tapestry, 103 x 79 in. (261.6 x 200.7 cm)

half-finished canvas. At key points, however—as decisions are made and proofs are pulled—he will be on hand to give his approval or direct the making of changes. Process is the guiding principle of all his work, but in these collaborative projects it takes on a special importance.

Self-Portrait, 2006 being woven on an electronic Jacquard loom

President Bill Clinton, 2006. Oil on canvas, 108 1/2 x 84 in. (275.6 x 213.4 cm)

Chapter 24

From the Oval Office to the Kremlin

At Chuck Close's most recent New York show, which opened at Pace Wilden-stein's Twenty-fifth Street gallery[21] in May 2009, there was a room of paintings and a room of jacquard tapestries. The paintings included self-portraits, portraits of family members, of artists, and, less predictably, the forty-second President of the United States, William Jefferson Clinton. The daguerreotype-derived tapestries included more self-portraits, portraits of art world figures, and also the portrait of someone more commonly found on the covers of supermarket magazines, Brad Pitt, who was in attendance at the private viewing.

A couple of days later, in his studio, Chuck brought up the topic of his subjects, and viewers' reaction to them.

"I know that people are asking, how come Brad Pitt's in the show? The reality is, things change—my life has changed. When I made those early paintings, I was painting people I knew—people I happened to see all the time. Outside of SoHo nobody knew who they were, but today if you look at those first black-and-white pictures you see Richard Serra—famous sculptor . . . you see Phil Glass—famous musician—big stars in their own worlds. I didn't know that was going to happen. And later on you'll find Bob Rauschenberg, Jasper Johns, Roy Lichtenstein, Cindy Sherman, and a lot of people who are hardly anonymous. My world has changed. My life is different. I still have the old friends, and they're as special to me as they always were. Some have become well known and some haven't—but now I lead the kind of life where I meet a lot of different kinds of people and some of them happen to be famous. *W* was doing a story on Brad Pitt, and Brad requested me to take his photograph, because he wanted someone who wouldn't flatter him. I had no problem about turning one of those pictures into a tapestry because I like Brad and I respect the seriousness of his involvement with art and with architecture."

The story of how the Clinton portrait came about is more complex and is better understood in the context of White House invitations Chuck has received over the years. A number of these were during the Clinton years, the occasion of the first being a ceremony paying tribute to the American Academy in Rome, while others were connected to conferences dedicated to the handicapped, learning disabilities, and various cultural issues. Three events stand out, however.

Chuck Close photographing Bill Clinton in the White House, 1996

The first of these was the photographic shoot conducted in the Oval Office in 1996. Chuck had been active in fund-raising during Clinton's first run for the White House, and the purpose of this session was to shoot Polaroids that could be used to generate an edition, or editions, that could be sold to raise money for the President's reelection. For the occasion, the Oval Office was transformed into a studio with protective covering draped over the carpet, lighting equipment dotted about, a temporary black backdrop placed in front of the Resolute Desk, and most important, the presence of the giant Polaroid camera on its wheeled dolly.

"We were setting up—very absorbed with what we were doing," Chuck remembers. "Leslie and Maggie were there, and Maggie, who was still very young, wasn't

Bill, 1996. Polaroid photograph, 26 1/2 x 22 in. (67.3 x 55.9 cm)

at all impressed by the surroundings—she would have preferred to have been almost anywhere else. Then the President arrived. You somehow expect him to make a grand entrance with a blast of trumpets or something, but he just walked in very casually with some staff members in tow. The first that I knew he was there was when Maggie looked up and spotted him and said, 'Oh . . . *my* . . . *God!*' He got right down on the floor and started playing with her, then spent a lot of time with his arm around Leslie."

In this relaxed atmosphere, Chuck went to work. As the Polaroids were pulled from the camera, one by one, and allowed to develop, they were clipped to a board leaning against the marble fireplace so that they could be studied by the President and the artist. The session turned out well, but the photos were never used for their intended purpose because it was pointed out by the White House legal staff that photographs taken in the Oval Office could not be used by a sitting president for campaign purposes.

The second occasion was a candlelight dinner held under canvas on the West Lawn of the White House in May 1998. The event celebrated the announcement of a "Gift to the Nation" being made under the auspices of the charitable foundation Friends of Art and Preservation in Embassies. Chaired by collector Jo Carole Lauder, wife of Ronald Lauder, himself a former ambassador, the FAPE had hatched the program of making what was described as a Millennial Gift to the Nation in the form of 200 works of art by important American artists. The dinner was highlighted by Dorothy Lichtenstein presenting the President with the program's inaugural gift, a 1990 painting, *Reflections on Senorita*, by her husband Roy, who had died not long before. Chuck then presented an edition of woodcut portraits of Roy Lichtenstein to be distributed to 150 embassies around the world.

Addressing the assembled guests, Chuck remarked that his gift both celebrated Roy Lichtenstein and honored Hillary Rodham Clinton's efforts to have contemporary art take its place in the White House. He also remarked on his desire to see "pictures of artists in our federal buildings instead of just officials," and he inserted a dig at Congressional Republicans whom he blamed for polarizing support for the arts and for attacking the freedom of expression.

In his response, the President gently chided Chuck for these latter remarks, saying "There still is, albeit smaller, a deep level of bipartisan support for the arts." That out of the way, he thanked Chuck "for this wonderful gift and making Roy be here in a way tonight." He also took note of Chuck's habit at that period of listening to Aretha Franklin while working (by then his soap opera era was over), saying that, given the energy of Chuck's work, he was tempted to issue an Executive Order instructing all agencies to play Aretha's music from 9 to 5 every day.

At this dinner Leslie was seated next to the President, Chuck sat at the First Lady's table, and Georgia was seated with Chelsea Clinton. The Closes were also guests at a follow-up dinner on the South Lawn, in June of the following year, to celebrate the full implementation of the FAPE program. This was attended by a number of other artists, including Robert Rauschenberg and Jasper Johns, and Mrs. Clinton, in her remarks, spoke of having been entrusted with personally delivering one of Chuck's Roy Lichtenstein prints to the American embassy at the Hague.

National Arts Award Dinner, December 20, 2000:
Chuck Close, President Bill Clinton, First Lady Hillary Rodham Clinton, Leslie Close

Chuck's final visit to the White House during the Clinton administration was as one of the winners of the National Medal of Arts for the year 2000. The National Medal of the Arts was initiated by Congress in 1984 and is awarded each year to a small number of distinguished artists, or patrons of the arts, nominated by the National Council of the Arts, an advisory body to the National Endowment of the Arts. Recipients have ranged from Martha Graham to Bob Hope to Smokey Robinson, and in 2000 the list included, along with Chuck, Maya Angelou, country singer Eddie Arnold, Mikhail Baryshnikov, jazz legend Benny Carter, playwright Horton Foote, National Public Radio's Lewis Manilow, Claes Oldenburg, Itzhak Perlman, Harold Prince, and Barbra Streisand.

Chuck was amused to discover that he had been passed over in previous years because of his earlier political activities and his travels as a young man, which had attracted the attention of the FBI. While in Europe under the Fulbright Program in the 1960s, he had visited—more than once in some cases—countries that were then behind the iron curtain. These expeditions had been noted, as had the *Betsy Ross Revisited* scandal during his University of Washington days, and the furor surrounding his alleged "urine" art while teaching at the University of Massachusetts. A few years later, his leadership role in the art community in the wake of the Kent State shootings had been carefully monitored. Those big fat cameras with telephoto lenses, outside the NYU Student Union Building in the spring of 1970, had been fully loaded.

Chuck's recent political activities have been more mainstream in character, but equally passionate in intent. He has been very active in fund-raising, organizing art auctions that contributed millions to Al Gore's presidential campaign and Hillary Clinton's run for the U.S. Senate. (The Hillary Clinton lapel button, featuring one of Chuck's photographs of her, has become a collector's item.)

In August of 2005, Chuck photographed Bill Clinton in his Harlem headquarters for the cover of *New York Magazine*, and was particularly taken with one of the resulting Polaroids.

"Clinton is very seductive," he later told Alastair Sook of the London *Telegraph*. "When he looks into your eyes, he has an almost laser-beam-like lock-on thing he does. He makes you feel like he's really connected to you."[22]

Chuck believed that he had captured this look in that particular photograph, and felt that it was an image he could use as the basis for a painting. Making a portrait of a former president was about as far from his original principles as could be imagined, however, and he did not rush into the project. The nearest Chuck had ever come to accepting a commission was his 1997–98 portrait of Jasper Johns, painted at the behest of financier Ian M. Cumming, and presented by Cumming to the National Portrait Gallery in Washington, D.C. Chuck felt he could undertake that assignment because Johns is an artist he knows and admires, so that this was a painting that he might well have initiated without any outside intervention. He saw it as an opportunity rather than as a commission.

It was Cumming once again who raised the possibility of Chuck doing a portrait of former President Clinton to be presented to a national institution. This time Chuck was more hesitant. Given the subject, he found the commission hard to refuse, but in accepting it he imposed conditions. He would make the painting on the understanding that if for any reason it did not come up to his standards he would have the right to destroy it. And he would only make the painting if Clinton approved of both the idea and the actual image.

The latter was taken care of when Chuck brought a selection of photographs to Hillary Clinton's birthday party at the home of Richard Holbrooke, former Ambassador to the United Nations, and showed them to Bill Clinton. To his relief, Clinton picked the one that he had singled out.

To paint an art world celebrity like Jasper Johns is one thing, but to paint the likeness of someone who for eight years was the most powerful man in the world presents an entirely different kind of challenge, full of potential pitfalls. Chuck Close has never been accused of indulging in flattery in the way he portrays his subjects, yet over the centuries the concept of pictorial puffery has become so attached to portraits of powerful men that viewers might read it into the painting even if it were not there. One way of avoiding this would be to go out of one's way to be unflattering. Lucian Freud's 2001 portrait of England's Queen Elizabeth might be taken as an example of that approach (though in Freud's case the refusal to flatter is habitual). The idea of being *deliberately* unflattering, though, is as alien to Chuck as its opposite.

Having agreed to make a portrait of Clinton, then, he went about the painting just as he went about any other, except that, as he liked to joke, "I had to be careful his teeth didn't look like Chiclets." As things turned out, Chuck was happy with the finished painting, which is neither particularly flattering nor unflattering, though he did remark to a studio visitor, "He's going to hate it."

At the time of this writing, Bill Clinton has not yet seen his portrait, which is destined for the National Gallery in Washington and has already been exhibited in London, St. Petersburg, and New York. The occasion for the London showing was Chuck's third exhibition at Jay Jopling's White Cube Gallery, which has become his principal overseas outlet. Jopling launched White Cube in 1993 in a small space on Duke Street St. James, the heart of the traditional London gallery district, near the Royal Academy, and the Christie's and Sotheby's auction houses. The gallery quickly made a name for itself by representing many of the noisily controversial "Young Brits"–Tracy Emin, Damien Hirst, Jake and Dinos Chapman, among others. Chuck's first White Cube show was a selection of photographs. Soon the gallery expanded to a much larger space in Hoxton, in London's East End, where in 2003 Chuck had his second White Cube show, though he did not attend the opening which was scheduled days after Leslie was diagnosed with breast cancer, causing much consternation, especially since her mother was also suffering from breast cancer at the time. (Both are now in remission.) Instead of being in Hoxton, then, the Closes found themselves spending time at Memorial Sloan-Kettering Cancer Center in Manhattan.

By the time of Chuck's third London exhibition opened, on October 2007, White Cube had expanded to yet another location, a custom-built modernist structure tucked away behind Duke Street St. James' august facades, in Mason's Yard, an urban oasis accessible by narrow alleyways. Scheduled for the eve of the Frieze Fair—London's biggest art event—the private viewing was a lavish affair followed by a celebrity-studded party at the Ritz Hotel. The British media responded enthusiastically to the show, which included paintings and tapestries, and plans were put in place to ship the paintings that had been included, along with a couple of newer works, to St. Petersburg, where Chuck had been invited to exhibit at the Hermitage Museum. It was an event he eagerly prepared for.

When considering his achievements, it becomes easy to forget the level of Chuck Close's disability. In addition to being confined to a wheelchair, his compromised immune system means that he is prone to all kinds of illnesses. Many people in his condition become virtually housebound, or at best confined to making limited neighborhood expeditions. Along with maintaining a career, however, Chuck has remained a fearless traveler, relishing trips to places as far afield as Russia, either to attend his own exhibitions or to visit or revisit the world's great museums. He had not made many trips abroad in his early New York years, but in the 1980s, he and Leslie traveled to Europe several times, although the primary purpose of these visits had been to allow Leslie to visit English gardens as part of her research, and museums were given relatively short shrift.

After the Event, however, as soon as he felt fit enough to take extensive trips, Chuck began to make up for lost time. As can be imagined, these expeditions involved an enormous amount of preparation since a quadriplegic faces difficulty merely getting on and off a plane. Reservations must be made in hotels that have adequate wheelchair access, not something that can be taken for granted in all countries. Power chairs must be rented, and nurses placed on standby. Nothing is easy. If no van fitted to accommodate wheelchairs is available, then the quadriplegic is faced with the problem of getting in and out of taxis or others kinds of conventional vehicles. The cost alone would make such trips unthinkable for most people in Chuck's condition, but, even given the fact that he is able to meet such expenses, travel of this sort is still a formidable undertaking.

Carol Johnson, a nurse who has made a number of trips with Chuck, both abroad and in the United States, explains some of the routine challenges.

"You'll get to the departure gate and find that there's no Jetway so you have to arrange an alternate way to board the plane, or the airline hasn't provided an aisle chair—the kind that's narrow enough to go down the aisle of a plane—or they haven't reserved the seat you had asked for, the one next to the door. Even when everything goes right, you're holding up other passengers, and of course they're impatient and it's difficult for them to comprehend what's taking so long.

"Then there's the bathroom problem. Sometimes Chuck travels with a male nurse but, if he's with me, do we go into the men's room or the women's room? Most of all you pray that Chuck doesn't have to be catheterized during a flight, but once we had to do it in the seats with flight attendants holding up a blanket."

Sometimes Leslie would accompany Chuck on these post-Event expeditions, but more often not since she found his voracious appetite "to see everything" exhausting. On a number of trips he has taken Mark Greenwold—who shares that drive—as a traveling companion. Greenwold had his own first experience of the great museums of Europe in 1987 when he was awarded the prestigious Rome Prize Fellowship from the American Academy in Rome. He has since had the opportunity to revisit Rome with Chuck, and other cities they have explored together include London, Paris, Madrid, Venice, Baden-Baden, and Munich. (In 1994, the Staatliche Kunsthalle in Baden-Baden was the site of a Chuck Close retrospective that was installed later that year at the Kunstbau Lenbachhaus in Munich.) Probably no one has looked at more paintings in Chuck's company than Greenwold. Luckily their tastes do not often clash—both love the Flemish masters and detest Goya—though Greenwold remarks that it is an advantage to be in charge of Chuck's wheelchair when doing the rounds of a museum.

"Chuck is highly selective. He wants to get from the Velázquez on one side of the gallery to the Zurbarán on the other, and if there happens to be some exquisite little still life by some minor master you've never heard of somewhere in between, he might not want to bother. If I'm pushing the wheelchair, I can control the pace and stop to look at anything I want to."

Mark's most vivid memories of these trips, though, are of the times when pace was irrelevant. In Padua, for example, the pair of them spent the best part of two days in the Scrovegni Chapel gazing at the frescoes in Giotto's cycle depicting the life of the Virgin and the life of Christ—masterpieces that ushered in the Renaissance.

"Coach parties full of school kids kept filing through the place," Greenwold remembers. "It didn't matter. We just stayed there, hour after hour, totally carried away."

In Kolmar, at the Musée d'Unterlinden, they had a similarly transporting experience in front of the panels of Matthias Grünewald's Isenheim Altarpiece, and at the Louvre both were in tears when confronted with Jan van Eyck's *Madonna of Chancellor Rolin*.

The St. Petersburg show, mentioned above, was scheduled to open in February 2008, a time of year when the Russian climate renders travel intimidating for anyone, let alone a quadriplegic. Wheelchair access is unheard of, even in the best hotels, and navigating snowy sidewalks is made intimidating by the fact that the partially ploughed roadways—even Nevsky Prospekt—are spread with dirt rather than salt, generating a filthy sludge that is thrown up by the wheels of passing vehicles. Chuck was not, however, disappointed by the Hermitage itself and its extraordinary collections (though his traveling nurse had an unpleasant surprise one day when she stepped outside for a cigarette and found a man—apparently freshly shot—sprawled bleeding in the snow. A soldier standing over him demanded to know if the victim was dead or alive).

Chuck's own most disturbing experience of the trip came when he was traveling from St. Petersburg to Moscow, where he was to have talks concerning a possible exhibition at the Pushkin Museum. At the St. Petersburg airport he was separated from the rest of his party by officious airline employees, who seemed sullenly determined to make his life as miserable as possible for the offense of being in a wheelchair. He was left in a kind of gulag, outside an office, having been given to understand that the four uniformed people inside—two hostile-seeming men and two disinterested women—would see to it that he would rejoin his party in the departure lounge in time for the flight. He waited but nothing happened. Occasionally one of the lugubrious functionaries inside would stare out at him, but still nothing happened. He tried to attract their attention. Someone finally emerged from the office, but did not speak English and nothing came of it, nor did anyone seem to care. With the flight's departure time rapidly approaching, Chuck began to panic. Eventually, though, two burly policemen arrived. They lifted Chuck out of his wheelchair and, grabbing him under the arms, dragged him face-forward up two long flights of stairs, his toes bouncing on each step. At the top of the stairs, they propped him against a column and went back for the wheelchair.

Chuck reached the departure lounge just in time to board the flight, only to discover that there was no Jetway permitting wheelchair access. Instead, he was taken outside onto the concrete apron and—perched upon, but not strapped into, an unstable wheelchair—he was loaded onto the platform of a scissors lift which raised him, through a freezing, near gale-force Baltic wind, to a narrow ramp across which he was wheeled—inches to spare on either side—to a hatch and into the plane.

"I have never," he says, "been so terrified. I thought I was going to die."

In Moscow his spirits were somewhat revived by the treasures of the Push-kin Museum and by a private tour of the Kremlin for which his guide was the daughter of the original cosmonaut Yuri Gagarin. Even so, he returned to New York swearing he was through with foreign travel. His resolve lasted a matter of weeks.

Chapter 25

Inspiration Is for Amateurs

The scope of Chuck's travels gives some sense of his undiminished appetite for life, which is matched by his appetite for work. Given that it takes him months to make a single painting—over a year in some instances—his total output is surprisingly large. As we have seen, this is because he explores multiple avenues at the same time, helped by the fact that throughout his career he has tended to work something akin to regular office hours.

"Inspiration," he's fond of saying, "is for amateurs. The rest of us go to the studio and just get on with it."

This in itself is an expression of art as process, the theme that runs through his career. For all of his success, and for all of the unwanted drama that have transformed his life, Chuck remains the same artist who moved into the freezing loft at 27 Greene Street in 1967. He continues to manufacture objects in much the same way as the sweatshop workers who toiled in that space before him, with manual repetition a principal ingredient. His work differs from theirs in that the end product is hung on museum walls and he gets to enjoy the full benefit of his labors. He is free to take pleasure in making something the old-fashioned way—by hand—and even in his collaborations with printmakers, which inevitably involve some technology, he likes to be as hands-on and pragmatic as possible, often overcoming problems by coming up with solutions that he describes, with satisfaction, as "low-tech."

Chuck jokes that he has been in the art world long enough to see painting pronounced dead several times. No one could be more devoted to painting as an activity than Chuck Close, and I believe it's fair to say that he revels in it more today than ever. That he does so may have something to do with the kind of paintings that he has been making during the past two decades, which allow free rein to his gifts for inventive brushwork and juicy color; plus, the fact that he is able to make paintings at all, given the disaster of his paralysis, is itself a source of continuing satisfaction.

Naturally he regrets the loss of manual dexterity and tells of an afternoon at the Metropolitan Museum of Art, a few years ago, during which a melancholy realization set in.

"I wandered into the galleries where the early Flemish masters are hung—Robert Campin, van Eyck, van der Weyden, Petrus Christus, Memling—wonderful artists. And I realized that many of the painters I love the most—Vermeer too of course—did these small, highly-detailed, delicate paintings that are so perfectly rendered you almost can't see how they were made: the very opposite of what I was doing. And it hit me that physically I would never be able to do anything like that again, even if I wanted to. It was a sad moment."

These are the words of someone who feels that he once possessed the gifts to use a paintbrush to set down absolutely anything that he chose to, as he chose to, and they cast an interesting light on his devotion to process. As Leslie pointed out, prior to becoming a quadriplegic Chuck habitually confronted himself with self-imposed problems to be solved and limitations to be overcome. This certainly helped emphasize the idea of process as the means to an end, but it also suggests that one reason for Chuck turning to process was as a way of keeping his own virtuosity in check.

Coming to artistic maturity in New York in 1967 was very different from earning the right to be called a master in Flanders in the first half of the fifteenth century, though that era too was one of radical change. The Flemish artists of that period were building upon the pictorial naturalism that had emerged in the work of miniaturists like the Limbourg Brothers, and doing so in the context of new discoveries regarding perspective and optics. Those were exciting times for artists, but everything pointed in a single direction—towards the perfection of illusionism.

In 1967, by contrast, a number of paths could be taken. Color field painting was still a strong presence, while other nonfigurative painters were experimenting with the possibilities inherent in shaped and extended canvases. Minimalism was in its heyday and conceptualism was on the rise. Someone who made the choice of pursuing process art could decide to follow any one of several directions, since the process selected would determine the outcome. The art made by Richard Serra is very different from that produced by Sol LeWitt, and neither resembles Chuck Close's work in the least, though all three have much in common in terms of underlying principles.

Bob, 1990. Oil on canvas, 72 x 60 in. (182.9 x 152.4 cm)

What makes Chuck's work so different from that of his fellow process artists is the fact that he was able to match this latter-day New York art world philosophy to the concerns that had occupied the talents of those fifteenth-century paint-ers in cities like Bruges and Louvain: the exploration of illusionism. That was something that had fascinated him since he analyzed those covers of *Time* and *The Saturday Evening Post* through his grandmother's magnifying glass. This paid off when he realized that by turning to the mechanical illusion created by the camera, he could resolve the apparent conflict between illusionism and the obsession with flatness that had gripped advanced artists throughout the modernist era, and especially since the revolution of Pollock's drip paintings.

Chuck has built his career on finding ways of fabricating images in which the tension between photographic "reality" and the flatness of the canvas—the struggle between the chimerical quality of illusion and the concreteness of abstraction—is always the dominant dynamic. His achievement has been to revisit the *discovery* of illusionism found in the works of those fifteenth-century Flemish masters, and to rethink it in terms of modernism. (This is especially apropos if one is prepared to accept, as he is, the notion that artists were making use of the camera obscura six centuries ago.) In a very real sense, his work encompasses the arc of western art from van Eyck to de Kooning, Pollock and Johns, and even Warhol.

Chuck Close's portraits are not the kind of paintings that you look at casually, thinking, "That's rather good." They grab your attention because of their monumental scale, then hold it because each of them contains so much information, and each bit of information is constantly transforming every other bit of information, shifting from description to abstraction as the viewer's position changes. Many early modernists—Wassily Kandinsky, for example—talked of making paintings that had the fluidity of music and its freedom from imitation. Seen from close up, Chuck's prismatic grid paintings come as near to being visual music as anything one can imagine, each dab and swirl of paint a note in a vast sea of orchestral texture. Yet from a slight distance, this chromatic texture shapes up into something more thematic, peppered with pictorial leitmotifs. A few more steps back and the music dissolves into description of the most sophisticated kind. (Appropriately, some viewers talk of performing a dance in front of a Close painting, moving to and fro so as to experience all the nuances of this play between the lyrical and the figurative.)

Nobody looks at a painting with the intensity of the artist who made it. Chuck Close's paintings, however, are made in such a way—and this again is a function of process, and especially its incremental aspect—that they challenge anyone who encounters them to at least *attempt* that kind of intensity. This is what gives them such a hold on the viewer. They do not readily reveal their secrets, and yet one hungers to uncover those secrets. It's possible to visit these portraits again

Leslie, 2002. Oil on canvas, 72 x 60 in. (182.9 x 152.4 cm)

and again and discover something new each time (or rather it's impossible *not* to find something new). Understanding them demands active involvement in the way they were made, as well as enjoyment of the finished product. This is true of the prismatic grid portraits, where the surface of the finished paintings provides evidence of the process, but it is equally true of the continuous-tone portraits precisely because in those the method of fabrication has been so perfectly concealed. In either case, comprehension of the process adds greatly to appreciation of the work.

While the likenesses of non–art world celebrities like the Clintons and Brad Pitt may garner special attention, Chuck has continued to make portraits of fellow artists like Lyle Ashton Harris, Cecily Brown, Lynda Benglis, Robert Cottingham, Inka Essenhigh, Andres Serrano, legendary dancer Merce Cunningham, and contemporary Chinese master Zhang Huan. Along with these have come more portraits of family members, including Georgia and Maggie and both of Leslie's parents.

Chuck's paintings and prints of Leslie make a study in themselves. Here is a face he has known better than any but his own, making the treatments especially interesting. In the first major version—the six-foot-tall watercolor made in 1972–73—Leslie, her eyes turned slightly away from the viewer as if her mind is elsewhere, is shown at the age of twenty-four but looking older. This is the face of an attractive woman, but no effort has been made to strengthen that perception. Certainly this is not the portrait of a muse. Rather, the painting adheres to the mug shot principle of the early portraits with no clue given to the fact that this might be the artist's wife unless in that there is something subjective and wistful about the image—qualities not found in other portraits of the period.

In a 1977 pastel derived from the same image, the grid of colored dots softens the image and restores Leslie's youth and attractiveness. In a small-scale 1986 watercolor, by contrast, and in the Japanese woodcut that derives from it, Leslie's face dissolves into patchworks of color that—especially in the case of the print—are as near to being abstract as anything Chuck had made up to this point.

The most spectacular of Chuck's portraits of Leslie is the very large fingerprint version produced in 1985. This is a magnificent painting, but once again it is far from flattering. The head-on angle and shallow depth of field make it appear that Leslie might have an incipient double chin (which was not the case), the lighting makes her nose appear shiny and her teeth gray, and the fingerprint technique itself tends to make her skin seem coarse (which it is not).

In his post-Event portraits of Leslie, the fragmentation found in the 1986 water-color and woodcut becomes explicit, and Chuck employs it with an inventive free-dom only occasionally approached in other portraits (notably some self-portraits), perhaps because the familiarity of Leslie's face permits him a license he does not take with most subjects. Or perhaps that familiarity frees him from the demands of descriptive fidelity imposed by his prosopagnosia. Whatever the reason, the portraits of Leslie are always fascinating in a way that might be described as be-ing as much psychological as aesthetic.

In 2002 Chuck created a likeness of his wife that utilizes a diagonal grid. In this incarnation, her face is tightly cropped and turned towards the viewer in such a way that her head tilts at an angle to her shoulders. The background is reduced to narrow parentheses of darkness. The lighting of the face is difficult to interpret, making this one of the least explicitly photographic of Chuck's recent portraits. There is a liquid aspect to the way in which the features are evoked, with fluid shapes overflowing the grid lines as one patch of color seems to spill into the next. There is something almost cartoonish about the treatment of the eyes, and the handling of the lips is extremely sensual, incorporating a pair of brightly colored hearts.

Despite those symbols of ardor, this is the most unflattering portrait of his wife that Chuck has ever painted. It's dangerous to read into a painting thoughts that may not have been present, or at least not intended at the time, and in this image Chuck was clearly exploring some of his perennial aesthetic interests—the concept of allover painting for one—and some of his contemporary concerns, for example an interest in imagery that seems about to dissolve. Even so there is much to ponder in this portrait. While indeed cartoonish, the eyes splinter into fragments in a way that is almost sinister. The mouth is sensual, but it seems to have been bruised out of shape, the lower lip swollen, the distortion at odds with the hearts imprinted on it. This is a painting awash in ambiguity, intimate yet curiously distant, as if someone familiar had morphed into a total stranger. In hindsight, it's tempting to see this portrait as hinting that the Closes' relationship had changed, and not for the better. Is there perhaps an undercurrent of anger here, blended with a sense of loss?

Chapter 26

Portraits of the Artist

In his essay for the catalogue of Chuck Close's 1998 MoMA retrospective, Kirk Varnedoe compared the pugnaciously punk 1968 black-and-white *Big Self-Portrait* with a more recent likeness in which the artist appears as a prosperous citizen, courted by museum directors and wealthy collectors.[23] There is nothing particularly novel about this passage from bohemianism to establishmentarianism. It is a journey that has been made by many successful artists in all fields. Picasso, in the first flush of success, moved from the ramshackle surroundings of the Bateau Lavoir to the glittering world of Maxim's and lavish balls in the *hotels particuliers* of the Avenue de la Grande Armée. This did not mean that old friends, haunts, or habits were abandoned. Most important, there was always the studio as a refuge. In the studio, the rules never change. It is the place where the artist is most at home, where trusted cronies come to visit, and where he carries on the activities that define who he is.

Yet that shift referred to by Varnedoe cannot be ignored. In an earlier chapter, I pointed out the evolution that is apparent when comparing *Big Self-Portrait* with a large 1976–77 black-and-white watercolor self-portrait. During that decade from 1967 to 1977, Chuck went from being a Young Turk to becoming a family man—or, more accurately, the image of himself that he presented to the world *by way of his art* was subjected to that transition. Anyone who knew him throughout that period would attest to the fact that Chuck's underlying personality did not undergo any great sea change. It is also true to say that the sneering punk of *Big Self-Portrait* was a heightened version of the Chuck Close you might have run into at Fanelli's or Max's at the time it was painted. The real Chuck Close was an altogether friendlier and friendlier-looking person. The family man image found in the later of these two portraits is somewhat truer to the real Chuck Close you might have encountered eating lunch at Jerry's on Prince Street circa 1977.

Chuck's career began with *Big Self-Portrait*, and since then, he has created more than a hundred self-portraits—paintings, drawings, prints, photographs, tapestries, even holograms—enough for a major retrospective, which is exactly what ensued in 2005 when just such an exhibition, organized by the Walker Art Center in Minneapolis and the San Francisco Museum of Modern Art, opened at the Walker before traveling to San Francisco, Atlanta, and Buffalo. Co-curated by SFMOMA's Madeleine Grynsztejn and the Walker's Siri Engberg, this retrospective brought together eighty-five images of Chuck Close by Chuck Close.

The impact of the show was overwhelming, not only to visitors but to the artist himself, who of course had never seen all these images together before. At a preview of the San Francisco installation, Chuck at one point fled the fourth-floor galleries of the museum complaining loudly, "I can't stand it! God, I must be so e*go*ce*ntric*—painting myself so many times . . . All those faces! I'm getting out of here!" Five minutes later, he was back in front of a huge 1973 dot drawing, studying it intently as if he had never seen it before.

I recall thinking, at the time, of Chuck's habit of referring to the person in his self-portraits as "him"—an understandable distancing device, but one that does not work so well if you are surrounded by multiple examples. "Him" had become "them." It was as if apprehending these likenesses *en masse* was somehow appalling because it did not permit Chuck the opportunity to remove himself from the subject matter. How many people, after all, have ever confronted so many self-portraits—an army of surrogate selves—in one place? It is difficult to even imagine the experience. This would be nothing like going through an album of old snapshots. Rather, it would be like staring into a mirror at different times in one's life, years and even decades apart. I had the impression at the preview that Chuck was fully comfortable only when confronting a single likeness, one-on-one, and blanking out the rest. That was a more familiar experience. It put him back in the studio.

For the ordinary visitor, what gave this exhibition its singular impact was precisely the fact that it was the same face portrayed over and over again, but with so much variety in terms of scale and treatment. That variety enabled the viewer to grasp the importance of process in Chuck's work more strongly than was the case with the MoMA retrospective. The show was hung to emphasize chronology so that it also permitted the viewer to see how that particular face had changed over the decades, and to comprehend the changing ways in which the artist had portrayed it as it aged.

Thirty-seven of the self-portraits in that exhibition were made before Chuck's hospitalization in 1988, and forty-eight were made afterward. Of the latter, nineteen had been made after the New York retrospective, which is to say between 1998 and 2006, a period of just eight years. (Several newer examples have been added since that date.) His career began with self-portraiture, and it is striking that there has been a manifold increase in his attention to the subject as it has progressed. Moreover, whereas the pre-1988 self-portraits were variations on a handful of basic images, the more recent self-portraits—especially since 1998—are derived from a greater variety of maquettes.

The accumulated self-portraits can be seen as a visual autobiography that breaks down into three periods. The first centers on the inaugural *Big Self-Portrait* and includes a smallish number of drawings and maquette photographs made between 1967 and 1975. These present Chuck Close as an uncompromising anti-establishmentarian tyro, eager to make his mark and unwilling to take crap from anyone. They were made at a time when he was presenting himself as an artist to be taken seriously because of the originality of his vision. At the same time, they served to announce Chuck's arrival on the scene as someone whose face you'd better get to know if you wanted to stay *au courant*. To this end, they were effective promotional tools, sometimes—especially in the case of *Big Self-Portrait*—incorporating an element of theatricality. The extent to which this was deliberate is debatable, but nonetheless that was the effect produced.

The middle period is much more substantial in terms of length of time and quantity of examples, lasting approximately from 1976 until the New York retrospective in 1998, allowing for a degree of overlap at either end. The images produced during this period, especially its first half, are almost self-effacing. There is nothing theatrical about them. All of the drama is purely in the realm of how the artist transforms these rather neutral likenesses into successful works of art. Painted in 1986 and 1987, the self-portraits included in the 1988 Pace Gallery exhibition—the first prismatic grid show, and the last before the Event—were made from maquettes as unassuming as passport photographs. The other portraits in that show—whose subjects were Alex Katz, Francesco Clemente, Cindy Sherman, and Lucas Samaras—were distinctly theatrical by comparison. This tendency continued after Chuck's rehabilitation. Theatricality is often apparent in the portraits of others—John Chamberlain, for example—but did not begin to creep back into the self-portraits until the latter half of the nineties.

Since the 1998 retrospective—the third period—Chuck has produced a number

Self-Portrait, 2004–5. Oil on canvas, 102 x 84 in. (259.1 x 213.4 cm)

of self-portraits in which he presents himself with the same flair that he employed for Chamberlain, Lichtenstein, and other "name" artists, making no bones about his status as a full-fledged art world personality. This is true of works in all media—multiples, Polaroids, daguerreotypes—but especially in the paintings.

I am thinking in particular of one made in 2004–5, eight-and-a-half feet tall and structured on a vertical/horizontal grid. Working from a Polaroid in which highlights and shadows are firmly delineated, Chuck produced a painting that is extremely elegant in a manner that recalls the portraits of Hans Holbein (one of his great favorites). Indeed, the bearded face that peers out through circular glasses might belong to some humanist contemporary of Erasmus and Sir Thomas More. When he sat for the maquette, Chuck was wearing a black turtleneck sweater, and if the painting is seen from a distance this garment can be read as a surrogate for the black, fur-trimmed robes worn by sixteenth-century scholars. (From close up, the apparent field of black dissolves into dark swirls of subdued color.) Fragmentation makes this an entirely modern portrait, of course, and the incremental units are boldly handled, especially in areas such as the beard where they seem to read almost like software code. In its way, though—and without compromising Chuck's basic pictorial philosophy—this portrait is as theatrical as *Big Self-Portrait.* In the late sixties Chuck was laying down a challenge: "You're not going to forget this face." Forty years later he could take it for granted that many people would recognize that same face, now matured and groomed, and he frankly reveled in it. This is the face of a master by a master.

Looking at that face—the urbane face of a successful New Yorker—I am diverted back to a photograph of Chuck taken in Everett more than six decades earlier, the likeness—probably snapped by his father or his mother—of young Charles Close the boy magician. It's almost as if he is rehearsing for his later triumphs. Nonchalantly leaning on a cane, he wears a top hat and looks out at the world through round glasses (as in the 2004–5 self-portrait), a sporty bow tie at his throat. At first glance, he is the picture of confidence—a 1940s comic-strip version of a juvenile plutocrat—yet on close inspection it can be seen that he is not quite looking directly at the camera, as if perhaps a touch self-conscious—not yet quite the master of that head-on stare one knows from his paintings. This, after all, is the kid who cannot engage in sports and must rely on his instinct to entertain. He may already know that he wants to be a painter, but first he must turn himself into someone who will be noticed.

We know from friends that by the time he reached junior high school Chuck was a charismatic kid who had the chutzpah to show up at school in a Tarzan costume with a monkey on his shoulder; on the other hand, according to Chuck himself, he was also the learning-challenged student who sometimes chose to be invisible in class. Moving on to high school, we find the yearbook photograph that shows him onstage in the role of a professorial caricaturist: once again, the top-hatted embodiment of confidence, the Chuck Close his contemporaries knew—Chuck the performer, Chuck the gifted artist, Chuck the kid who played sax in the blue-and-gold uniform of the pep band on Homecoming Day. Yet he was a student whose grades were insufficient to win him a place in a good four-year college and who was forced to take advantage of open enrollment at the junior college level and scramble for a way to fulfill his ambitions.

As we have seen, the solution to this dilemma proved to be close to home in the unlikely surroundings of Everett Junior College, where his talent was given the opportunity to flourish, and where he found an extravagant exemplar of extrovert behavior in the form of department head Rus Day. Day lived his life in costume, and Chuck, in his own way, did the same. From the beginnings of his career at EJC, he sported a beard, wore a derby, and generally did everything he could to draw attention to himself (in which he was helped by his six foot three frame). At the University of Washington, he continued to cultivate the image of a dandy, as he did at Yale, where his ego flourished. Chuck Close the bohemian Beau Brummell was, coincidentally, also the Chuck Close who was trying his damndest to paint like Willem de Kooning.

Settled in New York, he embarked on a totally new track, inspired by the idea of exploiting process as a way of creating original imagery. Process art, as envisioned in 1967, was identified with the world of blue-collar labor, and it was at this time that Chuck's uniform became blue jeans, torn tees, and denim work shirts, though Chuck himself has another explanation for the change.

"That was when the whole hippie thing really began to take off. I'd been dressing like a hippie since the 1950s. Now that everyone in the East Village was doing it and it was all over the media, I didn't see any point in continuing. I didn't want to look like everyone else."

In any case, soon after his move to New York, Chuck abandoned the notion of costume as a personal statement. For the next twenty years he was intent on building upon what he had achieved with *Big Self-Portrait* and the other black-and-white heads. He still had a good eye for a juicy-colored tee-shirt, and he might indulge in a well-cut pair of white summer pants, but essentially he was all business and his wardrobe reflected that. He was no longer someone who "dressed up" precisely because he no longer needed to. His work spoke for itself.

It was not until after the Event that Chuck began to take an obvious interest in costume once more. Emerging in a wheelchair, after more than seven months of hospitalization, it was inevitable that he was concerned about how he would appear to the world he had been shut away from. There is a telling photograph taken at his artist's choice *Head On/The Modern Portrait* exhibition at the Museum of Modern Art in 1991. Immaculately groomed, Chuck *stands* in front of a wall covered with portraits—by Andy Warhol, Max Beckmann, Giacometti, and Alice Neel, among others—very erect, arms folded, all in black except for a red dress shirt, with dress pants gathered at the ankles, Turkish style, providing a *fashionista* touch.

The picture demonstrates that he is able to stand, if only for a short time—importantly symbolic at the time ("I am not a disabled artist")—but beyond that it shows an early incarnation of what will become his uniform, something that can be seen in scores of photographs taken since then, and that varies only a little whether he is visiting the White House or at work in his studio. (For daily life, all-black is the norm.)

Before his hospitalization, Chuck had been a rising star of the New York art scene, a popular and socially ubiquitous figure respected by fellow artists, collectors, and insiders of the gallery and museum world. When he emerged from the months of rehab, he found himself at the threshold of an entirely different level of fame, one that would make his face—and that uniform—familiar to a much wider audience. Chuck Close became one of the handful of art world figures who—in the footsteps of people like Pollock and Warhol—had achieved a kind of public recognition that meant they were known to people who had never seen their work in the original, or perhaps ever set foot in a gallery.

The fact that he is in a wheelchair contributes to this level of recognition, though Chuck is so personable and gregarious, and his work has become with time so accessible, that it is possible he would have achieved much the same level of fame if he had been spared the trauma of the occluded artery. On the one hand, he prides himself in the fact that he has taken professional risks in his career; on the other, there is ample evidence that since childhood he has craved recognition and was not likely to become the kind of artist who would be satisfied with the subdued respect of his peers. He does not conceal his hunger for acclaim, but paradoxically this hunger has always been moderated by an unforced, self-deprecating modesty. He remains the most approachable of public figures.

However lofty his ambitions, he probably never expected the level of fame that has accrued to him during the past twenty years, and in reality it was thrust upon him by circumstance. There was no way that the public could fail to be awed by his ability to come back from the level of injury he had suffered, and not just as someone able to function adequately in the world, but as someone who could rebuild an already distinguished career and take it to the next level. To return from the dead—and that is barely an exaggeration in this case—invests a person with a supernatural aura. To have been reborn in this way would guarantee anyone a moment of fame. For Chuck, a moment was far from enough. He was not about to let it pass; moreover, his outgoing and engaging personality, his intelligence, and his humor were perfectly suited to sustaining that moment indefinitely.

One can more accurately point to a sequence of moments that, as they accumulated, contributed to a level of fame that built steadily over almost a decade. One, already mentioned, was the 1991 MoMA *Head-On/The Modern Portrait* exhibition, which reminded people around the New York scene, and afterward in Los Angeles too, that Chuck was still very much alive and well. Later that year, at the Pace Gallery, there was an exhibition of recent portraits that demonstrated that Chuck was painting as well as ever. The image of Chuck in a wheelchair reached a wider audience in the 1993 movie *Six Degrees of Separation*, starring Will Smith, in which Chuck portrayed an artist called Andy. The MoMA retrospective was another key moment. By the millennium, Chuck had achieved full celebrity status, becoming a staple of the society pages.

Celebrity did nothing, of course, to alleviate the physical discomforts and inconveniences of being a partial quadriplegic. Nurses were still needed four times a day. Infections continued to erupt without warning, making life miserable and ruining carefully laid plans. There were nights of insomnia, wrapped up in scarves and sweaters against the cold that tormented him no matter how high the thermostat was set. These and a dozen other afflictions, some far worse, were part of his everyday reality, yet somebody meeting him for the first time would never be given any reason to suspect that he might be in pain or running a fever. When the subject of his disability is raised, Chuck has been known to reply that despite it he considers himself the luckiest person alive. At most, in another mood, he might dryly complain, "Can you imagine how sore your ass gets sitting in a wheelchair fifteen hours a day?"

Chuck finds consolation in his privileged social life, which brings him into contact with some of the most powerful and intellectually challenging people in the world, from presidents to the Dalai Lama. He likes to party, but his life away from the studio is colored by a sense of obligation that can be traced back to his church upbringing. He no longer practices any religion but still invokes the notion of tithing, which he equates especially with time donated to a variety of causes. As noted in the first chapter, until recently he sat on the board of the Whitney Museum, and in 2003 Mayor Michael Bloomberg appointed him to the New York City Cultural Affairs Commission. He is a formidable advocate for anything having to do with the promotion of art education, at all levels, and for the encouragement of young artists. Other causes he actively supports include stem cell research, immigration rights, and efforts to assist children with learning differences.

All of this makes for a life that to all appearances—even in the studio, where he is seldom alone—is very public. He is well attuned to such a life, happily interacting with people, whether old friends or total strangers, journalists or television crews, or collaborators in some print shop.

If Chuck Close is someone who, by inclination, is totally at ease with life in the spotlight, Leslie Close is quite the opposite, though she too has been quietly active in organizations such as the Cultural Landscape Foundation, the Parrish Museum, and the Society of Architectural Historians Landscape Chapter. It remains a refrain of hers that she is a very private person.

"Chuck's physical condition already meant that there had been a huge loss of privacy in our lives. I clung to what little remained, but as Chuck became more famous, it seemed that that was being eroded too. I don't begrudge him his celebrity, but sometimes it was just overwhelming—I expected him to go to bed in his tuxedo. There were wonderful moments, but I just couldn't do it every night. I needed some downtime."

The most effective form of downtime for Leslie has always been working with growing things, and since leaving her job at Wave Hill in the eighties, this has been focused on her garden in Bridgehampton. The house is set on a substantial lot that includes a large pond and stands of mature trees in an area where rolling potato fields once ran down to the Atlantic beaches. The heart of the property is the kitchen garden, an eighty-by-sixty-foot rectangle, partially sheltered from inclement weather by the main house and by Chuck's freestanding studio. This is not a puritanically functional kitchen garden with tidily regimented rows of peas, beans, lettuce, and the like obediently waiting to be harvested. Herbs, vegetables, and legumes are amply present, but the garden blends function with fantasy in the form of a kaleidoscope of flowering plants—clematis, roses, sunflowers, and hollyhocks that stir lazily in the ocean breezes. These have been woven skillfully, but without evidence of studied artifice, into the organic whole, setting off the glory of tumescent leeks and cabbages the size of basketballs. This is as sybaritic as a kitchen garden can be, as pleasing to the eye as it is stimulating to the appetite. To see it in its summer glory—a pleasure ground for monarch butterflies, swallowtails, and workaholic bees—is to understand that it is a work of art in much the same sense as Chuck's prismatic grid paintings, incremental masterpieces made up of patches and dabs and dots of color, a complex entity that changes as you draw closer to one part or another, or step back to take it in it as a whole from the verandah that fronts the house.

"For me," says Leslie, "gardening is the most satisfying thing I can imagine. It's physical, it's spiritual, and it offers all the aesthetic and intellectual challenge and enjoyment that you'd find in practicing any form of art. I have a deep need to feel in touch with the soil and with growing things."

For Chuck the Bridgehampton house offered periods of respite from the seemingly ceaseless round of activity that his life in the city had become, though for a couple of summers after the Event he found it upsetting that he had been robbed of his old Hamptons' routines.

"It had always been about riding my bike to the village or to the beach, swimming in the ocean—things I couldn't do any more. Psychologically I found it easier to adapt to being in the city."

That phase passed, however, and the Long Island studio became a haven once more, a far more peaceful place than the New York studio, which was always buzzing with assistants, nurses, urgent deliveries, interviewers, and nonstop phone calls. There were friends and visitors who had flown in from other continents or else dropped by after a late lunch at Il Buco or NoHo Star. In Bridgehampton, he could work relatively undisturbed, with only a single assistant. Increasingly, he came to do most of his actual painting there, in some cases starting work on a canvas in the New York studio then trucking it out to Long Island to be finished (the Bond Street space has a deeper pit than the country studio, thus making it more convenient to work on the upper sections of a canvas in the city). Even in the summer, however, he would spend half the week in town, partly because he thrived on its energy but also because painting had become just one of his activities, if always the most important. The print shops and photo studios he worked in were mostly located in Manhattan, his gallery was there, and the Bond Street studio was the nerve center of what had become, to all intents and purposes, a small business empire, an enterprise with a need for attorneys, accountants, book-keepers, and that often requires him to be on the spot to make decisions. (The sale of paintings has always been central to how Chuck earns his living, but he makes an average of only four or so a year so, far more than most artists, he depends for income upon the sale of photographs, prints, and other multiples.)

Chuck's original Manhattan foothold, at 27 Greene Street, is just five minutes away, but the gulf between that first grubby, heat-deprived studio and the present streamlined hive of activity is enormous.

Chapter 27

You Start Off with a Blank Canvas

As this book goes to press, Chuck Close is sixty-nine years old. He has spent the past twenty-one years as a partial quadriplegic, a coming of age that is sobering enough, but that has done nothing to impair his creativity or even to slow him down except in the most literal sense.

"You have to play the hand you've been dealt," he says. "Sometimes it works out better than you expect."

Chuck emphasizes how art rescued him from the purgatory of underachievement and obscurity that might have been expected to result from his early learning disabilities, and once again from the oblivion that could have been his fate as a consequence of the spinal artery occlusion. Instead, the dyslexic child has become as an adult the recipient of a score of honorary degrees in addition to those he has earned, and the quadriplegic who escaped death by minutes or perhaps seconds continues to create extraordinary works of art. The impression Chuck Close projects today, as always, is one of unceasing activity, as he conducts a conversation with a visitor, simultaneously takes phone calls, yells out instructions to an assistant, then zooms off in his power chair looking for a missing transparency. Lunch might be eaten on the fly—a sandwich sent in from a nearby deli—though visitors are just as likely to be swept off to a favorite local bistro for a leisurely meal filled with lively conversation. Except for the occasional dropped phone, Chuck's physical impairments hardly seem to slow him in the least.

In reality, though, there are significant constraints. The nursing routine remains a disruptive constant. Infections flare up and antibiotics drain his strength. Demanding trips, like the expedition to Russia, take their toll. Since that particular journey, he has suffered from ailments that are peripheral to his core condition, yet serious because their impact is always worsened by his compromised immune system. For quite some time Chuck has been a victim of insomnia, on occasion sleeping no more than two or three hours a night, and has long been subject to fluctuations in blood pressure that have to be controlled by medication. During one endless night in the spring of 2008, soon after his return from Russia, he woke in a cold sweat—in itself not all that unusual—took his blood pressure, and discovered it was low to the point of orthostatic hypotension, a dangerous state in which the flow of blood to the brain and vital organs can be affected. The following morning, with assistance, it took him almost an hour to struggle into a pair of pants and get out of bed.

Over the next few days his blood pressure was subject to wild swings—off the chart both high and low—and frequent visits to doctors' offices culminated in a hospital stay during which a previously undetected cardiac arrhythmia was discovered, resulting in the decision to implant a pacemaker, which had the desired result of normalizing his heartbeat and reducing the swings in blood pressure. Additionally, in providing a record of the heart's moment-to-moment activity, the pacemaker showed that Chuck was suffering from sometimes prolonged episodes of atrial fibrillation.

As if all this were not enough, a couple of months later it was discovered that he was suffering from colon cancer. This came as a shock because a relatively recent colonoscopy had given him a clean bill of health. A compromised immune system complicates things, however, as his daughter Georgia, now a gastroenterologist, had pointed out, suggesting that he should be tested more frequently. Luckily, the tumor was caught at an early stage and a section of colon was removed without complications at Manhattan's Memorial Sloan-Kettering Cancer Center (where Leslie had been treated for her breast cancer several years earlier).

The day after he was released from Sloan-Kettering, Chuck sat by the pool at the Bridgehampton house, fielding phone calls from well-wishers and physicians. One in particular grabbed his full attention. After he replaced his cell phone in its holster, he seemed annoyed, almost angry.

"Stage two!" he said.

"Isn't that good?"

"I'd convinced myself it was stage one. That would have meant no chemo. Stage two, chemo is optional. It only changes the odds by a few percentage points. I'm not going to do it."

His spirits restored by that snap decision, he spent the rest of the afternoon and evening talking about art and photography and enjoying a barbecue. A few days later, however, he changed his mind about chemotherapy, having been advised by five different doctors that even those few percentage points were significant. Chuck would be taking a chemo cocktail that had many virtues, though it had been known to cause, in the long term, temporary nerve damage to the hands, clearly an undesirable side effect for a painter. Still, he had been convinced it would be worthwhile.

The very first day of the treatment, he felt a tingling in his hands. When he reported this, it was suggested to him that he must be imagining it—some kind of a psychokinetic response. The condition quickly worsened, at least he thought so, but the doctors remained skeptical. If this complication were to develop, they insisted, it would occur slowly over a period of weeks or months, not days. Chuck continued to experience stiffness and pain in his hands. Even when chemo was interrupted because of an unconnected respiratory infection, the pain did not go away.

Finally the doctors acknowledged that in fact there was no available data regarding the consequences of this form of chemo for somebody with Chuck's preexisting condition. It began to seem likely that his compromised nervous system might indeed have made his hands especially prone to the cocktail's painful side effect.

Chemo was definitively discontinued, and the pain very slowly subsided without completely disappearing. The nausea persisted too and was still dogging him a year later.

Chuck responded as he always does.

"All I can do when I feel shitty is paint. When I'm painting, I forget the worst of it."

Towards the end of 2009, even that solace was threatened. One consequence of being in a wheelchair for twenty-one years is that Chuck suffers from severe curvature of the spine, which has evolved into an acute condition that causes excruciating pain when he leans forward to paint (which being in the chair forces him to do, so that tragically the act of painting may have contributed to the condition). Attempts were made to rectify this with braces for his torso, formed from body molds. Wearing these proved to be just as painful—and very constricting into the bargain. Even had they worked, they would have provided only a temporary solution.

At the time of writing, Chuck faces the likelihood of surgery and a lengthy period of rehabilitation. Anything, he says, would be preferable to not being able to paint.

Making this series of recent health problems all the more challenging to deal with was the fact that, by the time they erupted, Chuck and Leslie Close were no longer living together, and the separation was not without acrimony. The trauma of the Event and its burdensome aftermath had been taking its toll for years. With time, it became impossible to ignore the stresses on the marriage brought about by the difficulties in adjusting to drastic changes in circumstance, and by the fact that Chuck and Leslie each viewed those changes from radically different viewpoints. This was rooted in their contrasting personalities—his gregarious, larger than life, hers protective of her privacy—and, as has been discussed, it had become a major issue during the period of hospitalization and rehab. During those dismal days at NYU Medical Center, each had displayed astonishing survival skills, Leslie attending to the day to day problems of crisis management—battling with the medical staff, fighting to hold her family together—Chuck following an entirely different strategy to keep himself focused on survival and the resumption of his career. Part of the tragedy of the situation was that it was the divergent demands of the challenges they had to face at that time that began to pull them apart.

Nothing in Leslie's experience had prepared her for anything like this. Chuck, on the other hand, had spent his early years battling with dyslexia and neuro-muscular challenges and coming to terms with the loss of his father. He believes these experiences had given him the resolve and means to fight his disability, but beyond that they seem to have blunted his sense of himself as a victim. Of course he had felt sorry for himself stretched out in a hospital bed paralyzed from the shoulders down, or lying in his own excrement on a gurney while he waited, apparently forgotten, in some bleak, institutional corridor; but somehow he was able—at least when it mattered—to retain the ability to see beyond those appalling circumstances. He managed to visualize himself making art once more, and the intensity of his belief in this possibility saved him from feeling victimized. Leslie too visualized him making art again—it was integral to her hope of a meaningful future for herself and her family—and she fought to make it happen, but it could not diminish her sense of having been treated cruelly by fate.

Chuck and Leslie had desperately hoped that things would be better when the institutional nightmare was over, and for Chuck that largely proved to be the case. Not that there were not many times every day when he became frustrated and even enraged by his disabilities, but at least he was back functioning in his chosen world and making paintings that met his own high standards. He also developed the knack of minimizing the impact of his quadriplegia on others—discouraging pity—by treating it as another kind of "normality," rather like dyslexia. With friends, he would talk freely and openly—often with humor—about the condition's demonic knack of inflicting misery and embarrassment without warning or pity. Frankness liberated him. Nor was he about to shy away from doing something because some squeamish able-bodied person might find it inappropriate.

For Leslie it was very different. From her perspective, normality could not return because through her eyes, it seems fair to say, Chuck would never be "normal" again and that transformed everything. As he overcame the consequences of his disability, they seemed to weigh more heavily on her. The challenge that had faced him was to use his mental strength to overcome physical affliction, with rebuilding his career his clearly defined goal. As enormous and complex as that task was, it was sharply focused (like one of his early paintings). Leslie's challenge was far less focused because it lacked a specific goal upon which everything else depended. Her rewarding and potentially stellar horticultural career—the public face of it, at least—had ended too soon, though in the nineties she embarked on an ambitious project to write a history of American landscape architecture—for which she did a vast amount of research, but which sadly was never completed—and she still had her own gem of a garden to nurture. Most important, she was of course devoted to providing the richest and most fulfilling possible future for her children, but with Georgia becoming a freshman at Yale just a couple of years after Chuck was released from Rusk, soon only Maggie was at home. When her new, unwanted life began, Leslie Close was still a young woman, in her early forties. She found herself in a situation where rewards were hard to come by, and where much of the time she must have felt a lack of control over her own destiny.

In her interview in *The Portraits Speak*, taped on December 13, 1996, Leslie talked at length about her efforts to come to terms with her post-Event existence. In one passage she spoke about the need to have her own space, outside the home, "someplace to go to escape the nurse, the assistants, the physical therapists, and the illness itself. . . . The first few months that I rented [an] office, I would just go there and cry. . . ."[24]

For Chuck, the nurses, the assistants, the physical therapists were his lifeline. For Leslie they were intruders crowding out any possibility of normality, and they were reminders of the real villain of the piece, the illness itself. That, more than anything, was what she was fleeing when she sought the privacy of her office or her garden.

In retrospect, it seems that extreme contrasts in personality might eventually have placed a severe strain on the marriage even without the unthinkable complications imposed on the situation by Chuck's disability. That possibility would have been easier to deal with because it would not have been weighted with all the feelings of guilt and bad faith that inevitably followed the cataclysm. The role Leslie played in Chuck's recovery and rehabilitation, and in facilitating the restoration of his career, was immeasurable. Ironically, this may have made it harder for her to come to terms with the deterioration of the marriage because, in a way that must have seemed to her entirely unfair, Chuck was the beneficiary of her efforts while she felt mired in a sense of loss.

The stresses placed on the relationship were inescapable, and this became clearly evident to friends even as efforts continued to find a viable basis for the continuation of the marriage. Not long after Chuck painted the 2002 portrait of Leslie discussed in Chapter Twenty-five, the couple began to discuss the possibility of moving back downtown, partly perhaps in the hope that a return to old haunts would have a therapeutic effect on the relationship. A huge expenditure of thought and energy went into reshaping and retrofitting a newly built West Village penthouse—with harbor views to Ellis Island and the Statue of Liberty—that they finally moved into in 2006, after lengthy delays. This was the ultimate expression of their shared passion for reshaping homes. The never-used kitchen and bathroom of the penthouse, totally inadequate for the needs of a quadriplegic, were torn out and rebuilt from scratch. That was just the beginning. Floors were stripped, bleached, dyed, and polyurethaned. A gallery was created to protect delicate works of art from the sunlight that made the apartment so appealing in the first place, and a wall drawing by Sol LeWitt—a gift from the artist—was given a place of honor in the living area. The result was a minimalist masterpiece, but in the end the effort involved in its creation could not disguise the deteriorating state of the marriage. The situation was well on its way to becoming untenable and, not long after the move downtown, they sought marriage counseling which after a while led to the suggestion that they should consider a trial separation. That in turn led to a permanent break with Chuck at first living primarily in his studio while Leslie spent more time in Bridgehampton. Leslie continued to use the new apartment, and in 2008 Chuck bought another for himself—its terrace facing south over the roofs and water towers of SoHo—half a block from his studio and a half-dozen blocks from their first Greene Street loft.

By the fall of 2009, a legal separation was in the works. There is nothing easy about the breakup of a marriage, especially one that lasted as long as the Closes' and that was put to such severe tests. Inevitably there was anger on both sides, but, in Chuck's case at least, this was tinged with regret.

"All the professionals we've spoken to—the doctors, the psychologists, the physical therapists—have told us that almost no relationship ever survives the kind of experience we went through. It was only because of our tenacity, and stubbornness, and our determination to keep our family together that we managed to keep the marriage going as long as we did. But in the end the devastation was so complete that it reached the point where there was nothing left—no relationship.

"I take my share of the blame. We tried but we just couldn't make it work. We just saw the situation so differently. For her, it was the loss of privacy that made it impossible, for me it was the lack of intimacy and affection. I hope that we can move forward now and find a modicum of peace and happiness."

The marriage of Georgia Close to Dr. Benjamin Spencer, and the birth of Chuck's first grandson, Owen Close Spencer, on March 28th, 2009, has brought joy to both parties. Maggie Close is also doing well. She has been working at the research facility of the New York Stem Cell Foundation, and she is now enrolled in a post-baccalaureate pre-med program at New York University.

Dr. Ben Spencer, Dr. Georgia Close, and Owen Close Spencer

The City of New York and the New York art world have been through many changes since Chuck Close first emerged into the public consciousness in the late 1960s. He arrived on the scene at a time when Pop Art and Minimalism had made their initial breakthroughs and the art scene was as parochial as a small village. He was there for the rise of Conceptualism, and for the arrival of the so-called Picture Generation in the early 1980s. He witnessed the success of neo-Expressionism, the invasion of European stars from Italy, Germany, and elsewhere, the growth of video art and installation art, the acceptance of body art and gigantism, the arrival of the Young Brits and the birth of post-revolutionary Chinese art. He saw the sprinkling of galleries that existed in 1970 multiply with viral intensity into sections of the city previously reserved for crasser forms of commerce, and he watched as art departments from California to Connecticut unleashed on the world eager young MFAs primed to satisfy the needs of a new breed of patron that hatched from the worlds of digital entrepreneurship, leveraged buyouts, hedge funds, and old-fashioned real estate adventurism.

For the most part, Chuck has been receptive to these cycles of change, which he has observed from his unique vantage point, and he has done much to encourage and help young artists. He is one of the few who can claim to have bridged the divide between modernism and postmodernism, having contributed to the cumulative stage of the former while helping to usher in the latter. He began his career from a position of such startling originality and has displayed such a gift for reinventing himself that he has never seemed out of step with what was happening around him. The fact that his primary medium has been paint on canvas might have been expected to become an impediment to his remaining *au courant*, but I believe it has had the opposite effect. While other artists have strained to make their mark by pumping up startling but shallow ideas with the help of the aesthetic equivalent of steroids, Chuck has remained solidly innovative without breaking radically with the past. As a result, his innovations seem all the more impressive because they are perceived as advances in a continuum rather than as mere novelties. It does not hurt that the endless potential of painting is rediscovered every few years, having routinely been rejected yet again for the same old tired reasons which have changed little since they were first advanced by the Dadaists almost a century ago. At each point of rediscovery, Chuck is there, as relevant as ever, having produced fresh and challenging variations on his unchanging quest.

Painting remains Chuck Close's central activity, but it is his continuing engagement with the world as recorded by the camera that emphasizes his relevance. There are many artists who use cameras—whether Hasselblads, movie cameras, or video rigs—to make art. No one but Chuck has used *art* to investigate the character of *photography* with the rigor and depth of imagination that is found in every aspect of his work. Even his most straightforward photographs take on an analytical dimension because of the way they relate to the dialectic of the paintings.

Finally, there is the matter of portraiture. The human face—that forbidden fruit, a taste of which according to Clement Greenberg would banish an artist from the modernist Garden of Eden—has proved not only durable but also vitally relevant to the art of recent decades, as can be seen in the work of some of the artists Chuck has painted—Cindy Sherman, Lucas Samaras, and Francesco Clemente, for example—as well as others as varied as Roni Horn and Hiroshi Sugimoto.

Chuck Close's influence in the art world has been subtle. He does not have obvious disciples or followers, the character of his art being too personal to allow for such a thing, and at the same time it is too broad in its implications. Yet all of the artists mentioned above, and many more, can be thought of as having been to a greater or lesser extent touched by his influence. That influence asserts itself at a dialectical and philosophical level. His work is intensely retinal in terms of the pleasure that it affords the eye, but not at the expense of intellectual reflection. Because of his childhood learning disabilities, Chuck's intelligence evolved largely in pictorial terms (though his ability to verbalize it is formidable). As his more abstract intellectual skills evolved to match his pictorial skills, he was inexorably drawn to rethinking the language of representation, that mysterious dialogue between man-made marks on paper or canvas and the eye. To a degree, perhaps, that process can be captured in words, as I have attempted to do in these pages. More potently, it can be experienced directly and viscerally by standing in front of a Chuck Close painting and letting it work its magic.

For all the philosophical rigor of his art, Chuck does not dismiss the word "magic."

"You start off with a blank canvas," he says, "and day by day, week by week, you add a brushstroke here, a brushstroke there, and something comes to life in front of your eyes. What could be more magical than that?"

It is the kind of magic that was practiced 30,000 years ago in caves in France and Spain. Chuck Close has shown that it has lost none of its potency, and the fact that it has enabled him to overcome both childhood disabilities and the kind of physical trauma that would have destroyed most people, only enhances that potency which he sums up in a simple phrase:

"Art saved my life."

Notes

1. Smithsonian *Archives of American Art*, interview with Chuck Close, conducted by Judd Tully, May 14, 1987.

2. *The Seattle Times*, 1/2/08, "College honors former art chair with exhibit," by Diane Wright.

3. *Russell E. Day: Catalyst*, exhibition catalog, Northlight Gallery, Everett Community College (formerly Everett Junior College), 2008, p. 10.

4. There have been several editions of this title, including a *Reader's Digest* condensed version, the most recent being issued by Kessinger Publishing in 2007. A 1944 edition was given the alternative title *Why Japan Was Strong: Adventurous Investigations of an American Hobo*.

5. For an account of this incident, sometimes referred to as Bloody Sunday, see *Mill Town; a Social History of Everett, Washington, from its Earliest Beginnings on the Shores of Puget Sound to the Tragic and Infamous Event Known as the Everett Massacre*, by Norman H. Clark, University of Washington Press, 1970.

6. *Russell E. Day: Catalyst*, Northlight Gallery, Everett Community College, 2008, p. 38.

7. From the transcript of a conversation between Alden Mason and Lamar Harrington, taped January 13, 1984, part of an oral history commissioned by the Smithsonian Institute Archives of American Art.

8. In her 2005 book *Art and the Power of Placement*, Victoria Newhouse points out that Pollock's large drip paintings first made a major public impact when seen at the Betty Parsons Gallery, a relatively modest space that forced viewers into an unusually intimate relationship with the artist's wall-sized canvases.

9. Chuck Close interviewed by Robert Storr.

10. A review by Emily Wassermann appeared in *Artforum*.

11. On my first full day in the United States, in November 1967, I found my way to the back room at the old Bykert Gallery space on West Fifty-seventh Street. In one fell swoop I met Brice Marden, David Novros, Ralph Humphries, and Alan Saret.

12. Seventies SoHo, and lost landmarks like Food, can be revisited in Paul Mazursky's 1978 movie *An Unmarried Woman*.

13. *New York Times*, May 6, 1977.

14. *New York*, May 30, 1977.

15. *Time*, May 23, 1977.

16. Terrie Sultan, Richard Schiff et al., *Chuck Close Prints: Process and Collaboration*, Princeton University Press, 2003, p. 66. The catalogue for a traveling exhibition that originated at the Blaffer Gallery, the Art Museum of the University of Houston, this publication provides a detailed introduction to Close's work in the fields of prints and multiples.

17. Ibid.

18. *Chuck Close Prints: Process and Collaboration*, Terrie Sultan et al., Princeton University Press/Blaffer Gallery, The Art Museum of the University of Houston, 2003, pp. 111–12.

19. Serious respiratory problems would continue for months because the patient's diaphragm was partially paralyzed, so that his cough was very weak and "unproductive."

20. Robert Storr et al., *Chuck Close*, The Museum of Modern Art, New York/Harry N. Abrams, 1998, p. 25.

21. Pace Gallery became PaceWildenstein in 1993.

22. *Daily Telegraph*, London, October 6, 2006.

23. Robert Storr et al., *Chuck Close*, The Museum of Modern Art, New York, 1998, p. 61.

24. Chuck Close, *The Portraits Speak*, A.R.T. Press, 1998, pp. 172–73.

Acknowledgments

It goes without saying that this book, like the one that preceded it, *Chuck Close: Work*, owes an enormous debt to Chuck Close himself. Without him neither would exist, and the amount of time he has devoted to ensuring their success probably robbed the world of a couple of major paintings, for which I apologize. It would be impossible to overstate my gratitude to him, and also to Leslie Close who, under sometimes difficult circumstances, granted many insights into her husband's life and work, and in particular provided her crucial point of view on the traumatic event that transformed both their lives, and its often painful aftermath. Leslie Close is a very private person and I thank her for her openness.

Thanks are due too to friends and associates of the Closes who provided information, anecdotes and perspective that contributed to my understanding of Chuck's life and career. Some of these, including Donn Trethewey, Larry Stair, Mike Monahan, Seth Greenwald, and Elizabeth Sipprell, date back to his formative years in Everett, Washington, and Seattle, and were able to throw invaluable light on Chuck's personality and activities from junior high school to college, a period that, as will be seen, was even more crucial for Chuck than for most people. Others who supplied me with recollections are Arne Glimcher, Peter MacGill, Mark Greenwold, Robert Israel, Barbara Harshman, Klaus Kertess, Jane and Robert Cottingham, Bernard Chaet, Milo Addica, Carol Johnson, and my wife Linda Rosenkrantz who, in addition to invaluable editorial input, was able to unearth from her files transcripts of unpublished interviews she conducted with both Chuck and Leslie in the 1970s.

It would be impossible to overstate my debt to the individuals who make up the staff of Chuck Close's studio who were always available to assist me with anything and everything. Beth Zopf in particular has helped in a thousand different ways, but my gratitude extends to Manolo Bustamente, Michael Marfione—many of whose photographs grace both this book and its predecessor—Field Kalop, and Janie Samuels. Chuck's longtime studio assistant Michael Volonakis was able to provide unique insight into the period at Rusk Institute when Chuck began to paint again after months of rehabilitation. I'm proud to count all of them as friends. Special thanks are due too to Mark Glimcher of the PaceWildenstein Gallery, and the staffs of both PaceWildenstein and the Pace/MacGill Gallery—especially Aram Jibilian, Ola Czarnecka, Ken Fernandez, and Heather Palmer—who provided unsparing support on both books. Jay Jopling, Tim Marlow, and the staff of London's White Cube Gallery were also more than generous with their time.

Some of the most valuable information I received came by way of someone I never met or spoke to. I refer to Chuck Close's Great Aunt Bina Albro who in the nineteen eighties—at Chuck's behest—wrote a history of the Albro, Wagner, and Close clans which was made available to me along with other family documents. What made Bina's narrative especially valuable is the fact that she was close to Chuck's mother, Mildred—in some ways more like a sister to her than an aunt. Mildred Close, whom I met on several occasions towards the end of her life, is a key figure in this book and Bina's manuscript provided perspective on her larger than life personality.

Christopher Lyon of Prestel Publishing championed this double-barreled publishing project from the outset and he has been closely involved in all aspects of its development. I cannot thank him enough. Prestel's North America marketing director, Stephen Hulbert, has provided welcome support and I thank all the staff of the New York office, notably Ryan Newbanks and Ali Gitlow. In addition I have received full support from Prestel's Munich office and must single out Jürgen Krieger, Publisher, and Claudia Stäuble, Munich coordinating editor, for special gratitude. Mark Melnick has brought to the task of designing this book the same great taste and expertise that he brought to laying out its predecessor, which is in evidence on every page. Richard Weisman and his staff at Duke & Company must be thanked for their expert typesetting. Production has been handled by Friederike Schirge and her staff in Munich with diligence and care, and Mindy Werner, the editor for *Chuck Close: Life*, has been a joy to work with, making herself available at ungodly hours as the deadline for delivery of the text approached. Her input has been crucial and I owe her lunch.

Finally, my warmest thanks to Kate Hirson, Sam and Martha Peterson, Peter Williams, Richard Brockman and Mirra Bank, Judy Harris, Judith Stonehill, and Zeljka Ulan for the generosity of their friendship.

Photo Credits

Michael Marfione: cover; Wayne Hollingworth: frontispiece, p. 156; courtesy of Chuck Close: pp. 6, 9, 11, 12, 13, 16, 17, 18, 20, 21, 22, 23, 24, 34, 35, 44, 45, 50, 66, 70, 86, 89, 91, 98, 103, 104, 114, 126, 155, 160, 161, 164, 169, 178–79, 182, 200, 221, 226, 230, 232, 233, 254, 277, 331; courtesy of Everett Community College: p. 58; courtesy of Dr. A. Seth Greenwald: p. 74; Fred Gutzeit: p. 79 (left and right); Ellen Page Wilson, courtesy of PaceWildenstein, New York: pp. 81, 152, 154, 175, 176, 237, 243, 270, 286, 288, 290, 308, 318, 320; Garie Waltzer: p. 107; © G. E. Kidder Smith/Corbis: p. 112; Frank James: pp. 122–23; © Elliott Landy/MAGNUM: p. 132; Chuck Close, courtesy of the artist and PaceWildenstein, New York: pp. 136, 143; courtesy of PaceWildenstein, New York: pp. 145, 158, 210, 213, 216, 219, 236, 246; Maggie L. Kundtz, courtesy of Pace Prints, New York: pp. 196, 197; Douglas M. Parker: p. 208; Bill Jacobson, courtesy of PaceWildenstein, New York: pp. 238, 282, 293; Maggie L. Kundtz, courtesy of PaceWildenstein, New York: p. 246; John Back: pp. 264, 265, 275; Tina Barney: p. 289; courtesy of Pace Prints, New York: p. 294; Chuck Close, courtesy of the artist and Pace/MacGill Gallery, New York: pp. 298, 299, 307; Donald Farnsworth, Magnolia Editions: pp. 302, 303; Kerry Ryan McFate, courtesy of PaceWildenstein, New York: pp. 304, 326; Official White House photography: pp. 306, 309

Index